Awakening

Awakening

A Practical Guide to Zen Meditation

YOGI BRAHMASAMHARA

ROCKPOOL
PUBLISHING

Rockpool Publishing
24 Constitution Road
Dulwich Hill NSW 2203
AUSTRALIA

www.rockpoolpublishing.com.au

First Edition 2008
Reprinted 2011

Acknowledgements

Grateful acknowledgement is made for the willing permission given by the publishers below to reprint excerpts from their publications, as detailed. *Stumbling Towards Enlightenment* by Geri Larkin, Celestial Arts Publishing, 1997. *The Integral Yoga* by Sri Aurobindo, Sri Aurobindo Ashram Trust, 2003. *Cave in the Snow* by Vicki Mackenzie, Bloomsbury Publishing, 1999. *What is the Dharma?* by Sangharakshita, Windhorse Publications, 1998.

Printed in China by Everbest Printing Co. Ltd

Brahmasamhara Yogi.
Awakening : A Practical Guide to Zen Meditation / Yogi Brahmasamhara.
ISBN: 978 1 921878 00 8 (pbk.)
Meditation.

Cataloguing-in-Publication entry is available from the National Library of Australia
http://catalogue.nla.gov.au/
For information about legal deposit and government deposit, please contact the Legal Deposit Unit on (02) 6262 1312 or email mailto:legaldep@nla.gov.au Information about legal deposit can be found on the Library's website, http://www.nla.gov.au/services/ldeposit.html Legal Deposit in Australia. Alternatively, the Legal Deposit Unit can be contacted on (02) 6262 1312.

Cover design by Seymour Designs
Typeface: Adobe Garamond
Photography by Julie Howard

There have been three wise men in my life.
I lovingly dedicate this book to one of them – my
dear father, Alan, a man who first taught me of love,
kindness and compassion and whose life exemplified
those enlightened qualities.

Contents

Little Stories of Encouragement

Without You ...

... it wouldn't have happened!

When we buy a book, we know that a particular person is the 'author'. Sometimes we'll buy a book *because* of that author. The reality is that an author is just one cog in a large wheel that delivers a book into your hand. That is so true for *Awakening* because I have had the privilege of loving support, direct and practical help, inspiration and encouragement from so many precious people, many of whom may never know the extraordinary gratitude I shall always feel in my heart for them.

Foremost, I bow to the lovingly tireless Ananda Beverley Manning, who co-ordinates the running of our first Meditation Sanctuary in Sydney. She has graciously taken an increasingly heavy load of work to lighten mine, so giving me the most treasured gift of 'more time'. Appreciation also to the many who now give of their valued time every week helping so willingly, and to the Sanctuary's loved 'Mother', Janene, who so often graces the Meditation Hall with beautiful flowers. My dear son Pete Grayson is also always so cheerfully available with technical and web support.

A book manuscript doesn't just flow beautifully from the pen (sadly!) but is often raw and in need of some loving massage and literary attention. Accordingly, deepest appreciation is held for Sue Close, a meticulous reader while being fiercely supportive, and for Karin Spirk for her letter-by-letter proofreading and her kindness, wider help, support and encouragement. My eternal gratitude to Yeganeh Atri for her 'care-full' and considered reading and particular gratefulness as well, to John Cole for wise editing, perceptive comments and his confidence-boosting belief in the worthiness of the project. Ros Burton's experienced observations were also invaluable in helping me 'sort the wood from the trees'.

Dear Teacher Alex Rossi was gracious in her support throughout, as well as being the perfect, meditative 'model' for the photography. Special mention must go to Sam Davis, a precious student who has grown to become a Precious Teacher and who also gave me the gift of time by venturing into the 'wilds' of other suburbs and creating further Meditation Sanctuaries so more and more people have Authentic Meditation available to them.

A loving '*Namaste*' to the very many who stood close to the sideline, cheering us on.

Finally, thank you to Lisa Hanrahan of Rockpool Publishing for her seemingly endless patience, encouragement and resilient belief in this book.

Bless you all. Together we created a book for others.

Brahm

Author's Comment

Reading this Book

This is a book on the original, pure and natural practices of Authentic Meditation. In being written for the modern seeker, it unveils the Way for people to genuinely enhance the fullness of their wellbeing and reach back into their 'original' capacity to be enthralled with the living of their life as a genuinely magnificent Being ... the true 'purpose' of meditation.

I suggest that you read it completely through once, but *without* dwelling on the actual exercises or being tempted to start them before you've read the whole. In so reading through it first, you will gain an overall perspective of the Great Journey into meditation – a little like being able to see the complete vista of your town if you stand on top of the nearby hill, rather than trying to glean its layout while standing in the middle of your street.

Having read it through and perhaps finding yourself interested in, or even excited by, the possibilities of Authentic Meditation, *then* go back and commence with the first exercise.

The 'Little Letters of Encouragement'

Scattered throughout the book are a number of letters written to me by students at various stages of the Journey. Invariably, these dear people had suffered in a dark place of unwellness of one kind or another, some for many years. Each, in their own way, eventually came to the practice of meditation, a few as a hopeful, final resort.

I shall leave them to relate, and you to read, the extraordinary effects that the practice of natural Authentic Meditation has had on their lives. But I make special mention of them here to acknowledge the wonderful courage they have shown in daring to 'put pen to paper' in the first place and, then further, by allowing me to include their letters in this book so that their gift of enlightening courage may be shared by others. You too, may find their Path into meditation ('this seductive and strangely compelling place', as one wrote) as inspirational as I have.

Prelude

The 'Story of Nathan'

'I have given myself 31 days to be enlightened!'

I remember, it was late when the phone rang. A Sunday evening, wintry cold and an icy wind. I had been writing for hours while the rain murmured, soft against dark windows – mellowing, trickling, whispering – friendly company as lulling as the rhythmic cadence of monks chanting. I hesitated to answer … but I did. Perhaps a student.

It wasn't. The voice on the phone was that of a stranger.

I initially assumed the stranger-voice to be yet another seeker who'd stumbled across 'meditation' and who wanted to find out more about it – like *now!* I was right in a way. He *was* a seeker but this stranger was rather different to most with his grand mission to 'become enlightened' (not so exceptional) but with the very specific time limit of 31 days (utterly startling!). For a minute I was speechless … and a little sceptical.

He took my silence as an opportunity to cheerily introduce himself.

'Oh, by the way, I'm Nathan.'

He was well-spoken, if a smidgen intense, but seemed genuine enough. I began to ask a few questions on whether he'd practiced meditation before and what he actually thought 'enlightenment' was.

Waste of yogic breath!

Nathan went straight for the spiritual jugular. He was in no mind to be messing around with chatting over meditating for stress relief or 'all that yogi mystical powers stuff' (his words). He didn't want any 'babble' about 'seeking for meaning' or 'practicing for wellbeing' (his words). He hadn't rung for a discussion on the 'ordinary stuff of meditation'.

After his little monologue, he asked whether he could meet me 'as soon as possible please!' Clearly, the countdown towards his enlightenment had already been triggered on the mission clock and the days and hours were wasting by. Bemused, curious, I agreed to meet my midnight caller at the Meditation Sanctuary the following Tuesday evening.

* * *

Tuesday came. About six o'clock. Cool evening. The orange rays of sunset through crinkle-glass windows painted liquid colour-shapes all over the polished floor – mesmerisingly beautiful, enthralling … meditative.

I was alone in the Sanctuary's large Meditation Hall … always invitingly peaceful under its lofty-apexed ceiling of wooden boards supported by hewn old beams woven high along the length of the room. The sweet vibrating mono-notes of a Tibetan bowl being played resonated softly and the fragrance of smouldering incense sticks, gifted from a student's recent visit to an Indian *ashram**, dwelled faintly, their waif-thin twines of smoke wafting upwards into nothing.

Right on time, he bounded into the Sanctuary. Late 20s I figured. He seemed tall (I was sitting). He had a pleasant, open face and black curly hair and was dressed in a smart business suit. He literally marched across the hall, hard leather heels echoing sharp-hollow cracking sounds around and around the walls – a secular novelty from the usual reverential padding of bare feet. He thrust his hand out and said, 'I'm Nathan!'

I was immediately struck by the broadest, most beautifully engaging smile; the smile you see on the happiest of Buddhist monks, the radiant smile that simply makes you want to smile back, because you can't help it.

I couldn't help but laugh a greeting. Then I asked him to remove his shoes, gesturing that he sit on the mat in front of me. Intriguingly, he easily assumed the masterful yoga lotus posture, usually impossible for the unpracticed and which must have been – umm – 'less than comfortable'

---

* As defined by the revered Guru, Sri Aurobindo, '*ashram*' literally means the 'house of a teacher or master of spiritual philosophies'.

in pin-striped suit trousers. My overall impression was of a large, bounding puppy, eager and joyful … just for the sake of being joyful.

I had a tiny thought-spark of the ancient story of a young man, Siddhartha Gautama (later to be known as the Buddha) who, in his early years as a prince, was isolated by his father from any exposure to suffering or death. Fleetingly, it struck me that sitting before me was another man, seemingly fresh with innocence who, like Gautama, had probably experienced little suffering in his young life.

'So, you want to become enlightened, and you don't have much time', I began.

'Yes, will you help me?'

'Why do you want to become enlightened?'

'Because I've been meditating for the last two years and I figure that's enough time but, I don't seem to be getting anywhere'.

'Where do you want to "get"?'

'Well … enlightened of course! Isn't that what it's supposed to be all about! After all, the Buddha apparently sat under a tree for just a few days to get enlightened so it can't be all that difficult.'

'Have you tried that?' I asked.

'Tried what?'

'Sitting under a tree like him – doing nothing but … just sitting. If it worked for him …'

I divined the first, nano-faint trace of doubt in Nathan's sunbeaming smile.

'No', he said. 'I can't *just sit* and waste that much time in one go. There must be a quicker way. Will you help me?'

'Why do you want become enlightened?'

The smile definitely dimmed. I *knew* he wanted to say 'you just asked me that!' but I could feel his mind working out that my repeating the question maybe, just maybe, wasn't doddery old forgetfulness.

'It's my next step.'

'How about telling me about the last step'.

So Nathan began to unwind his 'story'. He'd been successful at school, highly achieved at university, happily married to a lovely woman with a child on the way and now held a senior management position with an international finance group. Already promoted far beyond any expected position for one so relatively young, his progress through life had been 'just as he'd planned!' Everything had come to him easily. Like the young prince, he really hadn't wanted for anything or suffered in any way at all.

But, he told me, it had been 'about two years ago' that he'd begun to become aware of the possible life-path ahead … further promotions, more money than he'd ever need, bigger houses, more 'boys' toys', more children, more everything – all too easy, no challenges, just … boredom. After that, retirement, ongoing boredom – death! It all seemed too one-dimensional somehow. He had begun to feel unsettled that, despite his smooth passage through life, somehow he was 'missing the boat'. He *just didn't know which boat he was missing!* Years later, he was to tell me that, 'outwardly things were great but inwards was depression, anxiety and a real dissatisfaction with so-called success.' He recently wrote that 'so many so-called successful people are 'basket cases' behind the scenes, as if they have Attention Deficit Disorder of Life.'

Nathan's story that evening wasn't typical because *everyone* has their own 'story'. What *was* deeply familiar though was his 'feeling of something missing'. Over the years, I have heard similar comments from so many students. People from all walks of life, different religious backgrounds and cultures, young and old, rich and poor have sat with me and told me of their being dissatisfied, of finding happiness elusive; that they can't manage their daily life (even when they have most everything they could want or need); don't really know who they are; have no sense of purpose or meaning; can't find any lasting contentment; or, the real cutie, are just 'plain and simply bored'.

Just like Nathan, so many people have difficulty making sense of their 'missingness'.

Not long before writing these words, I had a long and loving discussion with an old man of 90 who lives in an aged-care residence far out in the Australian bush where we both had grown up. We were chatting over what he called the 'psychology of people' and had meandered along to discussing this sense of inner 'missingness' that so many seem to experience, 'even for a whole lifetime'. He talked about how this subtle discontent, if unexplored, untended and left unresolved, can lead to damaging negative thoughts and often destructive behaviour … the mirrored reflections of undefined suffering.

He illustrated this by talking of the terrible effect on others of the deeds of 'world leaders gone wrong' … all the way through to some of the elderly ones in the residence still 'living in sadness because they are *holding on to old sufferings*'. Then, as he slowly stirred his tea, he looked at me very directly and said, *'they don't hear themselves crying'*. My father is a wise man.

Nathan's sense of an indefinable 'missing something' was a silent inner cry. He was really saying that 'there *has to be* more to life than this; there *has to be* more to existing than just enduring it. Surely, there must be another way, something *other*, something more I can do, some better purpose or meaning. *There has to be more to me than this.'*

But somehow Nathan had slowly become aware of his inner tears and had awakened to a point of knowing that nothing in the 'ordinary' life was going to wipe them away.

'Will I make it?'

'Make what?'

'Enlightenment of course!'

'You still want to accomplish this in 31 days?'

'Yep … please. Will you help me?'

'Dear Nathan, you are already closer to it than you know, but I'm afraid you are unlikely to make it in *31 years*.'

Radiant smile replaced with genuine look of shock. You see, Nathan was another who'd 'done' some meditation and heard just enough old myths about 'enlightenment' to imagine it to be a quick 'n easy panacea for all ills – like taking an aspirin and waiting for five minutes. Without doubt he saw it as the perfectly right 'something' to overcome the 'missing something' and then all would be better.

'Why in god's name not?'

'Because you want it so much.'

'Of course I *want* it!'

'But your *wanting* is so overpowering that it has become the very barrier to achieving it. Only when you give up the desire, only when you completely *let go*, not only your magic 31 days, but also the whole idea of becoming enlightened, will you possibly give yourself half a chance of ... *being enlightened.*'

Nathan just stared at the floor for a while shaking his head. This was not good.

'What about the other half chance?' A grin re-emerged as he thought he spotted a loophole.

'Well if ... *if* you can ever let go this heavy burden of desire – this weight of 'wanting' – you may then unveil that half chance ... if you are prepared to go on a very long journey.'

'Where?'

'Well, nowhere actually. You might say that it is a journey over a Path that isn't actually there ... until you start walking ... and then just keep walking without expecting to get anywhere. This Path is called practicing meditation ... authentic meditation ...'

'But I've *done* meditation for two years already!'

'... and, unless you stop the desire for some kind of instant miracle or answer, you might well meditate for the next 50 years, and still be chasing your tail looking for ... what was it you wanted again?'

'Enlightenment!'

'Aahh yes! Well, you certainly have a few yoga techniques under your belt, such as sitting in the full lotus position, but you haven't actually put your foot on the real Path yet. However, we have a new class starting on Thursday and you'd be very welcome to come along if you wish.'

'How long will it all take then?'

'Oh, perhaps the rest of your life. But it is a journey only to be started by those with the courage to ...'

Nathan stood up mid-sentence, shook hands goodbye and walked to the door, shoes in hand. After he'd put them on and was about to go out, I called to him.

'Nathan! Why 31 days?'

He turned back. 'Well initially, I gave myself a month, 30 days, until I remembered that some months have 31 days. I thought I might need the extra day!' He flashed the Nathan smile and was gone. Last laugh to him, I thought, and wondered whether I would ever see him again.

* * *

Thursday evening. The Meditation Hall was dotted with many eager freshlings when I walked in. I went to the teacher's mat and sat. There before me, right in the front, was Nathan, smiling broadly. He had decided to turn up with his 'bags packed' and so, that night, for one young man, a most extraordinary journey began.

This book unfolds the Way of the Great Journey that Nathan decided to travel and, if you also choose to put your foot on this Path, you too may discover its enthralling ancient secrets and perhaps experience for yourself … *what happened to Nathan?*

Chapter One

Meditation – a Way Out or the Way In?

'Master, what is Meditation?'
'I love you – you love me –
I love you – you hate me –
I still love you.'

– Yogi Nilakanata Baba*

It is crystal fresh this morning, just perfect for sitting at one of the footpath tables and enjoying a hot cup under the plane tree outside Galantes, my favourite coffee house. Two vigorous little silver-eyes fluff and chitter for a moment, heatedly debating the bird-rights over a preferred sunny spot before, best friends again, they disappear rowdily into the leafy thickness.

People materialise from behind suburban doors and begin to stream along the footpath, rushing by to wherever they go to be busy again. Many have foreheads already furrowed with worry over the 'doings' of the day that hasn't yet started. Once more, I play my 'spot-the-happy-face' game and once more I lose. The little ones of the tree reappear, flit and flirt ... loudly gleeful for a few seconds before quieting. They are happy. No-one noticed.

---

* Words of Yogi Nilakanata Baba, speaking at the Kumbh Mela – the ancient Indian religious festival held every 12 years and attracting more than 50 million people.

Of course, the 'furrowed ones' think they know the reason for the head-down, hard road of the daily grind – their long haul of working, gaining, getting, acquiring, owning, achieving, 'succeeding' – whatever it is they believe will make them happy. But, in the main, so many seem *not* to be happy, or even at ease with their lot.

It suddenly occurred to me that I was sitting in a microcosmic metaphor of our 'existence experience' – tiny pockets of happy chittering sprinkled with transient moments of sun-soaking which, although real, present and freely available, slip by mostly unnoticed by a busy populace intent on 'just rushing' … like Nathan, seemingly without meaningful purpose or direction.

On the big wide world scale, this rippling, scurrying undercurrent of human discontent is unmistakably reflected in so many ways. It shows up in our habitual nation-warring. It is revealed in our headlong, greedy effort to destroy the precious planet's environment, almost as an act of subliminal, collective self-harm. It is underlined emphatically by our permitting half the globe's people to exercise wanton gluttony while glibly, thoughtlessly, allowing the other half to starve.

At the individual level, this busy, breathless era is mirrored in the rampant rise in 'sufferings' such as depression, increasing melancholy, a myriad species of anxiety and an expanding array of related physical illnesses. Undeniably, people are also becoming more insular and isolated because of a cynical, gratification-oriented, media-driven, spiritual barrenness stealthily tiptoeing through our global communities.

However, wafting through this widespread disquiet, I am beginning to hear little murmurings and whisperings of people awakening to the realisation that their tread-milling through a life of *more, more, faster, faster,* is not really experiencing life at all. Rather, it is more like being entrapped in life as prisoners of a laughably bizarre illusion that happiness can only be achieved by the mindless pursuit of 'more than enough'. I am beginning to see that Nathan is far from alone in his indefinable dissatisfaction – his sense of *missingness* and significantly, far from alone in his inner plea that there 'has to be more to life than this … that surely, there *must* be another way'.

There are clear signs beginning to emerge that, although rattled and dazed by the sheer emptiness of the social milieu we have created, increasingly large numbers of people, like Nathan, are seeking a way, *any way*, that might provide relief from their inner whisperings of disquiet … a way that might perhaps, offer at least a hint of 'true' purpose, direction or inner comfort. Is *joy* or *tranquillity* going too far?

Come sit with me for a while and have a coffee while I tell you of some of the 'signs', just here in my own busy neighbourhood, of people's seeking for something deeper, something … 'other'. On this street alone, for example, there are three 'traditional' churches, one or two now reaching out to the modern flock with more relevant, contemporary approaches. There's a newish mosque three blocks over, a Buddhist temple and library a few minutes drive away and a Hindu one just over the railway in the next suburb.

There is a minimum of three centres in this area alone offering modernish variations of yoga. Within five minutes walk, there are two 'wellbeing' stores offering an imaginative array of 'alternative therapies' from astrological readings to reiki. There's a busy gym down there on the corner and a counselling centre in the main street with psychologists, counsellors and one psychiatrist/psychoanalyst, all with diaries chock-a-block filled with the stressed-out needy. There's an adored doctor who truly cares, a chiropractor and an osteopath, yes – also in this street. Oh, and bingo for the aged every Thursday morning down at the hall.

The Meditation Sanctuary is not far away either – just up the hill and around the corner. It's the lovely old building with the hedge growing around it. Another sign of what a needful lot we humans have really become is the fact that hundreds of people are now coming along to the Sanctuary each year to 'learn' meditation. That number seems to climb exponentially as every new year brings further global tensions and individual strain, leaving people feeling as helpless as a leaf in the gutter being turned over and over by the whim of the winds.

The myriad reasons people tell me for their wanting to 'learn' meditation vary widely from the relatively comical (will you teach me how to levitate?) to the intensely sincere, world-wandering, perpetual 'seeker' still looking for the 'right' guru* to lead them to … whatever they think they are looking

---

* The revered Indian philosopher and yogi, Aurobindo, defines a 'guru' as *one who has realised the truth and who himself possesses and is able to communicate the light*.

for. All, in their own way, are further little signs of folks being disillusioned with the treadmill of their ordinary life, suffering as a result of it – and wanting to do something about it.

Whatever people's reasons for wanting to come along to meditation however, they almost all have a mindset glued to one of countless preconceptions and time-misty myths that have hovered over the very word 'meditation' for centuries. The preconceptions I have heard from would-be students range from simple descriptions such as 'I think meditation might be a good way of unwinding stress a bit', to the more fervent ones attached to a notion that meditation is some kind of extraordinary, complex, quasi-supernatural practice reserved for mystics and monks – as if meditation is a kind of exclusive club reserved for the very wise.

Their mind-pictures of the 'truly wise' are mostly spawned by television programmes or photographs that depict ascetics with long hair and beards who spend years sitting on a mountain or in a lonely cave with legs entwined like a grapevine. Or, they envisage mysterious monks who've withdrawn to a life of austerely practicing ancient secrets behind the walls of a mist-shrouded monastery!

Many folks, of course, do come along with genuine intent to 'learn', somehow feeling, believing or having heard that meditation might help in their quest for emotional, psychological, physical or perhaps even spiritual wellbeing. Many are now referred by a health practitioner of one kind or another, for exactly the same reason. Still others have a friend, relative or workmate who's *done it* and they *want what he or she has got* … whatever 'it' may be.

It is fair to say that most 'beginners' and indeed, some who perhaps have practiced previously, tend to be attached to one or other of the myriad preconceptions abounding about meditation. What they do have in common though is the fact that they are all 'looking for something' but, like Nathan, many really don't know just what that 'something' is. For this reason, the very first time we are together, I suggest they drop their thoughts on 'what they think meditation is' into an imaginary box at the Sanctuary's door so we can 'begin at the beginning with clear mind'. Whether you are new to meditation or indeed are an experienced practitioner, may I humbly suggest you do the same for a little while.

* * *

A long time ago, I had the great fortune to meet and then spend some years practicing with two great masters; an Indian yogi who was a master of *rajayoga* (meditation) and an old Japanese monk who was a master of Soto Zen, considered by some to be the most 'pure' or refined form of meditation. These two extraordinary men guided, encouraged (and sometimes, dragged) me along the Way of Authentic Meditation.

From the beginning, they showed me that meditation is a Journey along an extraordinary Path of awakening, revitalising and renewing the sleeping Self ... the *true* Self that tends to become lost in the dross, drudgery and suffering of a life lived without meaning or inner quietness ... a life spent without any sense of awe and wonderment. They guided me to a Realisation that meditation is *the Way* that so many experiencing the 'missingness' are seeking ... the Way of living life as it is meant to be lived ... *being enthrallingly awake to it, every tiny precious moment of our eternal existence.*

For years, they led me through their pure, authentic 'forms' of meditation ... reacquainting me with the gentle, utterly natural practices of profound and perceptive Nature-skills that every person had in abundance as a child ... beautiful skills that become smothered however, under the conditioned, stifling pressures burdened upon us to *be somebody* ... somebody who fulfils expectations rather than *just being* our truly magnificent Self.

They showed, through both their teaching and their lives, that meditation is the natural Way of reaching back into our innate well of light, insight and wisdom and that, in its practice, true balance, life direction, joy and lasting tranquillity may arise from within like a wonderful, natural cleansing spring. Ultimately, they taught that meditation can take you to a transcendent consciousness wherein your innate kindness, compassion, love, serenity and indeed, enlightenment, are *Realised*. Most importantly perhaps, they taught that Authentic Meditation is a simple and beautiful practice, not just for an elite, wise few of a 'spiritual nature' but ... *for everyone.*

These masterful men revealed to me that Authentic Meditation is simply the process of ... *Awakening.*

* * *

As a gesture of love for my Teachers and respect for their wisdom, I have written this book to pass on the wonderment of their meditation so that you too may practice letting go the unnecessary burdens of life … so that you too may begin to fully experience and cherish each precious moment of *your* magnificent being.

May your Journey *be* …!

Chapter Two

A New Way of Looking at Old Concepts

'The Path is yours alone.'

— *Brahmasamhara*

Many meditation masters admit that they struggle to communicate some aspects or 'concepts' of meditation effectively. They struggle because, they say, the meditative Journey in all its sweet simplicity, in all its converse complexity and its illuminating wonderment, cannot be 'taught'. It cannot even be fully verbalised, only individually 'experienced' by each practitioner *walking the Path for themselves*, even if they have a wise teacher or guide who has already walked the Path.

Indeed, students of meditation may sometimes puzzle over whether their teacher is the wisest person they've ever met or just 'plain crazy'. I remember, on asking my own first Master, the Indian Yogi, Bashayandeh, 'what does this or that mean?', he would often just smile or laugh enigmatically and say, 'you will see' … very annoying to a young man with Nathan-like impatience all those years ago! But then, days, months, sometimes years later, I would have an 'ah-ha' moment … an *awakening*, when I would say to myself, 'so *that's* what he meant!' I had *seen for myself*.

'Seeing for yourself' is, in Authentic Meditation, the only true Path to the eventual pristine clarity of awareness or 'waking up to what is'. Of course, my Teacher knew this perfectly well, so often did not bother with long-winded explanations that I would neither have listened to effectively, nor understood even if I *had* listened. He was really saying, 'the Path is yours alone. I can only guide you.'

The meditative Journey is an individual inner adventure and, in trying to describe or explain many aspects of it, our vocabulary is often just … well, frustratingly inadequate!

Perhaps that explains the contents of a little book on Zen Meditation I found in a back-street bookstore in Melbourne. Flicking open the cover, I discovered that all the pages were blank! My 'ah-ha' moment triggered loud laughter.

But, despite a teacher's difficulty in explaining Authentic Meditation, we *can*, nevertheless, draw on the experience of others who have taken the long Journey. We *can* be guided by their shining a light on the Path, if only to warn us of the potholes, give us a hand over the rough patches or put us back on our feet when we fall off a cliff and land, head-shakingly perplexed, on our backside.

If your guide just laughs at your perplexity, then you *know* you probably have a great and true teacher who simply 'sees' what you cannot yet 'see', while also giving you good-natured encouragement to 'just get up and get on with it.'

I may also struggle to communicate some aspects of the 'extraordinary' Journey with 'ordinary' words. I know, however, that *if you really dare to 'walk the Path' for yourself,* from time to time you too will get the exquisite clarity of 'ah-ha' moments. You will also say, '*now* I know what he was talking about,' because, you will have *seen for yourself* (and then perhaps fallen about laughing as well).

* * *

There are some concepts in meditation that are quite profound (and often profound because of their utter simplicity) for which we are simply 'stuck' with ordinary words in the endeavour to unfold their meaning.

Throughout this book, for example, I frequently use four key words – *'practice', 'letting go'* and *'experiencing'* – all describing 'concepts' that sit at the very core of Authentic Meditation. Now, in just reading those words, you will have had an immediate understanding of them flowing from a lifetime of using them 'normally'. However, in Authentic Meditation, the concepts these particular words convey go way beyond the everyday meaning of them. So in this chapter, I shall just do my best, using ordinary old words, to explain their meditative meaning so at least we start our Journey together from the foot of the same mountain.

The Concept of Practice

'I am not going to teach you anything! There is nothing to learn – only to practice.'

– *Brahmasamhara*

The concept of *practice* is as ancient as the beginning of disciplined activity when individuals or groups needed to develop skills in hunting and gathering food for their very survival. Across thousands of years, humankind has applied the concept of practice to myriad skills from throwing spears at an animal for the cave fire and weaving baskets for fruit collecting, to horsemanship, sword fighting and marksmanship or creating pleasing sounds from beautifully crafted instruments.

It is thought that the Indian monk, Bodhidharma, who introduced Buddhism to China approximately 500 CE, spent time in the renowned Shaolin Temple. There, legend has it, he created the first boxing techniques, about 18 different exercises, to be practiced by the monks who apparently were not the finest physical specimens of men because they spent so much time 'just sitting' in meditation. From these first practice techniques, designed to strengthen muscles, improve breathing and massage inner organs, the art of *Wu Shu* (later known as *Kung Fu*) began. Gradually, over the centuries, these ancient practices developed into various strands of martial arts, many of which still thrive worldwide.

Not only did the monks of the Temple become exemplars of fitness but also, over succeeding centuries, elevated the very concept of practice into the stratosphere of a high art form, practicing eight hours a day, six days a week, which they do to this very day. Interestingly, the same *intensity of focus* they apply to their long physical workouts is also applied to their practice of meditation because 'inner calm' is the spiritual rock on which both these disciplines are built and exist, hand-in-hand.

The 'Ordinary' Concept

Today, the concept of practice is familiar to just about everyone, particularly those involved in such activities as music or sport. For example, I once sat in to observe a master class for young classical guitarists in which a long discussion by an old Spanish master, Juan Martin (who had begun learning flamenco guitar at the age of six) concluded with a wry comment, 'practicing up to eight hours a day will achieve the *desired result*' (but thankfully he added, 'you should stop for a while when it hurts!').

The 'ordinary' concept of practice has several conventional elements. Firstly, there is *repetition*; then the *acquiring of techniques* through repetition; then further, accumulating those techniques to form *knowledge* and finally, the ongoing nourishing of knowledge to *develop mastery*, all of which may well be sprinkled with a little magic dust of 'ritual' and 'ceremony' along the way.

Ritual and ceremony can, in fact, be quite familiar elements in the ordinary concept of practice. The ritual in practice is the 'always' factor or a prescribed pattern of performance that eventually leads to the development of skills which were not previously present. For example, it may be the simple ritual of *always* commencing practice at a specific time for a precise period and *always* commencing with the same exercises. Ceremony, on the other hand, is usually an element of traditional practice or performance handed down from the ancients … such as the respectful bowing to an opponent before and after a bout in martial arts.

All these familiar elements of practice have some resonance in the meditative Journey, particularly in the early stages. For example, just crossing the first stepping-stones of becoming tension-free, or practicing 'right' breathing, involves the *repetition* of exercises to *acquire techniques* to regain (inner) *knowledge* and then, to *redevelop mastery* of these core skills. It could also be said that there is a hint of ancient ritual and ceremony in the way, for example, we may sit in the traditional lotus posture or greet a teacher and other meditators with respectfully bowed head and hands together in the 'prayer' position – the reverential greeting of the *Namaste**.

---

* *Namaste.* Derived from the Nepali and Hindi words *namas* – 'to bow' and *te* – 'to you'. In Nepalese usage, offering the *Namaste* is saying, 'I bow to the Divine within you'.

But ... there is a critical point of difference between our normal concept of practice and our understanding of practice within the meditative context.

Practicing to Achieve a 'Result'

In our usual understanding of practice, no matter what the pursuit or discipline, all practice is undertaken specifically to achieve a result or to fulfil a deliberate purpose. We do it to attain a goal or objective. In effect, the acquiring of skills through practice is *a means to a known or desired end.*

As a young man learning judo, I initially trained and practiced for about three hours every day. The intensity of my practice was openly motivated by the fact that, in many such martial arts, there are 'grades' of accomplishment which are signified by the wearing of different coloured belts. I became laden with *desire* to improve because, to a young man, the idea of being able to show off one's level of mastery in such an overt, ego-boosting way was like a juicy lure to a hungry fish! Then, upon my winning some ego-satisfying, minor regional championships and later, becoming an instructor, I progressively added even more hours to my already-severe practice regimen each week in an effort to satiate a rather blind craving to become a 'master'.

Now, so many years later, I see clearly that my practice then was really a matter of arduous endurance, suffered (including all the broken bones!) *specifically to achieve an end result.* Such unreasonable practice is often the unavoidable and quite foolish consequence of an irrational, inner 'compelling' to 'achieve' ... either for oneself, like me, or – much worse – to please others! I recall the story of a child prodigy being woken at 3AM every morning by his obsessive mother to practice the violin until dawn ... just because it was quiet at that time. The lengths we may go to in order to satisfy empty desire can be quite astonishing. Within the 'normal' understanding of the concept, practice can so easily become a driven, unhappy experience based on *must do* or *should do.*

It is a truth that the ordinary concept of practice is rarely viewed as a facet of a pleasurable discipline *to be enjoyed and deeply experienced in the actual doing of it.*

'Purposeless Practice'

Quite conversely, within the meditative context, the concept of practice is exactly that … 'a facet of a pleasurable discipline to be enjoyed and deeply experienced in the actual doing of it'. Masters of meditation call this *purposeless practice*. An old Zen monk explained this seemingly difficult concept of purposeless practice to his students in this way:

'I began swordsmanship at the age of 12, became a champion at 20, remained undefeated at the age of 30, but reached understanding when I was 50.'

He was telling them that one can practice hard enough to master techniques, achieve skills and even become a champion … and still not have the faintest idea of the core essence of the discipline. In this one story, the old monk offered his students a profound lesson. He was really saying that, in true practice, such as we undertake in Authentic Meditation, 'understanding' can only be fully 'realised' when practice is undertaken with no objective – when the desire for an 'end result' is vanquished.

True mastery of a discipline then, such as achieved in the old monk's 'understanding' or the elite 'inner skills' of martial arts accomplished by the Shaolin monks (or indeed, the profound 'levels' of meditation attained by Zen masters and yogis), can only be achieved by the meditative concept of *practicing for the sake of practicing* in which the exercises you practice and the techniques you acquire become the 'end' in themselves, *not the means to an end*.

My own Zen Master, the wizened and wise Japanese monk, Suni Kaisan, used to say that 'Practice *is* the Path – the Path *is* Practice'. He said that undertaking practice, '*where all is focused on the effort alone*' is, in itself, the Way or the Path that unveils *satori** (pure clarity of mind). 'At that point', he told me, 'you then possess technique or become your meditation'.

Martial arts masters are often asked by their students, 'how long before I become proficient?' The master will often answer, 'about 10 years', but then when asked the next impatient question, 'well, when can we start

---

* *Satori* used in Zen Meditation can also have the meaning of experiencing 'Perfect Presence' or the state of 'No Mind'. The Buddhists also call this exquisite clarity or purity of being, 'Enlightenment' or experiencing the 'Buddha Nature'.

to practice *real* fighting?', he will invariably reply with an enigmatic smile, 'proficiency will now take 20 years!' To the mystified student he may (or may not) then explain … '*the extra 10 years is to get rid of the desire first!*'

The young martial artists are always in a hurry to get to the 'real stuff' such as combat, just as I was in a rush to be graded to higher belts … both no different to seekers starting meditation for the specific purpose of 'getting somewhere' or 'attaining something'. As I suggested to Nathan, the *desire* to achieve a goal with any meditative practice is the very barrier to the achievement of that goal!

It takes time and genuine immersion in practice to *Realise* Suni's wisdom … that Practice itself is the Path. It then takes a unique, meditative 'Way' to illuminate this Path of *purposeless practice.*

Practicing the 'Ordinary' Awakens the 'Extraordinary'

The Way to understanding the concept of purposeless practice is really quite simple. It requires the giving of purely focused attention to 'just this moment' of practicing the 'ordinary'. This means practicing activities that are innately natural to us.

Through giving undiluted, undistracted focus to practicing such 'ordinary' activities as breathing, sitting, eating, drinking, moving and speaking, we can gradually *awaken the extraordinary* – the magnificence of our own essential nature. 'Is that all?', you may well ask. Well … yes, except that the giving of perfect focus to *just sitting* for example (which the Japanese masters call *zazen*), can require a level of mastery considerably beyond most other disciplines.

Meditative practice of the 'ordinary' does require discipline, although perhaps not as much as that of a Shaolin monk! I shall not ask you to dedicate eight hours a day to the Journey but, nevertheless, you must have a highly disciplined intensity of will to give true attention to the task. It is of little value to just dip your toe in the meditative practice pond to 'see if it works for you' or 'to see if you like it'.

However, do not let the need for discipline deter you from taking the first step, for even the greatest and wisest of gurus did not become 'enlightened' overnight, but experienced months, even years of practice (or their metaphorical 40 days and nights in the desert). One great guru, Buddha, said,

> *'no one can purify another ... it is for each of us with our own effort, with diligent striving to walk the Way that leads to blissful freedom. Having this knowledge is freedom ... is equivalent to perfection but it takes time and requires thorough practice and training'.*

Do not be concerned if all this sounds a little different to your 'familiar' concepts. Initially, the novel notion of *purposeless practice* was all very strange to me too as Bashayandeh challenged, tested and 'shook out' all the old comforting concepts I held. But, as you too become absorbed in the lovely naturalness of the meditative exercises in this book, gradually you will also just let go the wanting to 'get there' ... indeed, wanting to get anywhere! As you do, I assure you that the transcending benefits you progressively experience will become a continuing encouragement to make your 'new Way' of practicing ... *practicing the ordinary* ... a valued part of your daily life.

The Concept of 'Letting Go'

'The practice of meditation is to 'unlearn' – to let go all you have learned. Only then can you find your true nature.'

– Brahmasamhara

Students are usually startled when I say in class that 'the practice of meditation is to *unlearn*'. I can almost literally hear a collective, mental chorus of, 'well, why are we here then?' Their wide-eyed response is totally natural of course for, just as our ordinary concept of practice involves an 'end result', so too does our usual life understanding of the concept of *learning*.

We are all imbued with the concept of formal learning or gaining 'mind knowledge' from the very moment we begin to think. In reality, learning is a perfectly valid concept because we need 'knowledge' to conduct the doings of our daily life – to work effectively, to relate to other beings, to master tasks ... in other words, to just 'fit in normally' to our society. But, most of our formal learning is undertaken, purposefully and deliberately, in order to reach a goal or some kind of future 'end point' wrapped in our imagining as a reward, a result, an achievement or a 'success' *out there* ... somewhere beyond our self. It is for those very reasons that virtually all students initially come along to 'learn' meditation.

There is also another kind of learning called 'conditioning' or a process of 'mind-shaping'. In addition to our 'formal' learning we are, quite unconsciously, imbued with data, information, opinions, attitudes, points-of-view, belief systems and expectations through the influence of our environment as well as others in our life. As we grow up, we are exposed to this 'conditioning' from every aspect of our existence: the guidance of parents, the pressure of peers, the influence of teachers and leaders, the belief systems of the culture in which we are raised and even the mind-boggling input of mostly, trash-media ... all intrinsically imprinting 'knowledge' in our brain and all subtly influencing and shaping the 'kind of person' we become.

So, by the time we reach adulthood, we have an overabundance of 'stuff' in our brain that has been loaded aboard either consciously or 'unconsciously'. Most people then continue to soak up and store mental debris throughout their lives, like a burden of ballast they don't jettison until they die.

In Authentic Meditation, however, rather than fill our heads with even more information or 'learning', we do the opposite – *we practice how to 'unlearn' or 'let go' the debris or drivel that has turned our beautiful minds into garbage bags.*

For example, I tell students at the beginning of their Journey that 'you will not *learn* how to relax but rather, practice *letting go tension*'. Similarly, you will not *learn* how to breathe properly but practice *letting go* bad habits of breathing acquired through the stresses and strains of ... just living. You will not *learn* how to 'still your mind', but practice letting go your deeply imprinted habit of continual and chaotic mental chatter (which I call 'unmastered thinking'). In so doing, you will *let go* the main stumbling blocks to again unveiling the truly 'awakened consciousness' that awaits you in that beautiful mind of yours.

This meditative principle of 'letting go' is applied to literally every step on the authentic Path, from the very first moment you set out, to ... well, as far as you wish to travel! Eventually, you can even *let go the concept of letting go*, which the Zen Masters refer to as attaining a state of *No Mind*. By that, the Masters don't mean that one who attains this 'level' of meditation walks around 'blank of brain' but rather, that letting go mental chaos enables life to be lived with what I call *uncluttered consciousness – a glorious state of unchanging awakeness*. Eventually, through mastering the illuminating practice of just *letting go,* you awaken to living as your authentic, loving, compassionate, wise and fulfilled 'being' – your magnificent self!

This is the essence of the different concept of meditative 'letting go' we shall explore through the exercises and practices in this book.

The Concept of Experiencing

'You will begin experiencing unchanging awakeness and clarity of consciousness … the very moment you let go seeking it.'

– Brahmasamhara

I am often asked by new meditators grappling with the 'novel' concepts of *practice* and *letting go*, that 'if we just practice the *ordinary* and there is supposed to be no purpose to it, *what is the purpose of doing it?* What do we actually *do?'* My answer to them is that '*doing,* in your present understanding of it, gradually becomes less and less meaningful because, as you immerse yourself in practice, you begin to shift from the thought of *doing* to the understanding of *experiencing.'*

For example, I mentioned earlier that Authentic Meditation is ultimately about living your life as a serene, deeply aware person of gracious kindness and wisdom. These are not attributes that we attain by *doing* meditation, but existing core qualities that are subtly unfolded *from within* as we *experience* the letting go of all the life debris (from body tension to mind clutter) that has clogged up the 'access Path' to our original, essential nature.

The 'knowledge' of *awakening through experiencing* is a core concept of Authentic Meditation. In fact, the ancient Zen masters spoke of '*experiencing the Way'* and said that, over time, becoming absorbed in the Great Journey may again enable you to *experience* the 'original unity' ... the perfect wholeness of the self that we can reach back into by letting go the life-wasting, illusory pursuits that occupy our 'outer' being most of the time. It is then, the wise ones say, the 'self' actually 'dies'. By this they mean that the 'ego' or I-consciousness is suspended or let go so that being 'whole' or completely 'awakened' again becomes our natural way of existence. They say that, through ongoing meditation, *experiencing* this letting go of the I-consciousness then gradually enables the inner light of the pure being to shine clear and true (didn't a great guru, Jesus of Nazareth, once say, 'do not hide your light under a bushel').

Then, experiencing this inner illumination through practice can enable the meditative one to unveil the reality of the original Self – insight, wisdom, love, kindness and compassion – in a manner previously unimaginable to them (unless for example, they converse with a very young child who would, I am sure, explain it to them ... probably by pointing at a lizard and saying, 'look Daddy, look Mummy!'). I think all little children are Zen monks.

After a lifetime of 'doing' everything for the purpose of attaining a goal of some kind, awakening the 'luminous inner being' by just *experiencing* can be a bit of a difficult concept to grasp. Many struggle with it for a while. I did. But, I assure you that, through simply sinking into your practice, meditation becomes an increasingly elevated experiencing of the very process of 'letting go' until it becomes an uninterrupted, enthralling experience of *just ... being.*

Experiencing meditation in this way is *experiencing life* with a crystal clarity or, so very simply as that same great guru said, 'seeing as a little child sees.'

Finally, the masters tell us that, in reaching a point of *dwelling* in this illumined state as the natural way of 'being', the meditative person is said to actually progress from *experiencing* to *becoming* their meditation or, *becoming* their true wholeness again. At that point, the meditative person becomes an embodiment, or a living expression of, their inner purity ... their compassionate kindness.

They then experience the enlightened state of their true being ... permanently.

* * *

Do I divine among you a few dear readers with puzzled looks and a little furrowing of brows because all such lovely sentiments sound like some Eastern mystical fantasy or airy-fairy fable? I agree, it probably does and long ago, when Bashayandeh occasionally let loose with the magnificent possibilities of the meditative Path in this way, my mind used to offer a little, silent, sceptical *'wahoo, good for you!'* ... until I actually dared to surrender to the 'hard yards' of practice.

Then, tiny step by tiny step, I slowly found that the 'magnificent possibilities' are not fantasy and fable but eminently available to all because, *they are already within us* just waiting to be unveiled and *experienced* after we let go our so-conditioned mental drive for 'doing something only to achieve something'.

All people – you too – at some time, have already experienced the meditative state of uncluttered consciousness, even if only for a moment, or a minute or two. Remember, for example, those times when you let yourself just sink into the deep sense of 'presence', 'completeness' or 'otherness', when you perhaps walked the cool, pre-dawn beach enthralled by the music of the waves, then stopped to watch the sun rising over the sea, all breathtakingly gold and purple. Perhaps it was when 'losing' your 'self' while holding your child or your 'heart-tie' close to you and being *lost in the loving*, or perhaps taking in the delightful aroma of a fresh rose for no reason at all ... those times you surrendered completely to just *experiencing the moment!*

Can you imagine being able to experience such moments more often, or every day or even *all the time?*

This is the unveiling of 'the original unity' or the 'being at one' that, in practicing meditation, arises from that lovely place within, whenever we choose to *just be in the experiencing* rather than 'seeking to do'.

The Desire to 'Measure' Progress

An issue often facing the new meditator is the conditioned desire to measure 'progress'. Many students look for mental milestones to tick off as they are passed and I often hear the cry, 'how do I know it's *working*, or how do I know I'm *getting anywhere?*' because they are still gripping on to the old concept of ... result.

The Zen masters will tell you that you don't know when you are getting anywhere because … *there is nowhere 'to get'*.

However, the experiencing of meditation, the experiencing of letting go, even though it may be called the Way, the Dharma, or the Journey or the Flowered Path as I often call it, or any other fancy name, is not a matter of 'time spent' in order to advance systematically. Rather, it is one of sinking into the Journey … just falling into the practice with willingness and openness of heart in which awakenings, insights and realisations can, and will, just *well up from within*. Sometimes this 'welling up' unfolds slowly, like gentle rain filling a pond but, at others, suddenly and unexpectedly, like opening a floodgate to irrigate a rice field.

These 'experiences welling up' are your 'milestones' and, when they begin to occur in your practice, they will seem to develop a kind of meditative momentum that will simply lift you to increasing levels of *awakeness*.

So, we do not sit and wait for 'something to happen' – we *just sit* – experiencing the practice, knowing that one of the succouring qualities of meditation is that nothing at all 'happens' until you are ready – and much more than you can possibly imagine does when you are.

Chapter Three

Preparing for an Inner Pilgrimage

'All things in the Lila can turn into windows that open on the
hidden Reality. Still so long as one is satisfied with looking
through windows, the gain is only initial; one day one will
have to take up the pilgrim's staff and start out to journey there
where the Reality is for ever manifest and present.'*

– Sri Aurobindo *(The Integral Yoga)*

Having made the decision to 'learn' meditation, or perhaps develop your
current practice, you are about to embark upon the most extraordinary and
meaningful pilgrimage that a human being can make – the pilgrimage *within,*
'where the Reality is for ever manifest and present'. If you so choose, you can now
take up the 'pilgrim staff' for yourself and set off on this inner journey. It *is* a
journey with all the vagaries and ups and downs of any other long journey.

Sometimes you will find the travelling as gentle as a breeze caressing the
heads of wheat in a field. From time to time though, it may be as slippery
as a rain-soaked road in winter and occasionally you may even stumble into
seemingly impossible cliff faces as steep and as breathtakingly difficult to
climb as a Himalayan mountain with its peak lost in forbidding clouds.

But no matter how easy or difficult the Path, it is there; it always has been
and always will be, winding its way to the 'Gate of your Inner Garden'. If

---

*   *Lila* – the cosmic or divine 'play'.

you load your backpack for this pilgrimage with an irrational intensity of will, some raw courage, mindless persistence and a willingness to just keep getting up when you 'fall over' … and dare to continue taking one small step at a time, the Inner Garden of the pure and magnificent Self awaits.

The Path of this greatest of journeys is right there within you, just waiting for you to take the first step.

The Journey

As with all journeys, you need to plan and prepare for this, the 'Great Journey'. Very simply, the better the preparation, the more able you are to travel with purposeful direction. As your travelling may last a few months, a year or perhaps years, or even become a permanent pilgrimage, you need to have some essentials in your 'backpack' that will serve you well. The lovely aspect to all phases of this inner pilgrimage is that no expenditure, other than time and commitment, is required – no passport, no tickets – in fact, as the masters mischievously hint, *no destination*, so no forward accommodation bookings! But good preparation will be of immense value to you so, in this chapter, I shall help you 'pack your bags' with the essentials so you are *ready*.

Creating Your Own Practice Sanctuary

When most people think of 'meditating', they usually get a mental picture of monks in a monastery, or an old yogi in an *ashram* or even a little group of blissful, angelic-looking people sitting in the middle of a forest with their white robes turned golden by the filtered rays of sunshine – all very lovely and poetic.

The reality is that you can practice even the most profound levels of Authentic Meditation *wherever you are*. There is utterly no need to find a monastery, an *ashram* or a sun-bathed forest (although you can meditate in such exotic places if you really want to!). I have so many students who have travelled the world looking for the one perfect place with the one perfect guide. I usually ask them, as I did Nathan, 'have you tried … *just sitting?*'

There is a well-known saying, 'when you are *ready*, the right place and the right teacher will appear … from within'. I then tell students that, when they tire of running all over the place like little lizards on a sunny day, *just sitting* (*zazen*) is 'like buying your ticket for the last spiritual bus leaving town!'

But, particularly in the early stages of the Journey, you do need a place for your 'just sitting'. So, the first essential is a Practice Sanctuary of your own – a quiet place, a personal space to which you can retreat and where you will not be interrupted. You only need enough room to lie full length but it should be a space which can be set up as permanently 'yours' for your meditation.

To begin with, choose a space indoors to reduce external distractions. I can divine my students smiling at this point, as our inner-city Sanctuary in Sydney is virtually under the airport flight path, 200 metres from a fire station and 100 metres from the Italian coffee-shop hub of the whole area. I tell them that, after a few weeks, they won't even notice the sounds of jets and fire engines or the aroma of roasted coffee. The freshlings always give me a dubious look but, sure enough, after a few weeks, there they are, invariably *just sitting* attentively without distraction!

However, it is preferable to start in a quiet place with gentle, natural light such as your bedroom, study, or a quiet corner in your living room where you can practice after others have left for the day.

If you have a hard floor, be kind to your tailbone and provide yourself with a comfortable flat cushion and a mat or spare piece of carpet big enough for you to lie down. If possible, leave them permanently in place, so that the space gradually becomes your little 'haven' for retreat. I have long used a lovely 'teaching mat'. It's just a small piece of Persian carpet. When I originally went looking for a needed new mat, I told the grizzled, old Iranian shopkeeper the purpose for it. He hand-selected a small, but beautiful off-cut he deemed suitable and just gave it to me. With a beaming, toothless smile he said, 'use it well'. Gratefully, I have.

Just about everyone asks, 'what about music?' Background music or quiet sounds *can* create a pleasantly soothing, mood-setting 'white noise' that initially, is much less distracting than the clamour in the streets. But the sounds you choose should have relative 'monotone-ness' such as monks chanting, continuous waves of the sea, the Japanese shakuhachi flute or the ringing sweet sound of Tibetan bowls being played. As your practice grows, your ability to melt into inner quietness will gradually lessen the need for background sound … until you eventually require none.

Incense? Yes, if you wish. Fragrant aromas are therapeutically calming so incense is a lovely optional extra. However if you have a breathing condition such as asthma or emphysema, the drifting smoke of incense may be distressing. Perhaps you might substitute it with a little bowl of scented oil (patchouli, for example) or burn an incense stick half an hour before practice so you can enjoy a lingering pleasantness without direct smoke.

Why not the beauty of a single flower in a simple vase as well? At the Meditation Sanctuary the Sanctuary's 'Mother', Janene, often scatters rose petals or places flowers around my mat and the Hall. I always have a handful of polished river stones arranged close by, just because they too are beautiful.

It really doesn't matter how you adorn your meditation place … just keep it simple and make it feel like *your* Sanctuary.

Over time, you will notice two effects of having your own haven for meditation. Even after the early exercises, your special place with its personal items will begin to feel welcoming as you associate it with increasingly pleasant experiences. Soon enough, you are likely to begin looking forward to going there rather than saying to yourself, 'oh, I *must/should* do my practice.' Later on your Journey and as your meditation develops, you will let go the 'need' to adorn your Sanctuary as you realise that all you need for 'just sitting' is a place to … just sit! Eventually, you will be able to let go your need for a 'created' Sanctuary as you awaken to the Realisation that you can meditate anywhere – because the *real* Sanctuary is within you. But for now, create a special sitting place to enjoy your practice … until you have travelled past the need for it.

Right Clothing

No special outfit or uniform is required for meditation. All you need is loose-fitting clothing – an old tracksuit or something similar. Some meditators, both men and women, wear Eastern-style, inexpensive garments such as sarongs and Indian cotton shirts because they are specifically designed to be loose, cool and comfortable, particularly in hot climates – and they are. Such clothing is perfect.

When teaching, I mostly wear a large-sleeved shirt and the ideal, inexpensive Thai fisherman's pants, or a longer, loose robe such as those worn by many Middle Eastern people, simply so I can still breathe and walk after hours of sitting on the floor with crossed legs.

In winter, don't wear layers of jumpers and coats. Best to wrap yourself warmly in a thick blanket, shawl or robe, again for comfort. Beanies are good for head warmth. One young student, Patricia, pulls a beanie down over her eyes for all meditations – instant inner Sanctuary! When sitting for your practice, you should also remove any tight-fitting objects, including your watch, belt, heavy rings, jangling jewellery and, of course, your shoes because they can all be distracting and uncomfortable.

Comfort versus Discomfort

For effective meditation, physical comfort is important. There are, however, many teachers from various 'schools' of meditation who suggest that discomfort, even pain, keeps you 'focused'. They even encourage you to 'sit through' pain so you can 'experience your bodily sensations and emotions'.

Authentic Meditation teaches exactly the opposite ... for very sound reasons.

It is just not possible to give dedicated focus to becoming deeply calm of body and truly still of being if you are worried about your legs going numb, or if your back is aching or if you are shivering with cold.

You should never allow a teacher of any aspect of yoga or meditation to encourage you to tolerate pain as part of your practice.

As my father would say, such teachers have the 'bull by the proverbial horns'. It is not rocket science to understand that pain is the body's way of telling you that something is lacking in the wellbeing department. Pain is your body-friend, your in-built 'early-warning system' telling you to 'do something' to alleviate the physical stress it is suffering. Do not ignore your lovely body – listen to it carefully.

Later, when you commence your meditative exercises, I shall guide you in the gentle, natural way of alleviating any discomfort *before* it becomes a distraction so you can attain, and maintain, true stillness of being.

Creating the Time to Meditate

I often ask students before a class, 'how's your practice going?' A frequent reply is, 'well ... I am not practicing as much as I should. I just can't seem to find the time!' As you may experience the same difficulty now and then, it is important to look at the aspect of 'time', very simply because without some of yours given to practice, *there is no Journey!*

Some potential students have concern about actually beginning meditation because of a preconceived idea of how much time they think practicing will, or *should*, take. Because they have heard stories of old, bearded yogis sitting in mountain monasteries for a large part of their lives and not doing much else, they think that meditation is particularly time-consuming and, of course, they feel that they are already 'time-poor', busily occupying every single moment of their waking life. 'Doing' meditation, to them, is potentially just another burdensome load in already wearying days.

Although I won't send you off to sit on a mountain, you do need to find a small window of time *daily* for practice and technique development, *particularly* if your life is choked with 'busyness'. I'm yet to meet a person who, with a true willingness to begin meditation, has not been able to create some personal time, even if it means sacrificing another 'activity'. Mostly, creating some meditating time is just a matter of simple discipline – rising a little earlier or through positive action such as having one less cup of coffee each day.

A classic time creator used by the Zen Masters is the principle of *get up when you wake up*. If you think about it, how much time do we often 'lose' lying snuggled in bed (yes, particularly if it is cold), becoming burdened in our mind with the imagined load of the day ahead, *before we even arise?*

As a boy, I was raised on a huge property, literally in the middle of 'nowhere' in outback Australia, a place so dry and stricken that we used to count the number of acres per sheep, rather than the number of sheep per acre as they do in fertile country. In winter, it was cold with below-zero mornings. We didn't have internal heating out there. We didn't have heaters. In fact, we didn't have electricity – just the kitchen wood-stove.

Rising each morning wasn't easy but I had to, for there was always work to be done before school. I was seven years old when I developed a little 'getting-out-of-bed trick' of counting to 27 and a half. When I had slowly counted all the way to the 'half', the discipline was to throw off the blankets then run to light the stove.

With their *wake up, get up* policy, the Zen monks have mastered that discipline to a fine art but, of course, without counting, *just getting up!* I regard that practice as one of the gifts of my life because, over the years, it has given me so much more … *time!* You can do it too (you *do* get used to it after a while) and there's your practice time created, saved and waiting for when you choose to use it each day.

Occasionally, I meet dear souls who won't allow themselves to 'find' adequate time for meditation because they fear the 'unknown scary things' that they *think* they may discover about themselves in just being … quiet. Having feelings of trepidation or doubt at the beginning of the Journey is a totally natural response for students on meditation 'L' plates and is a commonly experienced disquiet. In an excellent book, called '*what is the Dharma?*, an English Buddhist, Sangharakshita, wrote:

> *'It is perfectly valid, indeed desirable that one should doubt – one shouldn't take things on trust … This doubt is really an unwillingness to find out about things. You don't take the trouble to find out about the truth because, to put it bluntly, you don't want to. If you find out the truth you may have to put it into practice and that is going to mean change – by which it is natural to feel threatened. And one strategy one may use to defend oneself against change is to raise all sorts of unnecessary difficulties and objections. Underneath it all is the desire to keep things vague and unclear. If one allows to emerge a clear vision of how things are, one is going to have to act, one is going to have to change.'*

He is tough, but right. To me however, *that is the sheer exhilaration of the meditative Journey – the very opportunity you provide for yourself to 'act' and to 'change'.* If you are one who feels some apprehension before the Journey, let me reassure you that meditation is the gentlest of 'Ways' to let go all the barriers to an awakened, exhilarating engagement with your life.

When you begin to really experience your meditation, you will slowly awaken to just how much time (and life) you waste in a typical day on meaningless activity. The good news is that, as you do awaken to the time-wasting miscellany littering your daily doings, you just naturally begin to cast it all off, as if shedding an unwanted load. Students so often tell me they are amazed that, *the more they practice, the more 'free' time they seem to have … to practice!*

It was Gandhi, an avid meditator, who once looked at his schedule for the day only to find it impossibly busy. He is reported to have said, *'oh dear, today is so busy I shall have to meditate for two hours instead of one'*. One intolerably busy Sanctuary student, a hospital doctor, so rid his days of the 'life-wasting unnecessaries' that he now meditates twice a day – an hour in the morning before operating and again in the evening. Gradually, just as he did, you too will realise that your meditation time is so beneficial that you not only make it a priority each day, but discover that, in ridding yourself of life-wasting activities, you just seem to have so much 'spare' time for other meaningful activities. 'In this way,' I tell my students, 'you are able to experience four lives in one … without any frenetic rushing about at all!'

So, do as Gandhi did … *create some time* for your Journey. Then set out with light heart and let yourself look forward to every step of it.

Time, Length and Frequency of Practice

'There are no shortcuts – there is no other Way.'

Suni Kaisan

When to Practice?

Realistically, you can practice at any time of day or night. Many people prefer the early morning because their meditation 'sets the tone' for the rest of their day. Throughout the course of my own practicing, I have tended to prefer the early morning, more often than not starting at about 4AM. At that time, the world's pre-dawn silence, before the awakening of the birds, before the bustle of neighbours preparing for work and before the city's unwrapping itself from darkness, is a precious time of earthly clarity and stillness … just perfect for quiet practice.

However, you may be one who prefers to 'come down' from the inner demolition of another busy day by practicing in the evening. This too, can be beneficial, particularly for people who have sleeping difficulties. Others find that *just sitting* quietly in a park for 20 minutes at lunchtime is calming and restful.

The best way to discover the right time for you is to try different times of the day until you feel you have it 'right'. There are no rules ... as long as you *do* practice.

For How Long?

You will see that I nominate an approximate time for each of the early exercises. For the first few weeks or so, I recommend that your whole practice session lasts about 15 minutes. Then, when you are ready, begin to increase this by about five minutes each week. The ideal practice time to work towards is 45 minutes to one hour, which I consider sufficient for most of the Authentic Meditation techniques in this book. However, only use my suggestions as a guide until you find, and settle into, your own 'time rhythm' ... which you soon will. One dear student, Erika, found it hard to settle in her early practice for more than a few minutes. 'But', she wrote to me, 'I am making sure that I celebrate the fact that I have even come to the mat'. With that spirited attitude, she already has a foot firmly planted on the Path!

How Often?

Well, there is no 'I'll leave it up to you' on this one! As often as I remember (annoyingly frequently for some), I tell my dear freshlings that one of the most important words they will hear in the Sanctuary is 'practice!' The Journey can only be trekked by you and you alone and if you do not practice *every single day*, you are wasting your time. Life will go on, hand to brow, exactly as it was.

The level of your discipline to practice equates exactly to the quality of the benefits that you will experience – or not!

However, I do understand that sometimes life can unavoidably 'get in the way' for a day or even a week or more. If you lose the practice plot for whatever reason, just resume as soon as you can and rebuild your consistency. A very wise old Zen monk who lived and taught hundreds of years ago said, 'if you need to start 1000 times ... then start 1000 times!' I know that in my early practice alone, I got to at least 1003.

Remember Suni Kaisan's advice, 'the Path *is* Practice ... Practice *is* the Path. There are no shortcuts – *there is no other Way!*'

Letting Go Expectation

So often, people start out on their meditative Journey with high hopes and masses of expectations like excited children heading off on holidays. Their hopes and expectations quite often arise from their misconceptions of meditation – and then they become disappointed that the reality is different to or 'harder' than that which they had – well … expected!

I remember a powerful lesson given to me by my master, Bashayandeh. After his accepting me as his student, I went along to his little '*ashram-house*' as often as I could. One afternoon, I knocked on the door as usual and, on hearing 'come in', removed my shoes respectfully and opened the door to find him in the centre of the room. That afternoon though, instead of his resting quietly in meditation or reading, as I usually found him, he looked like a praying mantis on stilts … all arms and legs. His eyes were closed, his legs crossed in a full lotus position, but … his arms were stretched downwards holding his body in the air with its full weight distributed on his fingertips – the only parts of him touching the ground!

When you first see someone in this difficult *hathayoga* position, it is astonishingly impressive. As I had never seen such a yoga position, I sat in silent awe, expecting him to complete at any second. But he stayed balanced on his fingertips for another 10 minutes – without the slightest trembling. Then he completed, flexed his arms and fingers, and nodded a greeting.

Rather wide-eyed I said, 'what were you doing?' to which he replied, 'talking to my guru'. I slowly, warily, looked around the *empty* room whereupon he doubled over with laughter until his head was almost on the floor. He didn't explain his answer – just moved straight into his teaching for the day. I began to wonder whether my teacher was just a little 'crazy' but then, as I mentioned earlier, it is sometimes impossible to tell whether a true guru is the wisest or wackiest person you will ever meet.

It took me months of pondering to realise that his 'praying mantis' trick had all been a lovely performance to teach me a lesson about expectation – or, more accurately, *to have none*. Dear Teacher had waited until I knocked on the door before assuming the difficult posture and his 'talking to his guru' answer was a 'nonsense charade' – *deliberately* confusing.

But it was a lesson with a *wisdom gift* buried in it whenever I was ready to accept it. With his seemingly unreasonable answer, Bashayandeh was really saying, 'what did it look like I was doing? *See what really is – not what you think is.*' Of course, I was conditioned to *expect* him to always sit in his 'normal' posture and to *expect* clear and 'rational' answers to my idiotic questions! Being aware of that, my wise teacher had pulled the 'expectation rug' out from under me and metaphorically thrown it over my head!

This is an *awakening* strategy often used by Zen Masters, particularly those of the ancient *Rinzai* school. Masters will give seemingly ridiculous answers to a student's often-silly questions or, more usually, ask mind-baffling questions to which there appear to be no 'right' answers. These strategies are called *koans**.

For example, a classic *koan* question is, 'what is the sound of one hand clapping?' A classic *koan* answer was given by the Zen Master, Zhao Zhou Congshen (about 800 CE) in response to a monk's question, 'what is the meaning of Bodhidharma's coming from the west?' The master's answer was, 'the cypress tree in the courtyard' … as startlingly irrelevant, but equally attention-focusing, as Bashayandeh's answer to me of 'talking to my guru'.

In using the infinitely puzzling *koans*, the Master creates what is known as the 'Great Doubt' or the 'Great Inquiry' within a student's mind … the exact opposite to conditioned expectation. The student is invited to give his entire being to finding an 'answer' or a 'solution' to the baffling problem of a posed question or to unravelling the meaning of a seemingly unrealistic answer to his question.

However, the *koan* is not a puzzle so it *cannot be solved* … but the new student is not aware of this. The process of 'awakening' through pondering a *koan* can therefore be torturously slow and mind-bendingly difficult. For a while, the student will return frequently to the Master with (what he thinks is) a well-reasoned, *expected* 'right' answer, only to be told to 'go away and try again'. His effort to provide the right answer will eventually exhaust his mind and, after months of rejection, he may want to just give up and, more than likely, go to the master, utterly fed up and even wanting to quit the monastery altogether.

---

* There are thousands of recorded *koans* but only about 240 are thought to be derived from original masters.

I know a student who once spent weeks trying to 'solve the unsolvable' and, eventually, in exhausted frustration, packed his meagre belongings, went to his master, and told him in no uncertain terms that the *koan* he'd been given was 'rubbish' and as a parting gesture, yelled dismissively that the answer was 'probably a *^%#^* wet frog! ... whereupon, the master smiled gently and said, 'now you are ready for another *koan*.'

Sheepishly on the way back to my room, I was pondering an assault on the new mind-puzzle when I stopped, went back to Suni Kaisan and said with a grin, 'Master, I don't suppose the answer to the new *koan* is also a wet frog'. 'Aagghh,' he said, 'you have not solved the *koan* ... you have dissolved it! You are now free of your Mind. You are ready to go on'.

The *koan* no longer existed – there was only the teacher, this student and the present moment – life being experienced without thought, 'logical' reasoning or *expectation. The master's wisdom-demand had been for the disciplined effort, not the answer.*

The dissolving of a *koan* can, for some, be intuitive, rapid and sometimes, so potent that it may well be the moment of culminating clarity or the 'moment of enlightenment', when the mind's imprisoning attachment to conditioned dogma, belief systems, opinions and illusory expectations is let go forever. The student is 'hit' by, or grasps, the fundamental truth of 'what is'. This is called the Realisation of a *koan* (as distinct from the interpretation of a *koan*).

An ironic, defining feature of such a Realisation is that it is ... unexpected!

Sometimes, a student may just 'happen' upon a perceptive response (such as 'a wet frog') that 'seems' to dissolve the *koan*. However, one wise old master said that 'even though that is true, *if you do not know it within yourself, it is of no good to you*'. In other words, a student cannot feign or fake a response, because the truly wise teacher will seek further 'evidence' of the student's genuine awakening by the way the student has 'live experience' of the *koan* in daily life through his being mindfully present, having let go the mental clutter that expectation allows to proliferate like weeds in an unkempt garden.

Although my own teaching became more influenced by the Soto school of Zen (awakening by *just sitting – zazen*), I do mention *koans* from time to time when discussing the different teaching ways offered by the great teachers and masters. After one such discussion in which I mentioned the *koan*, '*What is the sound of one hand clapping?*', I received a letter from a very dear student, Beckie. She wrote in part …

> '… *so anyway, on Friday morning (first day of a long weekend), I got up and went for a walk to the park. I was walking along, and felt a pang of the empty, lonely feeling I often get when I am alone for extended periods and perceive that everyone else (except me) is all jolly and together and having a fabulous time. Quickly, it was replaced by a feeling of happiness, almost excitement at the next four days of entertaining myself, and just "being" with myself. I thought – hmmm – what is this new, accepting and pleasant feeling? And then I thought – this is "the sound of one hand clapping!" (meaning, to me – being alone and contented rather than empty and lonely). Out of nowhere it came.*'

Oh yes! Beckie's extraordinary experience was, in effect, an intuitive and powerful realisation of a *koan*. In one awakening moment, she 'unexpectedly' moved from the unspoken, rhetorical *koan* ('why aren't I as happy as others?') to becoming present in the moment, the very 'purpose' of all *koans*. In realising the *koan*, her 'state of being' shifted to being 'alone and contented' rather than 'empty and lonely'. (I must remember to tell her that the 'it' that 'came out of nowhere' was a 'wet frog'!)

Now, if you have puzzled your way through all that, I hope you find *your* meditative practice riddled with lots of 'wet frogs' and the occasional 'unexpected' …

* * *

It is when you sink into your practice *without expectation* that you will notice little things beginning to just 'happen'. For example, one day, for no reason at all, you may just become aware that you have been calm for a whole hour (and that's not really 'you', is it) or you haven't yelled at anyone for a whole morning (and that's *really* not 'you' either) or you've not had a negative thought for the last 10 minutes (and that's *definitely* not the usual 'you') – or that you are sleeping better or seem to have more energy, and so on – times 1000 individual possibilities.

This is a letter I received from a student who had been practicing for only nine weeks, but virtually *every day*. The 'every day' bit is, of course, the key to the 'consequences' of which she writes.

> *Dear Brahm,*
>
> *'I am meditating daily (I have only missed a few days in the last nine weeks) for about 10 minutes per day. My original aspiration for meditation was to calm down. However, I was unprepared for all of the additional consequences of simply being somewhat calmer. The effects have been subtle and profound. They include:*
>
> - *being less reactive to daily stresses*
> - *being nicer to my husband and children*
> - *liking people more*
> - *better communication with people*
> - *quietly happier*
> - *taking more risks with my work because I feel less anxious and more confident – therefore doing good work that I am proud of*
> - *better insight – letting go of rumination. Somehow, I have a bit of distance on things and can look at them with more detachment*
> - *feeling more connected with the world where I feel I am making a positive contribution although I have not changed any activities other than meditating.*
>
> *Although we have looked at many meditative techniques, I am still getting used to the steps to meditation and am now managing to meditate for perhaps one minute after relaxation, breathing, mantra* etc. But I have taken your advice and just will plod away daily. I am still amazed I can get so much from 10 minutes a day.*
>
> *Margo*

---

* A *mantra* is a word or phrase recited repeatedly, either silently or vocalised, for the purpose of quieting thoughts, thus bringing the mind to singular focus.

Under a great deal of stress when she first came to the Sanctuary, Margo was naturally quite amazed with the unexpected 'benefits'. She need not have been because she had clearly grasped the two most important essentials for an effective Journey. Firstly, she was practicing daily and, secondly, she was 'just plodding away', not expecting a 'result'. She was simply *practicing for the sake of practicing.*

The last word on 'letting go expectation' goes to a new student who confided that, for his whole life, he had found it difficult to 'just sit still' and indeed, at the beginning of his Journey, he was the class 'wriggler'. I told him that, if he just becomes absorbed in his practice, he would soon amaze himself with his stillness. He grinned broadly and said '*I really look forward to that – of course, without expectation!*' Humour on the Journey is also a necessity and I suspect that student Calvin's gentle wit is the mark of one who will travel his Path well (and, sure enough, a few weeks later, he was *just sitting* in stillness – quite perfectly).

So, don't *expect* to feel 'transformed' after every practice session as if you've had an injection of wellbeing! The meditation Journey can be long or short, gentle or turbulent. But, the 'travel secret' is to *give undivided attention to one step at a time* – with no thought of the next. The Path will surely unfold beneath your feet as you walk.

The Journey is Yours Alone

Authentic Meditation is Natural

Some folks believe that meditation is a mystical practice based on strange philosophies, concepts and rituals and that its practice will interfere with their mind. They sometimes even feel that a teacher may have power over them and that they may relinquish 'who they really are'.

None of this is true or valid in Authentic Meditation.

But misconceptions are rife. For example, a respected member of the clergy once asked me quite innocently, 'do *you people* practice black magic?' With my heart in jest mode, I smilingly answered, 'oh no, but – do *you people?*' Still can't understand why old thunder-face walked away without a pleasant farewell. Now, dear reader, if you don't have a packet of humour in your backpack, go put one in please – you will surely need it!

If you are guided by a genuine master of Authentic Meditation, you will quickly discover that all exercises and practices are purely natural. Your entire practice regimen will quite simply involve working on (and eventually mastering) the letting go of tension, natural breathing and quieting the babbling mind, all followed naturally by just being deeply 'present' within the subsequent Serene Stillness ... which is called *meditating!* You then practice taking these mastered skills into your life by being mindfully present as you attend and tend each moment of experiencing your magnificent existence.

These are all natural skills in which you were accomplished as a child. Not much black magic in that!

As to relinquishing yourself to the 'power' of a teacher, again, a true master will never ask to be followed or worshipped or require obedience to his or her ideas, concepts or philosophies (which the truly wise ones have transcended anyway). Conversely, authentic teachers, whether they are Zen monks, yogis, or even 'self-realised' advanced practitioners, will all tell you that their task is just to shine a little light on your Path which you alone can walk. The only 'power' involved should be the open sharing of their wisdom and the offering of their teaching and guidance with gentleness, insight, love, compassion and kindness – because, through their own Journey, *that's what they have 'become'.*

I unwittingly create a little 'stir' in class from time to time by pointing out that *not one person who has ever lived has had, or currently has, 'powers' of any kind greater than any other person who lives or who has lived.* Some people do indeed 'become wiser' and may even 'become enlightened' or be Bodhisattvas (enlightened teachers) but the truth remains that they are all ordinary people, the same as you, the same as everyone else ... and they are all magnificent people, the same as you, the same as everyone else. Those who seem 'different' have simply spent years of meditative practice 'reawakening' or 'unveiling' their innate 'real power' of compassionate love – as everyone can choose to begin to do at any time.

Many seekers nevertheless attribute mystical powers to their teachers (whether they be gurus, yogis or Zen Masters) and some even credit mind-readers, mediums, clairvoyants and suchlike out there in the neverland of the spiritual fringe, with 'gifts' above and beyond the ordinary. They do this because they *really want* the others to have special powers such as so-called levitation or astral travelling (as in the spirit leaving the body) or mind reading or getting messages from the 'dearly departed' or diagnosing illnesses from auras, or whatever. In the seeker's mind, some people's allegedly being able to exhibit such magical curiosities or 'powers' would prove that there *is* more to life than their perhaps dreary, painful experience of it. They are illusioned into the belief that such practices would be a 'true sign' of deepest spiritual possibility.

Such beliefs, of course, stem from truly lovely ancient myths, created long ago with then very limited medical and scientific knowledge, in an effort to try and explain, or give meaning to, our consciousness of existence (just as we are still doing today). Holding on to a belief that such myths are true, provides consolation to those needing desperately to believe in something 'other' – *something out there*. So, the myths themselves are perpetuated and, over time, have gathered and even maintained, a dusty credibility to this day.

Let me tell you a little story to illustrate how some lovely ancient myths can still hold sway in modern times. A young man came to me after class one evening. Shyly, he revealed that he had come to meditation with the express hope that, one day, I might teach him to levitate (the beautiful myth of being able to 'float up' off the floor through harnessing 'energy' by sheer willpower and meditative intensity).

Peter really wanted me to be able to levitate because, if he could learn it, he felt he would have tangible evidence of 'something other than the ordinary'. When I told him it would not be possible and said 'sorry about that', I could see from the little curl of his lip that 'sorry' wasn't good enough. He was quite petulant with disappointment. He clearly felt very let down by his Teacher.

'Nah', I went on, 'all that stuff is too easy. If' … I lowered my voice secretively and leant towards him a little … 'if you are really *that* interested and you want to try something truly magical – unimaginably difficult – almost impossible, even for a bright guy like you – something that only the "best of the best" can do … how about beginning to practice a power far, far greater than levitation, one that few have ever been able to even grasp.'

His eyes lit up like a Christmas tree with excitement. Obviously, I'd just been holding back on 'the real stuff'.

'And what's that?', he stammered. I replied, 'what if we practice the ultimate power?' ... his eyes widened further '... the power to be able to love unconditionally, to have compassion for no reason at all and to show kindness always and to everyone ... because you can't help it? That is a power that makes levitation look like kiddies-in-the-sandpit stuff.'

His face went completely blank for a few moments and then, to his credit and my joy, his petulance disappeared as quickly as it had appeared, and he suddenly beamed widely and kept just ... grinning. He didn't say anything because there was nothing to say ... he had really 'got it'. After a little while, he just stood up and, still smiling, said, 'see you next week'.

Peter stayed the course and became committed to *just practicing*. In so doing, he began to experience the truth of some of the lovely old myths that float around meditation ... such as, for example, the truth that levitation really means the uplifting of one's true being of love and kindness ... not flying up into the air. Peter's *awakening* had been a big one and his *real* Journey began at that moment.

Quite simply though, holding on to such dear old myths and beliefs supplants the need for the seeker to courageously contemplate *within* for the truth, as all the great gurus did ... *and told us to do*. Holding on replaces the spiritual hard work of *letting go* the carapace of conditioning and so permanently clouds the possibility of divine freedom available to all who dare to practice 'seeing for themselves'.

The true teacher, master or mystic (one who sees what *is* with unconditioned clarity) knows that his sacred task is to guide you in the letting go. Over time, he will become your Journey-companion, and may even be a dear and most beloved one, as Bashayandeh and Suni were to me. He might sometimes confuse you and even annoy you. Sometimes you'll think he's crazy and, for a period (maybe a lifetime), you might even regard him as *your* Master or *your* Teacher.

Be assured however, that the authentic teacher will always be guiding you wisely from a 'step' behind rather than saying 'follow me or worship me'. If you are asked to 'follow' a teacher, rather than being offered his wisdom to smooth your own Journey, then you are in the wrong place.

The English Buddhist nun, Tenzin Palmo, who spent 12 years meditating in a Tibetan cave (alone), speaks with deep understanding of teachers. She says …

> *'People can put off practice forever, waiting for the magic touch that is going to transform them – or throwing themselves on someone charismatic without discriminating whether or not they are suitable. We should just get on with it. If you meet someone with whom you have a deep inner connection, great, if not the dharma (Path) is always there.'**

Even the Buddha himself, great guru that he was, never demanded that his Teachings just be believed or trusted as the 'True Way'. He taught that each must see the Journey as 'yours to swelter at the task'. The Buddha wanted each *sadhak* (student of the Path) to *test his teachings*, not just blindly follow them. The mark of the genuine teacher is that they will tell you exactly the same: *test their teachings with your own experiencing of the Path.*

So, in practicing Authentic Meditation, know that no-one can interfere with your thinking, or create thoughts or ideas in your mind that you do not wish to have. *You* are always the 'owner' of your meditation and can end any exercise or meditation at any time you choose, whether in your sanctuary or in an external place being guided by a teacher. You are always your own Meditation master so never follow any instruction that is against your own wisdom or will.

The experiencing of the Journey is yours alone – and your inner being is always your safe space in which to practice and to peacefully enjoy.

'I Want It Now'

No-one has actually said to me, 'I want it now' in such a blunt way, but so many come to meditation literally jumping out of their skin with urgency, wanting to 'find out, fix it and live happily ever after – and by about Tuesday next if that's all right with you, Teacher!' Or, they come wanting to 'seek, know and grow' but, again, impatiently sooner rather than later. I meet many 'Nathans' (perhaps with not such exalted aspirations).

---

* From *Cave in the Snow* by Vicki Mackenzie, published by Bloomsbury.

I have to admit to you that, as a young man of 19, when I stumbled into 'meditation', I was the classic 'I-want-it-now' student. For many moons, my eagerness became a rock-solid barrier on my Journey – although I didn't see it until I hit it head on, travelling fast. Under Bashayandeh's vastly experienced guidance, I had quite rapidly become an accomplished practitioner of lots of lovely exercises and techniques and was just about bursting with pride over my very obvious 'progress'.

From the beginning, of course, Bashayandeh perceived my young pride in full flight and let me bustle busily onwards for a while until one day, farewelling me at the door, he said, 'you are doing very well.' which, in my ego-high mind, simply underlined just how easy this 'Journey thingo' really was and how lucky Master B was to have such a good student! Then he said, 'Now, I want you *not* to practice for two months. To you, meditation is like rote learning – you are highly accomplished in all the practical work … but *you understand nothing!* When you come back … *if* you come back, we shall start all over again.'

How's that for an ego-thrashing! Chastened, humbled and, yes, angry, I went away and did as he said – reluctantly. Why two months 'detention' I wondered daily? Well, I finally worked out that it was his 'wisdom way' of firstly pulling a young man out of his smug, self-opinionated comfort zone by making him feel agitated for weeks, while also giving him adequate time to realise (hopefully) that his progress was stuck on a big hook of pride and impatience. He needed instead to be deeply focused on just 'drinking in the wisdom' and practicing without ego-driven goals. When I went back, cap-in-hand after 'serving my time', he looked at me intensely and, after a moment, just smiled. I think he divined that I wasn't at all humbled – I was absolutely on-my-knees mortified! *My* Journey had really begun.

The important thing to remember is that there is no 'right' pace, there is no 'right' time for it all to 'happen' and there is no 'right' Path. There is only *your* time, *your* pace and *your* Path. So aspire not to be in a big hurry or rush. Do not force your progress, as meditation is not a contest or a race with time limits or goal posts. In meditation, you cannot force your mind to mastery – you soothe and calm it, *allowing your natural mastery to well up from within.*

Sangharakshita, in the lovely book I mentioned earlier, also wrote,

> '... it is the fact that people who are cheerful and ready to go step-by-step do actually go much faster and more surely than those who are impatient and in haste. Small beginnings are of utmost importance and are to be cherished and allowed with great patience to develop.'

So, the collective message of the wise, dear reader, is ... have patience!

Being Fit to Practice

Many folks turn to meditation at the Sanctuary because they are suffering physically, emotionally, psychologically or spiritually. Somehow they are missing their wellbeing. Over the years, I have observed that the dedicated practice of meditation helps so many dear souls 're-find' some degree of their wholeness and, for many more, their *entire* wellbeing. Nevertheless, in setting out on the Journey, there can be some old habits and behaviours that make 'travelling' a little harder than it need be. So I've jotted down a few more little 'hints' that you may find helpful in smoothing the Way as you begin to leave footprints on your Path.

Weariness

Firstly, when you practice, it is best that you are not over-tired because, if you are, you will almost certainly fall asleep. If you do, that's fine because your body is telling you that you need rest. Best though, to be alert and rested, so you can reap the full benefit of a practice session. Gradually, however, you will find the practice of meditation extremely energising and the need to drift into sleep during exercises will ebb away.

Stimulants and Food

Avoid stimulants such as coffee or strong tea before practicing. They will make your mind 'excited' and your body will be even more tense than usual with a stimulant on board. Similarly, physical exercise can give you a 'good-feeling high' (which is why it is recommended for people suffering anxiety and depression). As it is best not to be too stimulated before meditation, leave your 'body work' until after your practice or for another time.

'Should I eat or not eat before a practice?' – another very common question. The answer depends on the length of your meditation. If it is a short practice (say, five to 15 minutes), it doesn't really matter. For a longer meditation, you should not be 'starving' because you will be distracted by a grumbling tummy and a mind hungering for food. It is best not to have a large meal before meditating either, as that draws down the energy supply for digestion which makes you tired and paying attention more difficult. So, I suggest a light meal only and if you practice soon after waking, just have a piece of fruit or a slice of wholegrain toast before you commence.

Alcohol and Meditation

A rule that we have in the Meditation Sanctuary is 'no drinking of alcohol for a period of six hours before coming to class'. One dear woman told me about her 'practice' of having three 'little' soothing glasses of wine after getting home from work, before meditating in her personal sanctuary. She wondered why her practice was not going so well. I didn't tell her it was because she was 'half-smashed' but did suggest that 'from now on, it is either the wine *or* the meditation.'

There is nothing wrong with a glass of 'something stronger' occasionally but *alcohol doesn't mix with meditation*. Quite simply, your mind becomes foggy (I'm being polite now) and less able to achieve 'single-pointed focus', an imperative skill for meditating. I have noticed over the years that serious meditators tend to reduce their alcohol intake to 'occasional' or eliminate it altogether because they just no longer 'need' it for either stress alleviation or pleasure.

Drugs and Meditation

Of course, the above comments more than apply to 'party drugs' (what an inane and tragic misnomer). Taking drugs such as cocaine, heroin and 'ice', although perhaps being transient 'party-mood' builders, in reality, reflects a deep sense of inadequacy and inability to love the self and inevitably leads to partial (sometimes complete) destruction of both the body and mind. Smoking marijuana similarly reflects a desire to escape reality by creating a temporarily more pleasant one but it also has severe, long-term negative effects on the brain and body.

Naturally, you may choose to partake of any of these but, if you wish to happily continue with such practices, you are certainly not ready to seek deeper aspects of your 'self' or discover a far more enthralling Way to live through meditation.

Having said that, many people suffering from the consequences of substance abuse turn to meditation to help them see the *cause* of their excessive intake, to understand it and to gradually let it go, thus enabling their addictive or excessive behaviour to gradually melt away. I know, and have worked with, many so-called 'alcoholics' and 'drug addicts' who with patience, practice and, yes, some pain, have had the courage to embed themselves in meditation to the point of returning fully to their natural wellbeing, no longer 'labelled' negatively as 'alcoholics' or 'junkies'.

Prescription Medication

I am often asked whether prescribed drugs such as anti-depressants or blood pressure medication, will affect meditation. My principle on such questions is that you should never just stop medication that has been wisely prescribed. Some drugs taken for depression and anxiety may dull the experience of meditation but won't nullify practicing in the way other drugs, such as alcohol, certainly will.

Many students come to the Sanctuary (or are recommended by their doctors, counsellors or psychiatrists) to practice meditation so that they may use it as a powerful 'weapon' to help them overcome an array of stress-induced illnesses and diseases. I always suggest that they continue consulting with their doctors to progressively reduce their prescription drug intake as meditation perhaps begins to replace the work done by the drugs. In that sensible way, many have become, gradually and naturally, drug free.

The reality is that meditation, practiced with patience and an intensity of will, can have a remarkably 'healing' effect on a wide number of illnesses, from migraine to chronic depression and even serious diseases such as arthritis and cancer. I have many, many students who have experienced at least partial alleviation from serious illness and many others who have fully returned to their natural wellbeing, sometimes after years of debilitating suffering and prescription drug dependence.

If you have a medical difficulty, the soundest advice is to inform your doctors that you want to practice meditation so they can monitor your progress and adjust any ongoing medical needs appropriately.

Mental Disorders

Many 'centres of meditation' say that people with a psychiatric disorder of most descriptions (they often include depression and anxiety among the 'forbidden' disorders) should not practice meditation – and won't enrol them. I find that attitude to be deeply reflective of people who perhaps don't really have genuine expertise in, or understanding of, either mental illness *or* meditation and, seemingly, lack even a garden-variety of kindness and compassion. Certainly, if folks are suffering psychotically to the point of 'creating a different reality', they will not find benefit in meditation until, or unless, medical intervention has effect. But there are many people who suffer from such difficulties as anxiety, depression, bi-polar disorder or compulsive/obsessive behaviours of one kind or another (just for example) who are finding varying degrees of genuine relief through meditative practice.

Without question, many of the less well may find the Path a little more arduous and the benefits are sometimes hard won but the light I see in the eyes of so many such students, where there was once darkness, has made me aware that many sufferers can be helped, either partially or completely, by the practice of Authentic Meditation. This is wonderfully reflected in the brave and inspirational letters included in this book from some of my dear students.

Again, if you have been diagnosed with a 'mental disorder', the wisdom is to discuss the possibilities with your doctor first and certainly, when you feel comfortable with your meditation teacher, tell him or her as well. If they are genuine Masters, you will be greeted with warmth and they may well be able to guide you in specifically helpful ways.

Too Young or too Old?

Can I bring my children? Am I too old? What is the best age to start? These are typical questions I field just about every week. We are a society obsessed with age and tend to mentally categorise people and their capabilities (including ourselves) according to 'how old they/we are'. People so often take the narrower view that, for example, 'he/she is older/younger than me' and then respond to, and judge that person according to their own conditioned attitudes about others of a particular age.

It is from this conditioned point of view that the 'too old/too young' questions often arise. The short answer is that there is no age limitation to practicing meditation. The youngest I have guided is a little lady of nine and the oldest, a retired doctor aged eighty-four. The effectiveness of meditation in one's life is correlated with the intensity of will to unfold the magnificent self within, not one's 'age'. That simple.

I know people in their 50s for example, who look and act much older because they believe the myth that they are 'getting old' (in yogic terms, they haven't even started living yet). Conversely, one of my dear students, Sarah, barely past 20 years old in 'human time', constantly exhibits the wisdom of a long-in-the-tooth guru.

So dear reader, if you have aspiration to practice meditation, then practice meditation … no matter what 'age' you are! Oh, and why not forget about telling *anyone* how old you are – or not. Sometimes, people ask me my age and I always reply 'the same age as you' which, in the grand scheme of eternal existence, is utterly true because all matter in the universe (including our body) came into being at the same time – or perhaps, always existed! Matter does not get 'old', it only changes.

Age is an ageing and life-limiting concept! Just get on with being the very best and most joyful 'you' that you can be in this and every moment.

Potholes on the Path

The final item you need to pack for the Journey is a jar full of 'self-kindness'. If you become a 'meditator' you will, variously along the Path, fall into an amazing array of metaphorical 'potholes' or 'slip off the track' or even run headlong into 'solid cliff faces'. In other words, at some points along the Way, you are certain to become diverted by mental ruts or lost on sidetracks. You may, for example, find letting go tension hard to achieve at times, or the breathing work difficult, or stilling the mind just about impossible for a while. You may, like all awakened ones before you, wrestle for a good while with any thought of letting go habitual and hardened old opinions and attitudes, illusory though you really know them to be. When we find the Journey tough going, our conditioned tendency is to give ourselves a hard time or, worse, allow feelings of 'failure' to arise.

I shall say this only once … *failure in meditation doesn't exist!* The mental potholes, ruts and cliff faces you will surely confront are in fact, little 'signs' that you really *are* on your Path because if you weren't, you wouldn't experience any such difficulties!

The absolute key to dealing with 'troubles' on the Journey is, firstly, not to chastise yourself or feel that you have failed somehow or that you are not doing it as well as others are seeming to do it or, the big one – 'I *can't* do it'. Everyone slips back in their practice at some time and I would be very dubious about your progress (as Bashayandeh once was with mine) if you told me, for example, that your Journey has been 'smooth the whole way'. I have slowly learned that the very 'best' students and, indeed, teachers, are those who *have* slipped and experienced a few tumbles back down the mountainside. I have gradually discovered that the ones worth listening to are those whose wisdom and understanding have been honed, tempered and refined by their daring to face, struggle with and overcome the inevitable difficulties on their Journeys.

Secondly and practically, when you find the Journey toughening up as the incline steepens and that your practice is becoming difficult or a 'chore', simply go back to an earlier exercise you found easy *even if you go back to the beginning.* Rebuild your confidence and enthusiasm for the Journey by practicing that exercise until you feel you have mastered it once more and then move on once again. Remember, if you need to start 1000 times …!

The teacher of Bashayandeh, the renowned Guru, Sri Aurobindo, deeply understood the 'difficulties' and wrote encouragement to all students in his 'must-read' book, *The Integral Yoga*.

> *'If there is the will within to face all difficulties and go through, no matter how long it takes, then the Path can be taken.'*

The most potent piece of advice I can offer you for the entire Journey, dear reader, is no matter what difficulties happen along the Way, *always, but always, be kind to yourself.* Slipping back is natural until you have finally 'awakened' –

whereupon, the reality is that it is no longer possible to slip back. (When you have a few weeks, I'll be happy to sit and share stories of my little off-track excursions!)

Being Ready – A Master's Lesson

Year in, year out, people scramble all over the world seeking the *ashrams* of great gurus. *Ashrams* were traditionally found in India and now, increasingly (along with monasteries, temples and sanctuaries of various persuasions), are being established on all continents with seekers coming in their droves to find … whatever they think they are trying to find – perhaps like Nathan, the supposedly mystical 'Path to Enlightenment'.

This is a story Bashayandeh told me about a wise guru in an *ashram*.

The wise gurus know that people who flock to them are still seeking the Path somewhere 'out there' – outside themselves – and they are all usually in a big hurry. Accordingly, the wise ones often keep the wanderers waiting, sometimes for weeks, before they are granted an audience. The gurus do this quite deliberately, not to make themselves seem important (the real ones have long let go 'ego') but because the very act of waiting forces the people to just … stop, to cease running like mice on a treadmill from one place to another, from one 'teacher' to another. They are 'forced' to become absorbed in … just waiting.

If they become frustrated and annoyed in the waiting, so much the better because that is the perfect antidote for overexcited expectation. Those who leave the *ashram* because they have become restless, impatient and bored, unable to wait for their audience with the master, are obviously not yet ready.

Most don't realise that, in being required to wait, they have already been offered their first lesson. They have been guided to the beginning of the Journey, the foot of the mountain – the place of simply being still and 'present'.

For those who do wait expectantly to attend the wise ones, the early audience with a guru is then often spirit-crashingly disappointing because he may only say a brief sentence or two. He then sends the novice away with the instruction to consider his few words carefully, usually for another frustrating period of days.

In being given time to reflect, however, they have been guided towards their second great lesson – that the Journey inwards requires patience, contemplation and understanding of every little step before the next one becomes possible. For example, one guru, on being approached by an obviously enthusiastic seeker, asked a seemingly simple question, 'are you ready?' With the wave of a hand, he then sent the novice away … for another three weeks! The would-be student left, shaking his head at the guru's question. Then he became angry. Didn't the guru realise that if he wasn't ready he wouldn't have made such an effort and travelled so far to attend his *ashram* in the first place?

The three weeks having to *just sit* and do nothing but deeply contemplate the question apparently worked wonders. Bashayandeh went back 'ready' with a genuine spiritual aspiration and was to become a master student of the great guru who had asked the question – Sri Aurobindo.

Not all of you are physically able to visit an *ashram*, monastery or sanctuary, whether in your town or on the other side of the world. But there is really no need to because, as I said earlier, *the ultimate 'wisdom place' you seek is within you.* There comes a time when you need to realise that all the running around looking for answers *out there* is basically a total waste of life. There comes a time for all who aspire to inner illumination, to just stop … just sit and just be still, and contemplate the wise guru's question: 'are you ready?'

Chapter Four

Introducing the Three 'Essences'

Seeing the Whole ... not Part of the Whole

One evening, a student asked, 'what *is* meditation?' The question was directed to me but I gave it back to the class for discussion. Their answers were interesting and varied from 'relaxation, isn't it?' through 'concentration' to 'stopping your thoughts' and finally 'just living'. If I had cobbled all their answers together, we would have quite a good 'definition' of meditation, for they all offered a little part of the whole – but not the whole!

Some years ago, I was invited to conduct a master class in meditation at a classical guitar festival. In the class, we looked at ways that meditation can be used to overcome nervousness before and during a music competition or concert performance. After the session, a middle-aged woman approached me. She told me, with a little, pretend-not-to-be-proud flick of the head, that she had been 'meditating daily for 17 years.' She was clearly pleased with her zeal over such a long period of time.

I said, 'that's wonderful, how do you practice?'

She replied, 'oh, I do a *mantra*.'

'For the whole 17 years?' I queried.

'Yes.'

'What do you do *after* that in your practice sessions?'

'That's all I do – the *mantra*.'

I pondered for a moment. Should I tell her that Zen monks, the ultimate custodians of pure meditation, regard the repetition of a *mantra* as a valuable exercise – but for beginners?

Finally, I said 'Zen monks regard the repetition of a *mantra* as a valuable exercise for beginners', whereupon the poor woman burst into tears. After a few moments, I partially resurrected the unhappy situation created by my inadvertent insensitivity by suggesting, 'perhaps it is time to move forward now that you have such a good grounding.' We then talked about the 'how' of moving further along the Path and a happier woman headed off with some new practices on which to work. The important point is that she had held onto a valuable little technique extracted from the whole – *but with no vision of the whole.*

Given its popularising by the Maharishi Mahesh Yogi in the 1960s, so-called 'transcendental meditation' (TM) has been wrongly but widely regarded as the holy grail of meditation. Followers are far less cheerful when they realise that they have spent their hard-earned money practicing the combination of just two basic beginner techniques – *mantra* repetition and breathing awareness. These are certainly most valuable tools, but are not meditating – again, part of the whole but, not the whole!

I relate these little stories because so many 'meditators' I have encountered over the years, including some very well-known teachers and practitioners, have such little understanding of the enthralling depth of the 'whole' of meditation. They lack an understanding that 'techniques' (such as *mantra* repetition) are only stepping stones designed to help the genuine seeker into higher and higher reaches of the Path *with such techniques themselves being discarded when they have fulfilled their true task.*

All people with a true, burning intent to walk the Path to their inner divine magnificence can do so. It is not a journey for a chosen few, nor can it be achieved by learning a couple of minor techniques and then getting all purry and misty believing that you can then 'meditate'. You can't.

The Journey into meditation can only be accomplished truly and effectively by first preparing a place of inner stillness through practicing, and eventually mastering, classic and authentic core skills which I call 'The Three Essences'.

Mastering the Core Skills First

The Essences required are the ancient arts of *Letting Go Tension*, *Right Breathing* and *Stilling the Mind*, the latter, in itself, being regarded by many as meditation – but again, is not. These three ancient arts, although having been 'taught' by some yogis and Zen Masters from early times, are actually skills or 'Essences' that you already know … because you practiced them naturally from birth and as a young child.

Tragically however, these natural gifts get submerged under the debris of 'ordinary living', smothered by conditioned, mind-numbing busyness that we think we need for surviving and 'getting ahead' in the tumult of contemporary society. Quite simply, as we become immersed in the mad scramble of 'unawakened' existence (the Tibetans call this *samsara*), we gradually lose the wholeness of our own essential nature. We crucify our 'self' trying to be the human that we think we *should* be – rather than being the magnificent human we really are.

So, in the modern world, the overwhelming majority of people, over the age of about five, no longer have a clue about the natural Essences. People are never tension-free (don't know how to be any more), they do not breathe properly (don't know how to any more) and do not even consider the possibility of a still mind (and don't care what that even means).

Some may quibble over my emphasis on the Essences or even the need for practicing them *at all*. It is true that some seekers may reach a quite advanced state of meditative practice without formal 'retraining' in the Essences, usually through retreating, perhaps to a monastery or a cave and just … being still. But, unless they were initially exposed to yogic and Zen meditation practices, which emphasise mastering the Essences, they are mostly in for a very, very long inner pilgrimage of solitary practice. Their retreat might range from eight to 20 years or more, before some, perhaps only a few, reach 'enlightenment' or whatever they were seeking.

Others, particularly Western 'meditation teachers', give only lip-service to the Essences by saying to a class, for example, 'relax, focus on your breathing, quieten your mind and then pay attention to your feelings' (or 'think of a beautiful place'), often all in one sentence! But saying 'relax' to somebody who is tense and anxious and who doesn't have a clue *how* to relax is of very little value. Saying 'pay attention to your breathing' to a class full of people who are all breathing 'poorly' is useless. Just saying 'quieten your mind' also begs the question '*how?*' from students whose lifetime experience is a mind-babble of non-stop thinking (because that's how *everyone* thinks). My sadness is that, if introduced to meditation in this way, many dear people can find their first exposure meaningless, bewildering or, just plain hard to grasp – hardly riveting encouragement to set off on the Great Journey.

My own Master, the lovingly tough Bashayandeh, was both wise and right in *demanding* that I mastered the Essences and it was only after daily and dedicated practice of each of them that he told me I was ready to *begin* practicing the art of meditation. Now, as a teacher, I too consider them to be utterly necessary stepping stones along the Path in the early stages of the Journey.

Quite simply, without practicing the Essences, you will not be able to meditate authentically and effectively – probably ever.

However, through simply practicing, and gradually 'remastering', your old skills of tension-freedom, natural breathing and mind-quietness, you will be able to *create an inner base camp,* from which you can set out on the Journey with light heart and purposeful direction.

The Concept of 'Letting Go Tension'

Many people ask, 'will you teach me meditation *so* I can learn to relax?' to which I reply, '*no*, you must *first* be able to relax in order to meditate. You cannot meditate or be still of being if your physical self is riddled with tension. So, let's practice getting rid of the tension first.'

Such a question underlines the fact that 'relaxation' is also a widely misunderstood concept and many confuse it with 'meditation'. For many harried folks, the idea of a 'good relax' is perhaps taking a glass of wine and a mind-popcorn magazine into the spa, or having a cigarette and a cup of coffee to 'get a break' for a few minutes, or scrounging a few days away from the kids, or playing a game of golf – and so on.

Such activities all *do* have value because they temporarily ease the routine drudgery and stress of ordinary life. They may even be fun and experienced as 'body treats' or 'mind treats' that release, or at least mask, underlying tension. But their effect is always short-term. Once such activities are completed and the normal routine resumed, it is not long before the usual body tensions bubble to the surface again.

The profound level of tension-freedom needed to prepare for meditation is based on the core principle of 'letting go' that permeates meditation at all levels. Over the next weeks and months, you are going to practice letting go accumulated bad habits – and that starts with, not learning 'how to relax' but, practicing *letting go tension*, until you can reach into, and sustain, the tension-freedom of a blissfully sleeping baby, just as you once could, long ago. The *experiencing* of this level of tension-freedom is infinitely beyond, and certainly longer lasting, than any 'relaxing' body activity or mind-treat.

The Three Tensions

Our lifelong 'wellbeing nemesis' is tension or, rather, our inability to release tension. Within the context of Authentic Meditation, we speak of three kinds of tension: *natural, unnatural* and *stored* tension.

The first one, *natural tension*, is the use of energy stored in our muscles ready and waiting to make the countless millions of body movements that enable us to function 'normally' – from opening our eyes to running for the bus. When called upon, our muscles use the energy to create tension, which is converted to movement, and so our precious muscles beaver away diligently, silently and ceaselessly throughout the day, only tiring when the energy needs to be replenished for further 'action'. Natural tension is 'good tension' because, if we didn't have it, we would just fall over in a heap.

Unnatural tension is the same as natural tension except that it is held in the muscles for a longer period than required in 'normal' use. This happens as a result of the muscle action being driven by emotion – usually, but not necessarily, a negative emotion such as anger, pain, jealousy or fear. If, for example, a car swerved suddenly and dangerously in front of you, you may well have an initial response of fear followed by one of anger.

With the sudden arousal of a cocktail of hormones and chemicals 'injected' in response to (in this instance) fear and anger, the muscles of the whole body tense up – your tummy becomes knotted, the face scrunches up with annoyance and the shoulders lift with tension ready for a fight. Unnatural tension in your body also lifts the heart rate, increases blood pressure and forces your breathing rhythm to a quicker pace. Some folks will maintain this exaggerated tension in their muscles until the next traffic lights and then let it go rapidly by yelling a few 'home truths' at the 'bad guy'. For others, the tension will ease more gradually as the other car disappears from both sight and mind, and the body 'gauges' settle back to normal.

Tension can actually be held at an unnatural level for days, even weeks if the stimulus for ongoing energy is constant rather than fluctuating, such as by soldiers held in readiness for battle or by students worried over an imminent exam. But unnatural tension usually quietens when its initial cause ceases to be physically or mentally present (soldiers withdrawn from battle – students complete the exams). Mostly, unnatural tension can also be regarded as a 'good' tension because it is part of our body's natural, adrenalin-pumping preparation for 'action' ('fight or flight') at a time of need or stress.

Stored tension, within the meditative context, is seen as the long-term internalising of, or holding on to unnatural tension, rather than *letting it go*. I call it 'stored woe' because it is the carrying of unnatural tension for such a long period of time that it eventually seems to become part of you. It is tension most usually 'caused' by negative emotions, such as anger, grief, guilt, ongoing fear, long-term lack of recognition or reward or failure to meet expectations, all of which, I say, becomes metaphorically 'stored in your bones' and carried as a destructive inner load that just can't be put down.

This stored tension slowly, insidiously, becomes a permanent burden, damaging the very core of one's wellbeing. Stored tension is 'bad' tension because it manifests as unhappiness and suffering and has a profound negative effect, not only on physical and psychological health but also on the very way we behave, conduct our lives and interact with others.

At one level, stored tension can be manifest as a permanent, visibly physical 'tightness', reflected, for example, in people who constantly frown and whose woes have slowly become a 'physical badge', stamped on their faces and foreheads as deep furrows. Others store tension in the 'infrastructure' of their body. They are the folks forever complaining of body soreness and being 'stiff'. At a more complex level, it is stored tension, the deep infiltration of long-held, negative emotions into our (metaphorical) 'bones and being' over a lifetime, which is the root cause of most illnesses and diseases, both physical and mental.

Over the years, I have observed countless students of Authentic Meditation *lose* their frown furrows, *let go* their body pain and even *become free* of longer-term illnesses and diseases. I daily see people who practice meditation, gradually *transcending* the forlorn, agitated, worried, anxious, depressed and ill state of being they carried with them, so clearly manifested in lined, sad faces and lacklustre, often out-of-shape bodies lacking in any vitality or vibrancy at the 'joy' of existence. As the simplest example, I love saying to freshlings who've only been practicing for a month or two, 'do you realise that your face has already completely changed and softened since you started practicing meditation?' They tend to look slightly puzzled but then a wide grin usually follows my next comment, 'and every one of you looks five years younger'. The extraordinary point is that ... I am telling them the truth.

Throughout the book, I shall share many of the benefits of meditation with you but, in this introduction to the first of the Three Essences – Letting Go Tension, I just want to underline the indisputable point that our mental, physical and, indeed, spiritual wellbeing can begin to arise naturally from the very beginning of practicing letting go the stored tension saturating the body.

So, the first step on your Journey will be the practicing of letting go tension, one of the natural preludes to meditation. The level of profound 'relaxation' you will experience will be a revelation of a wonderful, blissful, physical stillness that few outside a purely meditative environment can ever experience. Even if you decide not to go on after practicing just this first step, you will have given yourself a 'wisdom gift' that will be of value, *if you practice it regularly*, for the rest of your life.

We shall begin practicing letting go tension as soon as we have a quick introductory look at the other equally important Essences.

Mastering Your Life Force with 'Right Breathing'

'There is no life without breath ... to half breathe
is to half live.'

– Ancient Saying of Chinese Masters

With every breath we draw, we take in the sanctity of our very being. Breathing is the vital instrument of our existence because each breath imbues us with what the ancient yoga philosophers of India called *prana* (or the Chinese Zen Masters, *chi*) – the *life-force*. They taught that *prana* or *chi* is ever-present as the essence of energy manifest in all things in the universe and we absorb it when we breathe, eat, drink and expose our body to sunshine. Without the ever-constant renewal of this life-force in our body, consciousness of life as we understand it just ebbs away. *Chi* is the energy required for life and the meditator can regard it as a vast natural resource readily available for our ongoing nourishment and wellbeing.

Of the ways we take in *chi*, our breathing is the most critical, as we need 'air' every minute of our life for continuing existence and wellbeing. However, almost all people have forgotten the ability to breathe naturally and beneficially long before they become adults and so pass their entire lives at a reduced level of health and vitality. How does this happen?

A little while ago, I wrote of the various ways we hold tension in the muscles of our bodies. These muscles include the muscles in our chest and diaphragm, the large horizontal muscle under our lungs. As these muscles become tense and tight when we are stressed and anxious, the lungs' ability to expand becomes more limited and our breathing falters in its natural rhythm. The average person naturally draws between about 10 and 16 breaths every minute of their life (about four times more than the meditative person), so it clearly doesn't take very long for ineffective breathing patterns to be established and become habitual if we lead a life of tension-filled stress.

As breathing occurs virtually unconsciously, most people usually just potter through life breathing inadequately, quite unaware of their lungs and the miracles they perform. You see, when we were born, we knew how to breathe perfectly, but gradually the stress of modern life has caused most of us to forget our naturalness in being able to use the 'full force' of *chi* available to us every moment of our life.

None of us is helped by our polluted environment, air-conditioned offices and homes and factories and trains and cars, all of which cause our throats to constrict and prevent our breathing in a deep, pure and nourishing way. Emotional swings, from excitement to fear or anxiety, mostly triggered by a frenetic lifestyle, also work against people, causing them to 'tighten up' with tension which gives free rein to that great breathing 'no-no' … *rapid and shallow breathing.*

Put simply, most people breathe poorly for their whole lifetime to the detriment of their health and calmness.

I shall tell you my own story of breathing. 'Right Breathing' became of critical importance to me long before I began my meditative Journey. As a young child, I suffered from asthma, being hospitalised many times and once or twice sailing very close to the eternal winds. I was allergic to wheat dust – just the right allergy to have for a kid being raised on an outback wheat farm. At 13, however, and still an asthmatic, I decided to learn judo, so wandered into town and visited the local *dojo* (place of practice). I was skinny, underweight and withdrawn, not the perfect specimen for vigorous martial arts! The teacher was a small, tough and gifted *shihan*, a black-belt master instructor. He listened attentively to my plaintive wish, took a long look at me and said, 'ok, but I shall not teach you *anything* until I have taught you how to breathe' … and so, a long and captivating Path had its embryonic beginnings.

I was later to find out that the Teacher himself had suffered damaged lungs from being gassed in war and he had largely been 'cured' through rigorous breathing training. He taught me the solid basics of Rhythm or Right Breathing and how to expel *chi* to advantage against an opponent in *randori* – freestyle sparring. I took to judo like a goanna to a chicken egg, and practiced my new breathing 'techniques' every day.

My physique and health began to change almost immediately. Less than a year later, my asthma had disappeared completely, never to return, although I continued to live in a wheat-growing area for several more years. Some time later and still a teenager, this sickly child had become supremely fit and sufficiently qualified to become a judo instructor. My *shihan* had patiently worked a minor miracle.

When I headed off on the next leg of my Journey, meditation, I was taught an array of yogic breathing techniques by Bashayandeh that were later refined by my next dear Teacher, the beloved old monk, Suni Kaisan, at his monastery. *But ...* the most profound lesson for my breathing skills repertoire came years later on a very hot summer afternoon. I had gone into the bedroom of my sleeping daughter, then a baby, to check that she wasn't suffering from the heat. I noticed her little tummy going in and out rapidly and had a sudden, awakening realisation that everything I had been 'taught' by the best-of-the-best masters was being practiced perfectly by a six-month-old child!

I realised in that moment that 'Right' or 'Rhythm' breathing is our natural, 'original' way of drawing life energy from *chi*. The problem is that virtually everyone has simply let this wonderful, natural skill be covered with 'life debris' – warped by our stressful ways of living.

To the potential meditator, 'relearning' to breathe as naturally as a baby is as important to the preparation for meditation as the Essence of Letting Go Tension. Indeed, the two were naturally integrated from birth but most people have forgotten both of these meditative fundamentals – how to be free of tension *and* how to breathe. Very simply, the better your breathing, the more solid the rock on which you stand to practice your meditation and the greater access you create to a more gratifying consciousness of your life.

Stilling the Unquiet Mind

The Third Essence needed for effective meditation is Stilling the Mind – quieting the incessant, distracting, undisciplined mental chatter or 'brain babble' that is constantly going on between our ears, masquerading as 'thinking'. Most students find this the most difficult of the Essences, but with right guidance and daily practice, it is a skill that literally everyone can do, eventually at will.

Being able to still the mind completes the repertoire of Essences that, when practiced together, begin to illuminate a 'serene space', within which the pure meditative element of your Journey can effectively commence. Stilling the unquiet mind is extremely important preparation for meditation because non-stop, erratic thinking is a huge barrier, a mental cage that locks us away from profoundly meaningful engagement with our lives.

Understanding the 'Thinking of Thoughts'

If you are not a practiced meditator, it is safe to say that you spend your entire waking hours with your brain engaged in the virtually ceaseless activity of … 'thinking'. It is as if your brain has a self-propelling momentum, processing endless data and then, just to amuse itself, constantly lobbing myriad combinations of those data (called thoughts) into your consciousness as a barrage of words and images requiring immediate attention. Along with these thoughts comes a constantly changing entourage of associated or 'attached' feelings and emotions that 'make' us feel happy or unhappy. The Buddhists beautifully describe the effect of this incessant mental fusillade as being like 'monkeys in a forest' – all chatter and screech as they jump from branch to branch.

Most people are completely *unaware* of their 'mind noise' – in fact, quite oblivious to the mental storm they process every second unless someone asks them, 'what were you just thinking about?' Nor are they conscious of the fact that the vast bulk of their so-called 'normal' thought is, in reality, random, aimless and indiscriminate or, what I call … *unmastered thinking*. Above all, most people are not at all aware that the unceasing load of thought (and associated emotions) can quite literally exhaust and burden them, both physically and emotionally, for their whole life.

The most poignant aspect of the unmastered way most people use their brain is that *we weren't born like that*. We all 'learned' or were 'conditioned' into wasting this great gift – 'trained' over our lifetime to fill our beautiful minds with detrimental blather that is now a galaxy away from the exquisite capabilities of perception and wisdom with which we started out on our life journey. What happens to the minds of humans is a tragedy (it happens to no other species) but we can undo the damage by 'letting go' unnecessary mental foam by just … *awakening!*

The Born Awareness

Let's go back to the beginning of you – and me. From the moment we begin life's journey in the womb, our five basic senses of smell, taste, sight, hearing and touch develop and, apart from sight, are mature at the moment of birth. From our earliest hours, our acute senses of smell and taste enable us to bond with our mothers and recognise the source of our sustenance. We soon use our hearing and touch senses to increase awareness of 'our world' and, within a few weeks, our sight becomes fully focused, adding to our (mostly) pleasurable experience of pristine existence.

At this time, and through our very early childhood, we relate to our world intuitively and instinctively, *feeling our environment* through a most pure 'senses awareness'. We *experience life with an uncluttered consciousness* because it is untrammelled and unspoiled by thoughts, memories, opinions, judgements or belief systems.

As we grow, however, we are 'taught' or 'conditioned' to abstract this original, pure sensitivity by our nurturers and others who put descriptive words, mental name-tags and definitions on all the elements in our outer environment and even begin to give word descriptions to our feelings. So we gradually learn or are conditioned to attach a mental-shorthand or 'word labels' to all our 'input' or, experiences. We begin to collect and store these labels in our young brain as data and gradually we begin to assimilate them – as thoughts. So, gradually, every single life experience derived from our senses and associated emotions is filed away perpetually as a 'memory', (positive, negative or neutral), ready to be dredged up and assimilated by 'thinking' and then applied when needed.

By mature childhood, the capacity to think has caused us to begin covering over or suppressing our original, innate ability to respond to, experience and appreciate our environment and existence with natural intuition as we once did in such a crystalline way. By young adulthood, our intuitive sensibility is essentially obscured. By then, we are accomplished at managing our daily lives by drawing on an ever-expanding, increasingly sophisticated 'senses history'. This history is stored as memories or knowledge or 'experience data' that give us direction in the conduct of our life.

Filtered Reality

This memory bank of stored facts however, is no longer just raw data. We have also gradually accumulated (or been *conditioned* with) opinions, attitudes, concepts and beliefs, all of which we have imposed upon, or attached to, our massive reservoir of accrued information.

This lifelong conditioning acts as a mental 'veil' or 'filter' through which we assess and, indeed, judge all events, experiences, people, information – in fact, absolutely everything. So, we end up living with a sense of 'our reality' that is constantly filtered rather than 'clear'. Our perception of our world is no longer pure as it once was. It is as if we look at a lovely green valley, but through the haze of residual smoke from a bushfire that burned there two days ago. The view is still there (pure reality – what *is*) but all hazy with smoke (the conditioned mind).

I'll give you a simple example of just how our perception of reality changes over time. When we were very young, *before* we learned that a flower had a label called a 'flower' and its colour had a label called 'red', we were able to experience the totality of that 'thing's' glorious existence with all our natural, unspoiled, intuitive senses – just a purity of consciousness – simply being fully *awake* to it. But then gradually our experience of the flower became increasingly thought-driven ('there is a red rose – isn't it lovely – oh, it's thorny') as the increasing number of labels we can attach to a flower sublimated our innate, pure understanding of its *isness*.

We learned to *think* flower, rather than instinctively *experience* flower.

In fact, we reach a point at which, in the same way, we *think* our entire life because we have, mostly unwittingly and unknowingly, smothered our ability to truly experience our moment-by-moment living with the clarity of consciousness, the awakeness, of the original young child we were.

The Underworld of Expectations

Then there is yet another layer of mind-conditioning called *expectations*. From early on in life, our stored experiences and influences (parental, social, cultural, religious, educational, peer, and so on), gradually assimilate into a variety of expectations – expectations that we create for ourselves, expectations that we have of others (particularly of people to whom we are close) and, the difficult one, expectations others have of us.

Expectations are a smothering blanket over much of our existence and become a motivating force for the way we conduct our life – and the way we learn to habitually behave as it unfolds. This is reflected, for example, in the *I shall be happy if/when* syndrome … as in, 'I shall be happy *when* I am married to the perfect person, have a university degree (two or three would be better), am rich, have three healthy children, paid off my own home, am loved the way I expect to be loved' and so on … endlessly … rather like dear Nathan.

Our expectations are so powerfully imprinted in our brain over time, that they become a *mindset* (a lovely word for a closed or 'unawakened' mind) – an unreal or illusory 'underworld' of the mind. What a mind-load our thinking places upon us to meet conditioned expectations and what a web of negative feelings we become entangled in when our expectations are then not met … which is much of the time!

Our unmastered thinking alone and the expectations that are progressively cultivated in our life, quite literally become a prison of mind-conditioning from which it becomes very difficult to escape because, not only are we unaware that it has a door that can be opened, we are mostly unaware that we are even 'locked in!'

* * *

I shall tell you a story.

Many, many moons ago, on a beautiful Sunday morning after breakfast, I gathered up my then six-month-old son, put a multi-coloured rug under my arm and went into the garden. I spread the rug and sat us under a beautiful liquidambar tree with its large-leaved, luxuriant foliage. I didn't take a big box of plastic toys to entertain him, as we were surrounded by wind-whispering trees, lushly coloured flowers, bushes here and there and a vegetable garden laden and dotted with ripe red tomatoes – all providing more interest and senses stimulation with their beautiful colours and lovely aromas than any collection of plastic toys.

After a very short while, a wonderful thing happened. A willy wagtail flew down and sat on the end of the rug, directly in front of the child and less than a metre from him, unusually close for an untamed little creature. The wagtail, when in full song, has the most beautiful and varied voice imaginable and that day it decided to gift us with its whole warbling songbook for an uninterrupted four or five minutes, while its fanned tail wagged vigorously from side to side. The child (and his father) was utterly entranced.

The look of wonderment on the boy's face was one of open, ecstatic joy – an enthralled, enraptured stillness. After a while, the boy *did* put his hand towards the bird, no doubt wanting to add to his sensory experience by touching it and probably … well … wanting to taste it. The bird then hopped about us for a while and finally, just moved on – whereupon the child immediately became engrossed with the pattern on the rug, particularly the red threads, which he proceeded to try and extract from all the other threads.

The point of the story is that the child *experienced* this nature-episode in a pure way – without a veil of interpretive opinion, entrenched attitudes or a mindset of belief systems or expectations. He didn't know the words for 'willy wagtail' or even 'bird' for that matter. So he didn't think – 'there is a willy wagtail – bit daring isn't he', or any such thoughts. Nor did he try to chase it away or want to put it in a cage or have any other 'thoughtful' or 'conditioned' response.

In fact, he didn't think about it at all!

He was just profoundly still of being, aware, deeply and purely conscious, utterly awake, focused completely *in the moment*, and blissfully happy. He experienced *mindfulness* (which I shall discuss in detail in Chapter 17), the purity of being utterly in the present, *experiencing that moment of his life as it happened* rather than thinking about it through a mirage of 'created', conditioned illusions or mental clutter. And when the bird flew away, he let that moment fly with it and gave equally enthralled, singularly focused attention to the red threads.

He was experiencing *a purity of meditation* – an openness of being that most people have long forgotten how to experience. The secret was (and is) his *crystal clarity of consciousness*. His whole being was *awake* – and he was only six months old!

Didn't a very wise guru say, 'unless you see as a little child, you will not enter the kingdom of heaven'?

The trouble is, by the time we become adults, the debris of just living has tended to cover over our natural ability for such enthralled spontaneity.

We *think* about the metaphorical 'birds' in our life. We are unaware of the 'rugs' we sit on, let alone excited by the 'red threads' in our life! We sieve our reality (or a lot of little realities playing in our mind as life-theatre) through a dense mind-filter, a *very* cluttered consciousness, the hazy smoke across the valley. It is our *unmastered thinking* that gets in the way of our being able to truly experience life by choking our capacity to be in awe at the wonderment of our existence in each eternal moment.

Now, as you go about your daily 'busyness', perhaps it is not always possible to be utterly aware of every tiny leaf on every tree at every moment but … did you notice the effect of the sun through the leaves throwing lovely dappled shadows at your feet, the smell of coffee from each of the cafes you passed, the smile of the baby over there intrigued by your silly hat/beard/sunglasses? … all of which were probably among the million mindful possibilities of the moment. Most people are really unconscious of any of those wonderment-chances simply because they are engrossed in mind-yapping about anything and everything that pops into their (half)-consciousness as they go about their day.

They simply *don't know how* to switch off the babble.

What about you? Were you 'here' today … really *here* … or 'lost in thought'? The truth is that virtually all people haven't a clue *how* to become aware of the moment let alone be enthralled by the very living of it.

You see, dear reader, as I said earlier, life-conditioning has shifted the whole dynamic of our existence to *thinking* our lives rather than *experiencing* our lives. We learn to see an illusion of reality; an illusion of what we 'think' is, rather than 'seeing' what really *is* … as we once could … as the child does.

We actually cease to experience much of life at all, other than in our minds.

The Effects of 'Wrong' Thinking

Oh, I can hear you thinking, 'now come on Brahm, we can't just sit around all day being enthralled by willy wagtails and red threads and dappled shadows and all that blah. There are things to be done – like, earning money for food, paying the bills and cleaning the house – for starters. Without thinking, we would not be able to function or even communicate'.

You are absolutely right of course. The ability to think is a gift from the universe … (or you can call it evolution – doesn't matter much). Our thoughts form and maintain our sense of 'being' – *of our existing.* The assumption of our own reality, in which we participate every day, is based on our thoughts – the erratic progeny of all our experiences. Our thinking forms the very base from which we function – from which we create a sense of 'who we are' as well as our 'place' in the world.

Truth is, dear reader, we *can* think – and we *need* to think. But this wondrous capability is not, in itself, the impediment to our being able to experience the reality of our magnificent being. The difficulty is the chaotically out-of-control nature of our thinking. The reality is that, over a lifetime, our minds have become something of a vast quagmire of directionless thought and thought-spawned emotions that have, like an old, untended vine, grown over and smothered the naturally intuitive, awake, able-to-be-enthralled self … as experienced so divinely by the child on the rug.

The Effect of Thinking on 'Happiness'

Being bogged down in our minds by conditioned thought is like living in a polluted city. It has a number of real and debilitating effects on the way we experience our life. To begin with, losing our ability to know, appreciate, effectively use and master our gift of thought unwittingly builds up a huge load of old mental garbage which spills messily over our whole life until we simply reach 'overload'.

This superfluous mental litter can manifest itself in so many ways. It can have relatively simple effect, such as in students so often saying to me, 'my thoughts won't stop'; 'my mind keeps me awake'; 'I can't let go thinking about so-and-so or such-and-such all the time' or, 'I am a compulsive thinker'. On the other hand, the far more serious manifestation of unmastered thinking is that, all by itself, it creates our experience of 'happiness' and 'unhappiness'. Most people believe that their emotional status (happy-unhappy, angry-excited, and so on) is always 'caused' by events, circumstances, random happenings or the behaviour and actions of others – stuff that is 'out there' – *external to their 'self'.* Not so, dear reader!

In some simple exercises you shall do later as part of 'Thought Awareness', you will discover the truth for yourself that, because your thinking is random and relatively uncontrolled, so too are your associated 'moods' and emotions. Your experience of happiness and unhappiness actually swings from positive to negative (sometimes as quickly as every few seconds), according to what you are thinking. As you will also find out, your mood can change even if you are doing nothing but just sitting quietly without any external stimuli of any kind, just the batty old brain ticking over in its muddled, monkey-leaping way.

Another and more complex effect of 'wrong' thinking is reflected in students who come to the Sanctuary because they are 'unwell' (in one of a thousand ways). We shall see later that not transcending the ongoing muddle of your thinking can gradually lead to dysfunction of your whole being and so people become worried, stressed, depressed, unhappy, discontented and even physically ill and diseased – all underlining the great yogic wisdom that *it is our mind alone that causes our joys and our woes.*

Worst of all is that unmastered thinking turns us into mental automatons. We just react automatically to our chattering thoughts and become subject to them. We become attached to them like a barnacle to a boat until we function as if we believe we *are* our thoughts. In so doing, we 'overgrow' and overwhelm the born ability to respond intuitively to our environment and to be present in this moment with our whole being. Our attachment to our thoughts and their associated fickle emotions becomes a prison wall of the mind separating us from the reality of our true being. Putting all that very simply, we exist in a world of confused illusions that become the 'distraction-barrier' to actually experiencing the thrilling vibrancy of our existence.

I said earlier that you must be still-of-being in order to create a 'serene space' within which you can begin to meditate. It is of little value practicing the letting go of tension and right breathing, if your brain resembles the struggling of a wombat in a wheat bag – all wriggly and lumpy, without direction or purpose.

So, in the Third Essence, we shall work firstly on understanding the thinking process. Then we shall look at the real effect of living in a state of permanent 'mental chaos' and, finally, I shall guide you in authentic, meditative ways to settle, quieten and then still your mind. The aspiration is to begin to master practicing meditative techniques that will enable you to *transcend the muddle* that has been, and is, your normal way of thinking.

In practicing letting go the mind-babble, you will eventually be able to melt into *the original silence of a serene mind* and, when layering this wonderment upon the first two Essences, provide yourself with renewed natural skills enabling you once again to begin experiencing life as joyously and enthralling as you did when you were a small child.

I shall now guide you step by step through the three Essences with classic exercises and practices passed to me by my dear teachers. If you dare, *really dare* to practice these Essences which prepare you for Authentic Meditation, your walking this 'part' of the Path can only have radiant effect on the rest of your life.

One Step at a Time

It is important that you practice the exercises in the order I suggest for the very simple reason that each is dependent upon your accomplishment of the previous one. Do be mindful that if I suggest an exercise be practiced for example, 'five minutes daily for the next two weeks', it is only a suggestion – but probably erring on the minimum time. Remember, you are always the master of your own practice – always.

Please do not be tempted to think, 'oh, this exercise is too easy, I shall just skip it and move on'. *Every exercise has purpose and meaning* and has been created and practiced over centuries because they 'work'. Remember Bashayandeh's lesson to me: *truly experience and understand* each step you travel. Do not just become a clever 'technician'. If you rush to 'get somewhere' instead of sinking into your practice for the sake of practicing, you *will* 'hit the wall'. You *will* 'slide down the mountain' on your backside. You *will* find yourself either disillusioned or 'lost on the Way' and you may well find yourself having to go back and start again, as I was once mortifyingly 'invited' to do.

So hasten slowly dear one – travel well! Time now to set out on your Great Journey.

* * *

A Little Story of Encouragement

Living in the Now

'When I had the great fortune to attend the Meditation Sanctuary several years ago, as an exercise I wrote a biography of my life leading up to that time. I recall I headed it *My Life as a Soap Opera!* Today, with the guidance and wisdom I have encountered, my previous life now seems so far in the past that it appears to be someone else's story.

Meditation has provided a period of serenity and peace in my life. The small, mundane tasks of daily living have become an enjoyable piece of a daily puzzle to be completed.

I find it difficult to articulate exactly how or when the changes in my life have taken place. There was no defining moment, no epiphany; just a gradual acceptance that everything and everyone on the planet has an importance to be accepted and loved.

The greatest visible change is an empathy that, at times, almost overwhelms. It is no longer a choice to offer kindness and understanding to others – the feelings I have are without thought or control … they just *are* … and my problems of the past are insignificant and a dim memory. The joy I receive from the small things I may do are an enormous reward for what I now consider is just doing the "right thing".

Health issues I have experienced are not seen as a disability but rather as something that "is" and a challenge to be overcome.

Having said all that, I realise that the Journey will go on and undergo changes as I continue with meditation as a necessary part of my daily life but now, I look forward to the future with anticipation.'

– John

* * *

Student John has indeed suffered physically more than most people could probably endure. I have watched a man slowly transcend physical difficulties as meditation opened a new 'Way' for him to regard his health issues and his life. I have watched a man develop unfailing good humour and equanimity towards his pain – a man who spends so much time now making others feel lighter of being. At the time of writing this, John was in recovery from major surgery and we spent our first 20-minute chat just laughing at all the 'funny things' that had happened to him – in the Intensive Care Unit! His practice of meditation has gifted us all at the Sanctuary with the true humour of a loving, wise and inspirational man.

Chapter Five

Letting Go Tension

'When there is an intensity of will for inner mastery, mastery
has already commenced.'

— *Brahmasamhara*

By now, you have set up your own sanctuary, the personal space in which
your Journey may unfold. So go to it and prepare it for practice – perhaps
light some incense and put on some gentle music.

When you are ready, lie down on your mat. Place a cushion under your
head if that will make you more comfortable. We lie down in the earlier
practices, as this is the easiest of the genuine yoga postures and perfect for
'easing into' your exercises.

Savasana – The Lying-down Position

The right way to lie down for meditative practice is the first posture of
hatha (physical) yoga – called *savasana*. In Photo 1, the student is lying on
her back, her arms are a little away from the body, with the palms of her
hands face down and ankles a little apart. Her head is straight with eyes
closed.

1. *Savasana*. The student lies on her back with no part of the body touching any other part. Importantly, the palms of her hands are face down.

The 'Keeping-Your-Mouth-Closed' Trick

Many students worry about their mouth falling open or even dribbling when they are deeply relaxed. To ensure your mouth stays closed, first open it a little. Press your tongue against the roof of your mouth, quite firmly, and then close your mouth with teeth slightly apart. In so doing you will have created a little vacuum in the mouth cavity … so it *can't* fall open, even when you are in deep meditation.

Falling Asleep

In the *savasana* position, some people tend to drift into sleep when they practice the tension-freedom exercises. However, if you do fall asleep, you have done so because you poor body is unfamiliar with being genuinely relaxed and quiet (and finds it a novel treat!) or simply because … you are tired. Never feel bad about anything that happens in your practice, as all exercises in Authentic Meditation are pure and natural. So, enjoy a little nap if needs be … and start again tomorrow. Eventually, the level of 'single-pointed focus' you master in your practice actually prevents you from nodding off.

Exercise 1. *Resting Calmly*

The purpose of this exercise is, firstly, for you to become familiar with the 'idea' of being in your sanctuary regularly; secondly, getting used to having a practice routine and, then most importantly, beginning to experience *just being quiet and still* – probably a fresh and guiltily luxurious experience for most new meditators.

> *So, lying down in savasana, begin with a mental check that you are in the right position. Close your eyes. The first exercise is simply to allow your body to 'sink' and soften into the mat and then just begin to rest awhile.*

After a few minutes, you will become aware that your body is not moving and refreshingly, that you are not actually 'doing' anything. Thoughts will flit in and out of your mind and you may begin to have little 'guilt trips': 'I *should* be doing this or that'. Instead, just give yourself permission for a little time out.

> *Continue melting your body into the mat, letting go the general tension until you think and feel that you are as relaxed as you can be. Endeavour to stay present with the 'feeling' of resting calmly and just melt into … enjoying the feeling.*

The Keys to 'Right Completion' – and a 'Secret' Golden Rule

Before we move on, I want to guide you in the right way to complete an exercise or meditation so that you retain maximum benefit from your practice. I call this important way of finishing, Right Completion.

The first key to a successful completion is to always 'draw back' from a meditative practice *very slowly and gently*. Never just suddenly jump up to go about your daily duties. You will be disoriented and will instantly wipe out any benefit, such as profound calmness, that may have settled upon you in your practice. The second key is (and this is the secret golden rule) *the longer the exercise or practice, the longer you take to complete it*.

Over time, you will realise that a right completion is equally as important as the exercise or meditation you have just practiced and is to be carried out naturally and gracefully. Completing an exercise in the right way enables the benefits of that practice to begin to 'spill over' into your daily life – at first, perhaps only for a few minutes, but gradually for longer periods of time until, of course, your experiences within meditation begin to have beneficial effect on every moment of your life. So now – the right way to complete.

Begin completion by firstly telling yourself (later, just by 'becoming aware') that you are to soon finish your practice. Keep your eyes closed and when you are ready, take a deep, slow breath (the extra oxygen gently energises your whole body providing the energy to begin moving). Commence by moving your fingers and toes, just a little – then a little more. Next, move your hands and feet, followed by arms and legs, but all very, very slowly.

Then it is time to take a lesson from the animal kingdom. So many animals, after lying fully relaxed, indulge in a slow, sumptuous stretching of the body. This has the effect of reintroducing the appropriate level of tension to the body so it is primed for action.

Stretch your body now – all of it – slowly, deeply and luxuriously, perhaps visualising a cat – you know, paws stretched way out front, back arched, back legs vertical and rigidly straight with rear end rather inelegantly stuck in the air (no, dear one, you don't have to mimic the cat – just do the 'human' version, unless of course …). Then, having stretched, when you are ready, open your eyes and slowly sit up.

Make it a daily feature of your practice to *just sit* for a few minutes reflecting on the experience you have just enjoyed before moving from your sanctuary. I want you to practice just this exercise for about a week and for around 10 minutes daily.

The Natural Tension Barrier

After practicing Resting Calmly for a week or so, you may think that you've 'got this relaxation stuff nailed'. The good news is that you *have* started the Journey. The reality is that, in terms of profoundly letting go tension, you haven't actually reached first base yet. You can, in fact, let go so much more tension … *about 75 per cent more!*

You see, we have a *natural tension barrier*; a level of tension beyond which, under normal circumstances of resting, your body will not let you 'relax' any further, except during the short period of very deep sleep or unconsciousness. Your body has been 'trained' or 'conditioned' over your lifetime to hold a level of tension so it is always primed for action or even just sitting in a chair without falling off. So, although you may 'feel relaxed' in your first practices, you are in fact enjoying only about a quarter of your body's capacity to become deeply still – at least while you are conscious. The key to accessing true stillness lies in practicing another yogic 'secret' technique. It is the virtually unknown practice of 'breaking through' the body's natural tension barrier, thus enabling it to reach a point of *no tension*.

To achieve this state of pure stillness of body, we deliberately create a 'false barrier', which is a level of tension greater than the body's 'normal' level. The false level of tension you induce is unfamiliar to the body so it becomes confused and 'forgets' just where the natural tension point was. This 'body forgetfulness' is exactly what you want to achieve so that, when you begin to practice Letting Go Tension seriously, you are then able to melt right through the 'old' tension barrier into increasingly deeper ponds of body stillness.

This is a most important exercise, to be practiced until it becomes second nature.

Exercise 2. *Breaking through the Natural Tension Barrier*

Lie down in savasana as before and let yourself fall into the body restfulness as you have been practicing.

When you are as 'relaxed' as you think you can be, slowly stiffen your entire body, tensing every muscle from head to toe simultaneously. Give special attention to your neck and face muscles, particularly around the eyes, mouth and temples until you have 'pulled a face' that (as I say to my students), 'even your mother wouldn't love!'

(Every time I used to practice this exercise, I would 'hear' my dear grandmother's voice saying whenever I pulled a funny face, 'don't do that dear because, if the wind changes, you will stay like that'. On the odd occasion of looking in a mirror these days, I suspect she was probably right!)

Do not stiffen your body to the point of straining or discomforting yourself, but when you have tensed all your muscles, hold this deliberately-created, whole-body tightness for a 'slow' 10 to 15 seconds. You can count if you wish.

Now, the most important phase.

> *Very slowly, almost imperceptibly, begin letting go all the tension but ... evenly throughout your whole body at the same time, rather than one part followed by another. So, for example, as you release the tension in your face, you will also be letting it gradually leave your thighs, and your hands – and so on. Your whole attention, your complete focus, is on your body. Try to be really aware of the feeling of tension seeping from you. Continue releasing the 'false' tension until you have let go as much as you think possible.*

Very importantly, you need to *take about a minute for the 'letting go'* part. If you feel you have done it too quickly, just tense up again for 15 or so seconds and start the 'letting go phase' once more.

> *When you then have let go as far as you think you can, just lie on your mat and try and become absorbed in the feeling of being relatively tension free. After five minutes or so, do right completion as you have previously – slowly.*

Practice this exercise daily for about a week but, in each day of practice, hold the whole-body tension for a second or two less than you did the previous day and also take a few seconds less to let go the tension over your whole body. So, at the end of a week or so of practice, you will probably be holding the 'full' tension for only about five seconds and then releasing it over about 30 seconds.

Continue to just lie absorbed in the feeling of 'no tension' after each practice. Increase this time a little each day until you are resting in this body-quietness for about 10 minutes before completing.

Directing Your Mind-focus

However, having broken through the tension barrier and relaxed as far as you think you can, you are still only about half way towards being completely tension-free. The next 'phase' is to practice letting go more tension by deliberately directing your 'mind-focus' around your body – to find and release tension literally from one end to the other; a quite exhilarating mini-journey for all you tense ones.

You have probably attended classes, read books or listened to CDs in which the teacher suggests that you 'relax' by focusing on your body one part at a time. Then, invariably, they instruct you to 'start relaxing your feet and work up the body towards your head'.

Although that follows the general principle of focusing your attention on just one part of the body at a time, such instructions are virtually useless because, firstly, unless you 'break through' the tension barrier as your practice starting point, it is not really possible to *ever* become more than about 30 per cent relaxed. You will simply get to where you were in your first exercise – Resting Calmly – very pleasant, but not profoundly tension free. The widespread practice of 'starting with the feet first' is really quite ineffective in allowing you to reach into profound tension-freedom which, as I have said, is a prerequisite for being able to meditate authentically.

An Ancient Secret – The 'Right' Place to Start

I shall share an ancient yogic secret with you, taught to me by Bashayandeh, a secret rarely written down but passed from master to master. In Authentic Meditation, you *never, but absolutely never*, start mind-focused, tension-freeing practice by giving attention to your feet first.

Rather, *you start at the opposite end.* You commence with the muscles around your eyes – *always!* The reasons are several and simple. By letting go the tension in the little muscles around your eyes alone, extraordinary effects are felt in the body. Your whole body will begin letting go about another 20 or 30 per cent of its tension – *because you can't help it.* It is an autonomic response. Then, quite amazingly, you will also find your breathing begins slowing quite significantly – *because you can't help it.* It is another autonomic response that adds a further, deep, calming layer across your practice of becoming still.

So, just by relaxing the muscles around the eyes first, you will have given yourself an extraordinary 'head start' on reaching into profound tension-freedom. I have actually had a number of yoga teachers write to me saying that, after practicing this 'new way' (it's about 2000 years old) with us in the Meditation Sanctuary, they have now adopted it in the little 'meditations' they do at the end of their *hathayoga* or pilates sessions.

You will only need to try it once to understand why we will start every practical exercise and later, practicing meditation itself, with this 'yogic secret'.

Focusing your Mind

From now on, I shall be using the term *bring your mind's focus* when asking you to give attention to a particular area of your body. This simply means the process of, firstly, 'thinking' of that area (say, your left hand), then giving your full, focused attention to it. In so doing, you gradually become so deeply aware of just that one specific spot, you will not actually be conscious of anywhere else. It will seem as though *your whole mind is 'in'* the particular place on which you are focusing. In Zen practice, this is called 'single-pointed focus'.

In your first efforts at single-pointed focusing, you will find miscellaneous thoughts popping in and out of your mind. This is perfectly natural and normal in the earlier stages. When you become aware of your mind going for a wander, don't 'punish' yourself. Just quietly bring your attention back to your area of focus and continue. This is one of the key principles for your entire Journey – gently guiding any meandering attention back to *just this*. Eventually of course, you will be able to hold your focus deeply and attentively on whatever you choose – at will.

Exercise 3. *Becoming Tension-free*

Step One: The Quieting

All your current exercises will be done while lying down in *savasana*.

> *Gently settle into the right posture, then tense your whole body but, now, only for two or three seconds before commencing the slow, ever-so-gentle sinking through your tension barrier until you feel as relaxed as you think you are going to be.*

Now, let's try some real magic.

> *Bring your 'mind's focus' to your closed eyes. Become aware of the little muscles around them, starting with the muscle group under your*

eyebrows and deliberately let go tension in that area alone. Keep on just letting go and, almost miraculously, you will experience a quite physical sense of the tension leaving those muscles.

Then move your mind-focus slowly to your temples – then under your eyes, deliberately letting go tension in each 'area' as your attention settles upon it. 'Feel' the muscles with your mind and 'tell' them to let go further and further – one by one. At the same time, you will feel the 'magic' of more tension dissipating from your whole body, as I mentioned a moment ago.

Eventually, you can be tension free around your eyes … permanently! The 'age' or worry lines on your forehead and around your eyes will take years longer to develop, if at all, because you will let go 'screwing up' your eyes or frowning with stress or concentration. More magic! Let's go further now.

After giving tension-freeing attention to your eyes, move your mind-focus to your forehead and, when you have eased the tension there too, move upwards to your scalp (yes, there are tiny muscles there!) then across the top of your head, down the back of it to your neck and then to one side of your head, followed by the other … letting go tension the whole way.

You will feel as if your 'mind' is taking a little journey – particularly as you backpack further around your body.

Now, bring your focus to the face starting with your cheeks, moving out to the muscles around the ears and then down your jaw line to your chin. Finally, let go tension above and below your lips and the lips themselves.

Pressing on now, we apply the same process of mind-focusing and letting go to the rest of your body but, as I have said, working down your body, from head to toe; remember, never the other way around.

So, shift your focus from your face to your neck, wandering your awareness all the way round it – starting at the front, then one side, the back and the other side, just allowing your neck to 'sink' into the mat as you let go all tension.

Many people hold vast amounts of tension in the powerful muscles across the top of their shoulders. Try pressing there right now. You will almost certainly feel stiffness and probably soreness as well. You can now practice 'using your mind' to let go all that tension.

> *Spending a minute or two on each shoulder, begin with taking your mind-focus from the neck slowly across the large shoulder muscles to the 'point' where your arm 'begins', consciously releasing the tension until you feel your shoulders seeming to 'just sink' into the mat. When you think you're done, (and this applies to all areas of your body), just try to 'let go' a little further. You will usually be astonished that you can.*
>
> *The next tension-freeing move is to your right arm, starting at the point of the shoulder and slowly, slowly 'washing' your mind-focus down through each muscle structure; upper arm, bicep, forearm, wrist, palm, back-of-hand, then all five fingers, one by one. When that arm is tension-free, do the same with the other.*

Important note! As you journey around your body on your tension-releasing campaign, try very hard to maintain the relaxed state in the areas of your body already 'treated'. To help with this, from time to time, just pop back to the eye area for a 'refresher let go', remembering that being deeply tension-free there has that magic whole-body effect.

> *Now move your awareness to your chest and, starting at your throat, 'walk' your mind-focus down through your chest to your abdomen and then lower abdomen – very slowly, just gently feeling the tension seep away. You can even say, 'let go, let go', in your mind if that helps you keep your attention 'on the job'. Then shift mind-attention to your back and do the same, from the nape of your neck all the way down to your buttocks – but slowly!*
>
> *Finally to your legs which you 'relax' as you did your arms – one at a time, giving particular attention to the large muscles at the front and back of your thighs, then down through your calves to your toes … all the while deeply letting go the tension.*

*When you have journeyed as far as the toes, just lie on your mat for
a minute or so, with your mind-focus on 'feeling the feeling' of a physical
calmness, now certainly beyond any level you have experienced.*

You will probably need to spend about five minutes on 'conducting' The
Quieting to begin to feel tension-free. Of course, the longer you are able
to spend on this key part of letting go, the more effective it will be. *Don't
complete the exercise just yet* as there are two more 'letting-go steps' to practice
before moving into a quite pure, tension-free state.

Step Two: Chasing Fugitive Tension

In the earlier stages of your meditative practice, you will discover that, while
you are letting go tension in one part of your body, some areas you have
already relaxed may become a little tense again. I call this Fugitive Tension –
tension that wants to escape your attention. This will occur naturally until
you become more fully practiced in holding a tension-free state in one area
while working on another but, in the meantime, you need to find the
Fugitive Tension … and deal with it.

So, the second part of the Essence of Letting Go Tension is 'taking your
mind for a walk' around your body until you stumble across muscles that
need relaxing again. This I call Chasing Fugitive Tension. They are likely
to be areas in which you feel 'knotted' or in which you 'naturally' store
tension during your daily life.

*So begin by taking your attention to, say, your right shoulder and 'challenge'
it – you can even mentally talk to it … 'I can relax you more – I don't
need tension there' … and so on, around key areas of your body.*

When you rest your mind in those areas, you will be amazed that you
can really physically feel more tension seeping away. Always complete
this step by returning to the muscles around your eyes and 'treating' them
again.

Step Three: 'Melting Chocolate'

The final step in reaching profound tension-freedom is once more broadening
your mind-focus to the whole body for a final, all-over 'let-go,' much as you
did at the beginning. I call this Melting Chocolate because, a few years ago,

dear student Hannah, on completing this final phase of the exercise, exclaimed that she felt 'just like chocolate melting over the floor'.

So, after chasing down the tension villains, imagine or visualise that you are 'melting' into your mat and across the floor – as if letting go the 'boundaries' of your body. Then just rest your mind in this beautiful tension-free state for five minutes or so or as long as you wish to enjoy it.

Completing a Tension-freeing Exercise

Complete this exercise as you have done previously, remembering the golden rule that the longer the practice, the longer you spend on completing. After being so deeply relaxed, you may need to spend up to five minutes gently bringing yourself 'back'. As always, when you have finished, just sit for a little while before leaving your sanctuary.

Increasingly, you will begin to discover a meditative wonderment – that the calm you have experienced in this lovely exercise will begin to last for a little while *after* you have walked away from your formal practice. As your days of practice pass into weeks and months, the sense of whole-being calmness derived from each session, will begin to extend further and further across your day and begin to sift into your life activities – *because you can't help it!* And this is only after practicing the First Essence.

Daily Practice of Becoming Tension-free

I suggest that, before moving on to the next exercise, your *daily* meditative activity for perhaps the next two or three weeks (as a minimum) is to practice all the elements described in Exercise Three. So, *each session* over this time becomes the practice of:

- tensing up (more on that in moment)
- breaking through the tension barrier using whole-body release of tension
- directing your mind-focus in The Quieting
- conducting the Fugitive Chase
- Melting Chocolate
- then ... just enjoying the deep physical stillness before slowly completing.

You will probably now be spending 15 to 20 minutes per practice on the First Essence. When letting go tension begins to become a familiar and settled part of your practice regime, you are ready to move on.

Letting Go the 'Tensing-up' Phase

Throughout this exercise, you have used the creating, then letting go, of 'false' tension as the ancient and highly effective way of breaking through the natural tension barrier to help you experience deeper calmness.

When the phases of the whole exercise are becoming increasingly smooth, the next step is to *let go tensing of the body altogether*. From that stage, you simply commence your practice by melting into restfulness and just proceed through the 'phases' of Letting Go Tension (The Quieting through to Melting Chocolate). You will have then trained your body to become tension-free without having to 'deceive' it by creating a false tension barrier.

'Smoothing' the Practice

As you practice this skill over the coming weeks, you will gradually find that all the phases of the First Essence gradually just seem to sweetly blend into a singular completeness of 'just letting go'. You will notice that the Quieting becomes naturally quicker and your chasing of Fugitive Tension will become pin-point accurate in defining and releasing remnants of tension.

You will develop a *knowingness* of where your body tends to hold its 'stored woes' and be able to just let them go completely. Not only that, you will find the blended letting go seems to be happening more quickly and naturally because, in 'real life', letting go tension is natural … you had just smothered the gift. Finally, as you go on, the whole practice of the First Essence will seem to become a gentle continuum without deliberate effort, in which the initial restfulness just melds gradually into profound, meditative tension-freedom. At that point, you are ready to move on.

This principle of, firstly, practicing each exercise by its composite elements and then gradually blending them into one fluid continuum, applies throughout your meditative practice from the beginning to … well, as far as you wish to journey.

How Long is 10 Minutes?

Of the questions I've been asked, that is one of my favourites. The student really was asking a sensible question which comes up quite frequently – 'how do I know when 10 minutes (or whatever) are up?' At this stage of your practice, you don't – and it doesn't really matter. At the moment, it is much better to estimate an approximate time rather than set a loud alarm to remind you to finish the session. Be careful not to underestimate time you give to your practice (for example, three minutes instead of 'about' 10). That would mean that you are rushing to 'get there' and that, dear reader, won't work. Conversely, and equally useless, is the thought that if you 'do' the exercise three times longer than suggested, you'll get 'there' three times faster!' *Wrong*, and you know why.

Later, when you are ready to practice a longer meditation but have a time limit, one suggestion is that you set a digital radio to a gentle music station so that after the time is up, you are reminded very softly and musically that it is time to commence completion. Another way is to select several tracks on a gentle music CD and conclude your practice when the tracks are completed.

When more advanced in your practice, you will simply 'know' not only how long you've practiced but also exactly what 'time' of day it is. Bashayandeh used to frequently, and quite literally, raise the hair on my neck with astonishment over his uncanny knowingness of what we call 'time'. I clearly remember a number of times waiting outside his door until the appointed hour for a teaching and, as I lifted my hand to knock, I would hear, 'Come in!' I knew he had no watch and I would discreetly search his room with my eyes for a clock – to no avail. Finally, I asked him how he knew I was there, to which I received the not-unexpected obliqueness of a Zen Master with his answer, 'you will know' (and indeed, you will … if you dare to walk the Path).

Quite often, we do a longer meditation in class and I tell the students the proposed duration for the practice. Then, on time, I tell them to 'complete when you are ready'. One evening, at the end of the meditation, dear student Lauren asked me, 'how do you always know exactly when the time is up?' Having previously told them of Bashayandeh's uncanniness, I was tempted to say 'you will know' but instead, just smiled for a moment and then slowly lifted my arm and pointed to the front of the Meditation Hall … where there is a clock on the wall! I was given a very quizzical look at first, but then she 'got it' and laughed.

A big lesson! The supernatural is ordinary – the ordinary is supernatural!

'Experiences' and Effects of Letting Go Tension

From the very beginning of practicing Letting Go Tension, you may experience one of a number of peripheral physical reactions, feelings or 'experiences' that, at first, may seem 'strange', unusual or even slightly discomforting. It is important to know that *any* unusual experience you may have while letting go tension is natural and harmless … because you are simply lying on a mat relaxing as purely as a newborn – not indulging in any weird or mystical practice.

Nevertheless, not having let go tension as deeply as this before, there will be some little unfamiliar 'encounters'. I shall describe some of the possible experiences so that, if they wander into your practice, you know they are 'normal' and you don't need to become distracted by them. If they arise, the idea is to continue your practice as intended, just allowing the 'experiences' to be there. They will soon pass as you deepen into stillness.

'Unusual' Experiences

One of the first responses is likely to be your nerves or muscles 'jumping' or twitching unexpectedly, like a fish jumping suddenly from a pond. Jumpiness or twitching simply indicates that the nerves and muscles are not receiving the familiar 'tension instructions' from the brain. It is a perfectly natural reaction and will quickly slip away.

Many people feel their skin tingling or perhaps becoming warm. This is a very good reaction and you feel warm because your relaxed muscles are no longer squeezing closed all the little capillaries and veins in your skin. By letting go tension, you are improving the blood flow throughout the body.

You may also feel as if you are floating or flying. Occasionally, this disorientation may cause nausea, although this is very uncommon. If it does happen, simply open your eyes to reorient yourself and, only when you have settled, begin again. If you prefer, finish for the day and try again the next. Any such experience will also soon pass.

At times, you may think or feel that you are really big or really small (I experienced this one quite often). In other words, you lose the normal feel of your body's dimension or proportion as you begin to quieten your sensory awareness. After a time, this experience may develop into losing the sense of 'body-self', beginning with not knowing, or not being able to feel, which way your hands are resting – face up or face down.

This loss of body awareness may occur in deep tension-freedom and certainly will arise in practicing deeper 'intensities' of meditation. Any experience of losing 'body-sense' can be a little disconcerting the first few times, because you naturally associate it with numbness. Know that you are not numb, nor have you become paralysed – you are simply slipping into the pleasurable state of deeper physical stillness.

Knowing When You are Tension-free

How will you know when you are as tension-free as it is possible to be? There is not an obvious answer to this question as each student will experience the effects of letting go tension in different ways. There is not an actual 'moment' when you can say with a deep inner sigh of satisfaction, 'got there!' because the instant you think *that*, you won't be '*there*' – you'll be flushed with pride, which intrinsically brings tension. However, any of the experiences I mentioned above are all definite little clues or signposts that your practicing is being effective in easing tension from your body. I personally felt comfortable moving to the next 'phase' of my practice when I experienced the fading of body-sense and you too will know when you are 'ready'.

Deeper Effects of Being Free of Tension

Each time you sink into deep relaxation and then become absorbed in the stillness, there will be deeper, positive physical effects on your body of which you will gradually become aware.

Letting go tension throughout your whole body has the remarkable and beneficial effect of both lowering your blood pressure and slowing your heart rate. When you move into deeper meditation practice, you will develop control over your body to the extent of being able to measurably achieve these 'body benefits' *at will*, consequently enhancing your entire wellbeing. You can, in fact, significantly slow your whole metabolism, much as a bear does when hibernating through the depths of winter.

Calming Emotions

To this point of practicing, you will have been mainly aware of 'physical' responses to letting go tension. But, in being single-pointedly focused on your body as you have been, your mind will also have begun to let go its 'monkey-jumping' or wandering off getting lost in thought. You have already, in effect, begun the practice of mindfulness, the yogic art of keeping your mind present – focused on the 'here and now'. For example, while you are 'being present' through deeply focusing the mind on easing tension in, say, your right shoulder muscles, the monkeys are really not able to bother you with either positive thoughts (a coffee would be great!) or negative ones (I really can't face work today). Because our erratic thoughts drag our emotions to the surface (in this simple instance, coffee = happy feeling, work = unhappy feeling), the deep focus on your body means that your thoughts are much less intrusive and so, of course, attached emotions are reduced in intensity.

Gradually, as you become more practiced, both positive and negative emotions will tend to meld into your body calmness, which, for a stressed or suffering soul, can be of immense relief. (At this early stage, I emphasise that letting go tension can provide *temporary* emotional relief to the sufferer but it won't, yet, by itself, overcome *the cause* of the suffering). Such relief on a daily basis can indeed provide a critical 'breathing space' in which difficulties and issues can be addressed, understood and perhaps eventually (with further meditative skills) let go forever in a mature way. However, even after just a few weeks of practicing letting go tension, you may well feel a rising sense of emotional calmness and some improvement in general wellbeing.

I do need to specifically mention the positive effect that just the practice of letting go tension can have, particularly for people suffering anxiety and depression – conditions that are mostly predicated on 'unbearable' tension or stress, however caused. Letting go tension as practiced so far can be used as a most valuable tool to help alleviate symptoms of these and related sufferings.

'Miscellaneous' Pain Relief Through Being Tension-free

When you reach complete body stillness, you are more than likely to find that, remarkably, you are not feeling any of your usual aches or pains. That is not to say that the *causes* of your muscle soreness, such as the bruising blows from the hard game on the weekend or the old arthritis aches and pains, are not still there but that, just at the moment, you are not *feeling* them. I said before, as you progressively let go tension, you are slowing down the messages from the nerves and muscles throughout your body to the brain – and that includes the messages relating to pain. When you are fully, meditatively tension-free, those messages virtually cease.

Directed Pain Relief

As you increase your ability to direct your mind-focus, you are actually beginning to develop 'control' over your body. So now you can begin to use the techniques of letting go tension quite deliberately for relieving various physical woes such as headaches or muscular and other pain. When you need to, set aside part or all of a practice session for pain alleviation.

In those sessions, commence with the Letting Go Tension phases until you have reached stillness. Then direct your mind-focus to the very core of the pain area in your body and, just as in the Chasing Fugitive Tension phase, give long and specific attention to letting the tension go in the painful spot or area until pain begins to subside.

One student was recommended to the Meditation Sanctuary by her doctor because her migraine was so chronic that it had been hospitalising her approximately every six weeks … for the past 15 years! She soon became a devotee of this 'pain-relieving' practice. At first, she noticed a slight lessening of symptoms. Within weeks, she experienced sufficient relief from the worst of the attacks to not require hospitalisation and then, wonderfully, a cessation of migraine events altogether. Within six months she felt sufficiently secure in her 'wellness' to take a three-month holiday in Vietnam! (I think I let out a little '*Wahoo!*' when I received her postcard from overseas.)

The 'Afterglow'

One of the deeper feelings you are likely to experience, as you nurture the art of letting go tension, is a physical peacefulness far superior to any effect achievable by any other form of 'relaxation'. Some students use the words 'joy' or 'blissful' to describe their being deeply free of tension. It just makes you feel *gooood!* As a result, you may well experience a kind of 'afterglow of wellbeing'. The afterglow may last only a few minutes early on in your Journey but, as you progress in your practice, the effect becomes increasingly long-lasting.

Eventually, when mastery is reached, this physical peacefulness can be with you all the time unless temporarily broken by circumstance (such as running to rescue someone from a burning house), whereupon it will soon return without conscious effort.

You may also begin to notice a greater fluidity and gracefulness in your movements simply because your body becomes less 'tight' as you let go stored tension.

Energy … the Renewable Resource

After longer sessions of becoming tension-free, you may have the quite unexpected experience of feeling wonderfully renewed or energised. This is not surprising considering that holding your body tense for most of your waking hours gobbles up energy and is, in fact, quite exhausting. So, letting tension go allows your natural energy to flow freely again. When you realise that *your energy is a renewable resource* simply attained by mastering the release of tension, you can begin to practice brief meditations for an energy boost whenever you need one.

Gradually, having additional energy will just become a natural essence of your life. You will find, for example, that many meditation masters are people who have accomplished a great deal more in their lives than others, not through being more extraordinary humans but only because of their practiced mastery at harnessing this quiet, ongoing energy while outwardly never seeming to display any undue haste or frantic busyness.

Aspiration without Expectation

It is important, however, to practice without expecting any of the experiences I have mentioned and without harbouring a desire for wellbeing or creating a deliberate goal of 'getting more energy' or whatever, because … it will not 'happen'. Remember, expectation and desire becomes a barrier on the Path. The idea is to just keep mellowing into each practice … for the sake of practicing.

Although I have said to let go expectation, all serious meditators will have an *aspiration* for their practice. The aspiration then, for the First Essence of Letting Go Tension, is to be able to do so *at will* until the practice is mastered when, just like a Zen monk, you will *possess* it. At that stage of the Journey, the body will have been trained in letting go to a point where it simply 'knows' the appropriate level of tension it needs for movement and naturally returns to a deeper level of physical calm when tension is no longer required.

Until then, dear reader, just continue practicing the unfolding of your potential mastery by working on Exercise Three … daily!

Letting Go the 'Unnatural' Unveils the 'Natural'

Melting into deep physical stillness can bring the dawning of the profound understanding – a true awakening – that *letting go a 'negative' such as tension in your body, has the corresponding effect of allowing a 'positive' experience to naturally well up from within.* So, for example, in practicing letting go the 'negative' of unnatural tension, you release your natural body calmness that wells up from within to flood the 'empty space' once occupied by tension.

The letting go of the 'unnatural' to allow the welling up or renewal of the 'natural' (for example, tension replaced by calmness, erratic thought replaced by mental stillness, 'ego' replaced by loving kindness, and so on) is the very core of your meditative Journey. Awakening to this understanding of the 'welling up' of your original naturalness is a meditative signpost that your feet are planted firmly on the Path.

* * *

A Little Story of Encouragement

The Secret of 'Just Practicing'

'Around the middle of 2005, I saw a brochure in the local supermarket for meditation classes. At 59, I'd tried meditating using instructions from books on and off for many years but never kept it up. This was the first time I'd seen a class that was close to home – so I rang and booked in for a "beginners" session.

It was winter, but once a week about 25 of us sat in a freezing hall directly beneath the international jet flight path, trying hard to hear what our teacher had to say while, above us, planes would pass over every few minutes.

I tried to relax, breathe and "let go" – didn't seem to catch on to it straight away. But I liked the teacher's style and was sufficiently interested to continue to brave the cold.

Although I wouldn't call myself a depressive personality, prior to beginning meditation class, I had been feeling down for some months and had reached a mental state of despair such that I wanted to quietly die and suffer no more mental anguish. If not for my lovely wife and family I would have done something very foolish. Several months after starting classes, I began to think that meditation just might offer a solution to my personal problems.

Eventually, I started meditating every morning and most days, in the evening as well. Oddly enough, my mental state improved little by little, and I saw some hope for the future. After just a month or two of regular practice, I found my depression had lifted considerably, and the irritability that plagued me when walking among people on the street or driving in traffic began to fade.

Now, after 18 months of simple daily meditation, my problems have fallen away. I no longer lie awake at night for hours worrying. I find it easier to deal with difficulties. My ability to concentrate is improving. Situations with work colleagues that previously could literally make me shake with anger and frustration no longer arise. Rather than ignoring beggars as before, I now reach into my pocket and give. My enjoyment of life is becoming richer.

Curiously, my taste for alcohol has disappeared, and I no longer daily consume vast amounts of chocolate. There is a sense of calm and peace during meditation that spills over into my daily life. I feel more positive and confident and – yes, happy!'

– James (actual name withheld for personal reasons)

Chapter Six

Meditation Postures

Up to this point, all the practice in your sanctuary has been in the 'lying-down' position (*savasana*). Now that you are familiar with the concept of 'letting go', all your formal practice from here on will be in one of the more classic, 'sitting-up' postures which enable the body to be a naturally and beautifully balanced 'base' for all meditation exercises.

The Lotus Position and Variations

The first posture, as shown in Photo 2, is called *padmasana* or the 'lotus position' of which there are several variations. The full lotus position with legs fully intertwined (feet resting sole up on the opposite thigh – as if tying them in a knot), requires some serious flexibility developed through

2. *Padmasana*, the classic lotus position, most usually adopted by exponents at a more advanced level of *hathayoga*.

3. Half-lotus posture, a 'softer' sitting discipline.

4. *Sukhasana*, the classic posture favoured most often by practitioners of *zazen*. This is the posture we usually adopt in Authentic Meditation.

much practice and is most usually adopted by exponents at a more advanced level of *hathayoga*.

This complex position is not at all necessary for meditation but we do use a simpler version of it, either the half-lotus (shown in Photo 3), with one leg resting on the opposite thigh or the more classic *zazen* position, *sukhasana* (Photo 4). It is classic, simple and comfortable. Even in a deep meditative state, you can't fall over!

To try this position, cross your legs gently and in a loose way so that one doesn't place pressure on the other. Experiment a little to find the best position. The back is neither rigid nor bent forward – just comfortable and very slightly arched.

The key to a balanced posture is the position of your head. It is most important to find the 'balance point' for your head so that holding it in position will require virtually no tension in your neck muscles. It is as if you are trying to balance a basketball on your finger.

When you think you have the right position, just relax the muscles in your neck. If your head begins to fall forward for example, then the right position is a little further back – and so on.

Kneeling Posture

Another posture adopted by some students is the 'thunderbolt' posture, *vasrajana,* shown in Photo 5. In this position, get on to your knees and then slowly sit back on your heels with the soles of your feet facing upwards and your toes pointing out behind you. The kneeling posture is more appropriate for shorter meditations as your weight is only distributed across your knees, shins and ankles, whereas in the sitting position, weight is distributed a little on your legs but mainly across that beautifully padded larger area designed for sitting!

Some students also put a cushion between their calves and buttocks in *vasrajana* (Photo 6) to make it more comfortable. You may also use a slope-topped little stool,

5. *Vasrajana,* the 'Thunderbolt' posture, also used in Authentic Meditation.

6. Making *vasrajana* 'more comfortable' with a cushion.

available in some yoga 'shops' that, in effect, replaces the cushion and raises the body a little higher.

I personally find these latter postures less balanced than the lotus position and certainly, if you have damaged knees, or have arthritis or are discomforted in some other way, this position is not for you.

Difficulties Sitting on the Floor

Some people initially have difficulty in sitting on the floor because of knee, back or other physical conditions (often just because they are not 'in condition' through years of non-exercise). A number of such students commence their early practice sitting on a chair but, after a few weeks, I suggest that they try sitting on the floor as best they can for just a minute before popping back into the chair. Then on the following day, I suggest they do the same but for say, two minutes – then increasing the 'floor time' little by little each day. I have found that almost all folks can genuinely stretch their muscles and tendons after a few months to a point where they can sit *comfortably* in at least the *zazen* position (*sukhasana*) for perhaps 20 minutes.

One dear lady, now a senior student, for the first six months of her practice flatly refused to try and sit on the floor, saying simply, 'it's not possible'. But one day, I glimpsed her sitting on the floor for a short while and getting back into the chair after a minute or so – and yes, you can write the rest of the story. Two years later, she is completing one-hour meditations in the lotus position without a muscle twitch for the whole period! Be inspired to try.

Sitting on a Chair

If you do have damaged joints, are elderly or perhaps disabled in some way, it is perfectly fine to sit in a chair or, if required, a wheelchair to practice. If you are permanently bedridden, you can practice all the exercises lying in your bed (trying hard of course, not to nod off). We have had several dear students come to the Meditation Sanctuary happily parked in their wheelchairs and one precious being suffering from MS even brought her 'bed' with her.

My discussing postures for meditation is simply to emphasise the need for you to be *comfortable and balanced* in order to maximise the effectiveness of your practice.

Moving When Uncomfortable

Until you are practiced in one of these postures, you may find that your back begins to hurt after a while, or your legs become stiff, sore or 'tingly'. This is normal and these stroppy little areas of your body may complain simply because they are not familiar with their new task.

Pain is your body-friend, designed to tell you that something is amiss and warning you to 'do something' to alleviate the physical stress or difficulty it is suffering. Do not ignore your body – listen to it carefully. It is your best friend. So, if you need to move, then move, but there is a right way to do it.

If you need to shift in your posture, do so when you *begin* to feel discomforted, not as a last resort when you are about to faint with pain. *The secret to moving is to do it very, very slowly* while endeavouring to keep your mind singularly focused on your practice at the same time. Moving slowly dissolves the distraction of pain before it becomes ... distracting! The body stillness (and later, any meditative state) that you have attained will not then be unravelled as it would by sudden moves which are an instant distraction that breaks down inner quietness.

So if you have pain in your back, for example, lean gently forward or backward – perhaps twist a little to one side and then the other – but almost imperceptibly if you can. If your legs start yelping a protest, either open the posture a little or stretch them out in front of you ever so slowly, while keeping your mind focused as best possible. When you are in a true tension-free state, you will find it virtually impossible to move rapidly anyway because, as I have said, you have slowed or stilled the messages from the brain to the muscles and nerves of your body.

If, however, pain continues after you've moved, stop the exercise altogether. Try again next time and then for a little longer each subsequent day until your body becomes familiar with your new demands of it. If pain persists, adopt a different posture until you find one that is comfortable. Later, though, endeavour to source the cause of the pain – if it is not just lack of fitness.

An alternative to moving, if you are uncomfortable, is to shift your focus to the area of pain and practice a 'directed pain relief' as I guided you in earlier. If you are just adding 'tension upon tension' in your effort to hold a 'right' *sukhasana,* you may find that targeted relaxation solves the problem.

* * *

In summer months, when there are a few mosquitoes looking for a victim among the tasty ones at the Meditation Sanctuary, I'm occasionally amused by the sound of a sharp 'slap' from somewhere in the group meditating peacefully before me. I know instantly that the 'slapper' is distracted by thought and external stimuli (although a mozzie bite may be a reasonable 'distraction') ... and has not reached the tension-free state. If they had, they wouldn't be able to move fast enough to slap!

I remember a story told by the Buddhist monk, Ajahn Brahm, founder of the Bodhinyana Monastery in Serpentine near Perth, Australia. He was talking of his own training in the forests of Thailand and telling about a day when he was meditating outdoors with another shaven-headed monk. Upon glancing at his colleague, he 'noticed about 40 mozzies feasting' on the monk's shaved head – and his fellow traveller didn't even move. Now *that*, dear reader, is seriously meditating.

* * *

The Mudras – Hand Positions for Authentic Meditation

The position in which hands are rested for meditation is called a *mudra*.

7. The most popularly recognised *mudra*. It is an ancient hand posture with religious and ceremonial tradition. It is not used in Authentic Meditation as it requires tension in hands, arms and shoulders.

Many yoga practices adopt a *mudra* with the top of the thumb touching the top of the forefinger, so forming a little circle or the more classic position with the top of the thumb placed *over* the top of the forefinger with the wrist resting on the knees (Photo 7). In some monastic practices, these and similar *mudras* have religious significance and symbolism in which the thumb represents Brahman or the Absolute and the forefinger represents the 'ego' or, as that was known for thousands of years, the I-consciousness. So, in the pictured popular *mudra*, the thumb 'erases' the forefinger or 'Oneness with the Absolute' overcomes the I-consciousness.

Although such *mudras* (and many others) may have significance in meditative practices with a religious base and indeed, 'look very yogic', they are not appropriate for Authentic Meditation because they require tension in your shoulders, arms and hands to hold the fingers together – and you have just spent weeks or even months practicing letting tension go!

There are two ways to hold your hands that require *no* tension in your body and are the *mudras* we adopt in Authentic Meditation. The first one I call the butterfly *mudra* (Photo 8). Both hands are held, palms facing up with one 'cupped' restfully on the other – as if you are holding a delicate butterfly or revealing a beautiful flower to a loved one. Then the hands are just rested in your lap. The other position (Photo 9) is resting the palms of your hands cupped on your knees. Be careful not to place your wrists on your knees because, after a while, the pressure on your wrists will restrict the blood flow to your hands.

You will find these more natural *mudras* restful, comfortable and tension-free, which is why they have been used by Zen meditation masters for centuries.

8. The butterfly *mudra* – the perfect hand position for Authentic Meditation as it requires no tension to maintain the hands at rest.

9. 'Hands-cupped' posture. A tension-free alternative to the butterfly *mudra*.

Chapter Seven

Releasing Tension in a Meditation Posture

Once more in your sanctuary, adopt your chosen 'posture'. I shall use *sukhasana* – the gentle *zazen* position for the purpose of my discussion.

In effect, the entire practice of the First Essence sitting in *sukhasana* is identical to that which you have been practicing while lying down *in savasana* – except that now you will be holding some tension in your back and balancing your head. As you are deeply familiar with the phases of letting go body tension (Restful Calming, Quieting, Chasing Fugitive Tension and Melting Chocolate), I shall not describe them in full again but just guide you more briefly to emphasise a few important points of practicing while sitting, because this is your posture from here on.

Exercise 4. *Letting Go Tension while Sitting*

Close your eyes, check that you are comfortably balanced and then, move your mind-focus to your body.

For just a day or two, you may wish to tense up all over again, slowly letting go the tension and sinking through the tension barrier to stillness. However, that is optional and you may choose to simply 'let go' until you feel calmly relaxed. From there, first move your attention to the muscles around your eyes in the Quieting phase, before taking your mind-focus down your body, exactly as you have been practicing.

However, when you reach your back in the Quieting phase, you will discover that you are holding added tension across that whole area because your body believes that it needs more tension to keep you upright. The reality is that, while sitting, you can actually let go about 80 per cent of the muscle tension held in your back without moving your body a single millimetre. Try it now.

When the Quieting phase takes you to your back muscles, stay focused there for extra time. Start from the nape of the neck and very slowly work down to your buttocks, just as you did when lying down. You will feel the tension gradually seeping from your back until it is quite deeply relaxed – except that you are still sitting exactly as you were when you commenced – perfectly balanced.

This is not really difficult at all. Be mindful of the little bird that spends the night sound asleep while perched on a branch, head under wing and often standing on one leg. This little creature has mastered the ability to *hold perfect balance using just enough natural tension* where needed. So you, also, being a little creature on this planet, can perfect the same balancing ability. As you will need this posture from now on (sitting on your mat, not on a branch … unless you really want to sit on a branch – in which case …!) practice holding the lowest level of 'natural tension' that your back requires for you to remain vertical.

Continue the Quieting until completed. Then, move your mind-focus to a full body 'sweep', seeking out the fugitive tension spots that crept back just to annoy you. Remember to give special attention to the muscles around the eyes and for a few weeks add your back muscles to your 'special attention' list. Complete with Chocolate Melting without your body moving – just as if you were lying down.

Just 'Sinking' into Tension-free Mode

To this point in your practicing of Letting Go Tension, I have guided you through the different phases of letting go, step by logical step. After you have become really familiar with each of the practice 'steps', from Resting Calmly to Melting Chocolate, it is time to begin to let go the process of practicing by steps. Remember, I have said that mastering meditation is about 'letting go', from the first tension-freedom exercise to as far as you want to travel on the Path.

Exercise 5. *Letting Go the 'Steps'*

This exercise is really quite simple. You allow each 'phase' of Letting Go Tension to just gently, fluidly flow into the next phase – and then the next.

> *So, in sukhasana with your eyes closed, commence the first step of Essence One (Resting Calmly) while, at the same time, resting your mind-focus on the muscles around your eyes. Then fluidly run your mind in tension-freeing mode down your body like a wave whooshing slowly back down the beach … rather than your awareness 'stopping for a coffee' at each body area and saying 'Hi, I'm here to relax you', as it has been.*
>
> *Continuing the flow of one phase 'becoming' the next, you will find that when the Quieting wave has seemingly washed through you, your focus will just automatically shift to fugitive areas still needing attention before just flowing into a whole-body, 'chocolate meltdown'.*

For a few practices, you will probably find that your mind continues to attend the different steps of the Essence, but soon the flow of one to the other will seem to 'take over' and become just a single-motion, beautifully natural tension release without much effort at all. The aspiration of the first Essence is to be profoundly, blissfully tension-free and, in time, you will have developed the ability to *just do it* – seemingly without 'thoughtful' effort. Continue practicing the First Essence in the sitting posture, until reaching tension-freedom in your sanctuary has become a natural part of your daily activity.

Chapter Eight

Taking Your New Skills With You

The standout problem in our society is the life-pressure under which we folks place ourselves (*yes, we do it to ourselves*), leading almost uncontrollably, minute-by-minute, to the suffering of 'uber-stress', stored tension, illness and disease.

If you just look about you, you will find that so many people in the hurry and flurry of today's streets and marketplaces wear stress on their faces like a roadmap of worry. With the growing of your practice, you may slowly realise that you may have been just like those people as well – *because you probably have.*

Just about everyone in the world seems to need the 'letting go skills' that you are practicing. The good news that I want to shout to the worried ones in the street, the high-rise office dwellers and indeed, the whole universe of harried folk, is that *it is eminently possible to become a 'quiet being', awakened to the very living of life the whole time* ... not just in the privacy of a secluded monastery or meditation sanctuary. The best news possible, dear reader, is that if you *are* on the illuminating Path of meditation, one day you may become the peaceful one – the 'illumined being' – I often hope to glimpse in the madding crowd.

* * *

To this point, all your practice has been in the familiar environment of your sanctuary. You will probably have developed a mental association between the sanctuary and being tension-free so even just entering it will begin to feel as comfortable and inviting as the lovely feeling of 'coming home'.

I said at the beginning of the book however, that *Authentic Meditation is ultimately about living your life* as a truly mindful, aware, awake and even 'enlightened' being, at one with your existence. The key to returning to this natural state of living with uncluttered consciousness, is to gradually go beyond just sitting and practicing the exercises in your Sanctuary, by enabling your experiences there to begin to sift and seep into your whole life.

It is so important that you don't just consider your Sanctuary experiences as 'nice while they lasted' and then let them go the moment you walk out, allowing any benefits to be overtaken by the busyness of – next! If you do, you defeat the purpose of your practice, leaving the benefits spilled and wasted right there on your sanctuary floor.

Throughout the book then, I shall sometimes conclude segments with guidance on what I call 'Active Meditation'. This, in effect, is the art of taking some of the skills you are redeveloping with you and gradually, weaving them as beautiful, new and colourful threads through the rough old fabric of your daily life. So, although your continuing training in the sanctuary will remain essential for much of your Journey, I shall also guide you in taking these skills 'outside' to begin to add awakened value to the quality of your active life.

Exercise 6. *Practicing the 'Yogic Secret' – Outside Your Sanctuary*

With Eyes Closed

One day, just sit at the kitchen table or another quiet and comfortable place in your home.

> *Close your eyes and, just as you did in your sanctuary, focus on the muscles around the eyes and let go the tension in them. Keep your awareness there, and then just move your focus to your forehead and face. Be aware of your whole body calming (the magic of relaxing around the eyes) and be aware of your breathing slowing. Just 'feel and rest' for a few minutes, then open your eyes, focus on an object for a*

moment while you adjust back to just sitting in an unfamiliar practice environment.

That's it! Easy. Just a tiny exercise but one that can have amazing effect if you just stop and do it for a minute or two, several times a day.

With Eyes Open

When that powerful little exercise is beginning to have a calming effect, you can take it a step further by trying it with your eyes open. At first, you may find focusing 'inwards' on your body a little more difficult because you are surrounded by a myriad visual distractions. But, as always ... patience.

Focus on an object in front of you (cup, orange, pen ... anything) and then, while staring at it, take your mind-focus to the area around your eyes and let go the tension as before. Again, endeavour to be really awake to the calming that will begin to wash through you. Continue deepening the letting go until you feel free of tension and then just hold there for several minutes while gazing on the object. To complete, slowly look away and just sit quietly for another minute or two.

The key to the effectiveness of this exercise is the first 'action' of really giving focused attention to an object to settle your busy mind in one place. Later, we will expand this practice into a more advanced meditative technique, so practice well now.

You will find that, at the beginning, Active Meditation doesn't seem to be as immediately effective as the practice in your sanctuary, because there you've had the advantage of being distraction free and, secondly, taking your whole body through the tension barrier before letting go tension around the eyes. However, do practice taking this exercise 'out there', particularly when you feel tense or stressed. You will quickly find it almost miraculous as calmness begins to infiltrate the old tense self. The more you practice this Active Meditation, the more effective it will be and for increasingly longer periods of time.

What a wonderful relaxation 'weapon' to possess – one you can take out of the mental holster anywhere, anytime.

Exercise 7. *Letting Go Tension in Daily Life*

When you are ready, you can venture even further into taking your meditation with you by beginning to let go tension in more areas of your body – again, wherever you are.

> *So if, for example, you are feeling tense in your shoulders, close your eyes, take your attention firstly to the muscles around them (because you always attend to them first), then move your focus to the selected area, just letting go until you know you are tension-free.*

Very importantly, you will soon have developed the skill to pre-empt body-tension and even anxiety 'attacks' whenever you have a spare moment, simply by closing your eyes and wandering your mind-focus around your body, letting go tension wherever you happen upon it. Later, when you are comfortable with this exercise, begin to practice it with your eyes open as well. After just a few days, you will find this whole practice much more refreshing and rewarding than taking an aspirin or having a good lie down.

But you must remind yourself to 'have a go' daily, not just now and then – which is quite useless. Perhaps write yourself some notes saying 'Let Go Henrietta!' (last word optional), and place them in a few key places around the house or on your desk. In my own early practice, I did exactly that until it all slowly became a rather beautiful permanent habit of just 'letting go' physical tension the very moment I became aware of it beginning to happen. I tell my students that if it worked for me as a quite recalcitrant student in my early days, it will work for anyone.

Exercise 8. *Letting Go Tension While Walking*

After becoming comfortable with stopping what you're doing to let go tension, you can then begin to introduce your letting go skills to your whole body as you continue to go about your daily business, no matter what you are doing.

Start simply. While you are walking along, for example, just bring your awareness to the way you are walking. Are you tense, quick and hurried? Are you dashing to get somewhere, unaware of what you are doing and bumping into people? Everyone has important appointments and everyone gets held up in traffic – including meditation teachers – but you can be in a hurry while, at the same time, being completely tension-free and, consequently, calm of body and graceful of movement. Try this now.

> *After bringing your awareness to your body while walking (and probably soon recognising that you are riddled with 'hurry-tension'), continue to walk but … slow it a little and deliberately spend a few moments giving attention to each step you take. Focus on letting go tension from around your eyes, face and shoulders – then your hands and arms. Try to let go some tension from your chest, tummy and back as well – yes, as you are walking along! You can let go tension from your legs while maintaining the same walking pace. True – try this too!*

I don't mean you to relax so much that you hunch over and walk like a gorilla with arms straight by your side or that you fall in a heap right there on the pavement – but enough to feel 'unnatural tension' beginning to leave you. Soon you will discover that you are losing the 'tension-jerkiness' in your movement and that you are moving more smoothly and efficiently. You may even begin to enjoy 'getting there' rather than wishing you 'were there'. Now, wouldn't that be something!

It really is so simple. While giving attention to easing tension from your body, you bring your attention to *now* – because you are focusing on your body and the true loveliness of its moving, not on all the hurry-babble swamping your poor brain. Immediately, the worried concern of getting there or meeting the deadline will settle – because your focus, and your 'intent', has shifted to the present. The purpose for your bustle is still there but you can arrive (at the same time as you would have anyway) without that horrible stressed look on your face and your body feeling like a taut violin string.

After practicing Letting Go Tension in your daily doings for a while, you will simply begin to feel a sense of 'ease' filtering across all your activities. The great irony is that, as you lose that minute-by-minute tension, your focus, or 'mindfulness', actually enables you to do more! You reach a point of tension-free efficiency in which you are neither losing or wasting time endlessly, nor bumping into people through being too brain-busy to 'see' them or 'bumping into yourself' because you are too busy, stressed and tense ... to see *you*.

The great beauty of this important practice is that it is so wonderfully 'portable'. You will find countless situations in life that create tension in various areas of your body. The kids, partner, next-door-neighbour's dog, work ... everything at times can be a 'situation' that just about 'drives you nuts' – or creates tension to sometimes unmanageable levels. You may find your stomach muscles too tense and tight before a performance of some kind or your arms rigid with tension after a long drive.

However, instead of letting such situations disturb your calmness, you will awaken to the truth that each one provides you with an opportunity to *take your practice with you*. The key to it all, dear reader, is *awareness* – being aware that you are 'tensing up' – that your muscles have exceeded the natural tension barrier. As your awareness grows, you will find that you can create specific tension-freedom at key moments while being right in the middle of the activity or situation that is causing, or may cause, you tension.

I shall tell you a story that illustrates just how far this skill can be taken.

A number of times I have talked with an impressive young woman named Karin Schaupp. At an unusually young age, Karin became an internationally recognised classical guitarist. One day, I was privileged to just sit in on a master class she was giving to senior guitar students during which she began to talk about 'relaxation'. I expected the more usual advice about 'breathing to relax' and 'focusing the mind' before a concert performance, and so on.

Instead, Karin talked about *releasing tension while playing*. She highlighted the tiny pause that occurs between each note played, no matter how fast the fingers are moving on the strings. She told the students that they can 'use' each of those fractional pauses to relax the fingers, wrist and arm to prevent tension building up and affecting the quality of the music. Now *that,* dear reader, is serious Active Meditation ... that really is creating tension-freedom right in the middle of an activity.

I had wondered how Karin became aware of this advanced skill in tension-freedom until she told me that she had been practicing meditation for years. I should have guessed. You may not be a concert performer (or you may be!) but, as I said, *being aware* of the tension moments so you can swing into letting-go mode is the key.

Just as Karin's tension-free playing has become natural to her beautiful performances, so will *your* developing art of Letting Go Tension begin to seep naturally into your life. You will gradually find your 'normal' tension level moving to a naturally lower threshold than when you started your training. One day, you will just 'know' that you have reached into that lovely inner space on your Path when you begin to *possess* the naturalness of your meditative tension-freedom as you go about your daily life. Then you will be able to let go the formal practice of it.

The First Essence will simply be, once more, a natural part of you – a natural part of the way you live … as it was as a child.

Being Free of Tension under Pressure

People often ask me, 'what about times of real difficulty, sadness or danger – surely you can't 'just be' tension-free then?' Well, yes, you can because, with practice, you build such an innate awareness of tension that you will spontaneously allow the right amount of natural tension to be present to help the body react quickly to danger, or manage difficult circumstances *without getting lost in the mind*, which creates the unmanageable tension. When you master meditative tension-freedom, you develop an instinctive 'knowingness' of when to hold needed additional tension and when to let it go. When you *possess* your tension-freedom, that knowingness is available to you at all times.

Perhaps being one of the countless people who leads a tension-soaked life, you may feel that unveiling such a knowingness is fanciful and only accessible by the most highly trained such as a Zen monk or a yogi. Not so. They too started their Journey at the beginning and travelled it one little practice-step at a time. They too travelled the Path that you are now travelling and no matter what others may say or want you to believe, becoming truly tension-free is not difficult. Awakening to the practice of Active Meditation is a realisation that can become literally life transforming. It simply requires 'the will to walk' the Path – daily.

It is now time to practice the calming art of the Second Essence, Right Breathing, which will be like having two scoops of calmness instead of one.

* * *

A Little Story of Encouragement

'A Letter from a Zen Woman'

'My story is not the inspiring tribute to meditation of a person in horrendously difficult circumstances who has come through the other side of some personal tragedy with newfound meaning for life. It's a little more mundane and ordinary but, hopefully, just as telling on how meditation (or learning how to relax and be a meditative person) helps one very normal, everyday, working mother.

I found myself enrolled in meditation after my doctor had prescribed anti-depressants for post-natal depression. My coping abilities had completely deserted me and the insomnia and headaches started just as my five-month-old son started to sleep through the night. The drugs helped with many of the symptoms but, to address the others was something I had to do myself. So, after eight months of sleep deprivation, I was keen to start meditation. I had seen it help a family friend after a heart attack as part of his treatment plan, so I was open to the idea. But, being non-religious, I didn't want any spiritual intonations so thankfully, the Meditation Sanctuary proved a "suitable fit".

My drug regimen at the time included 75 mg of anti-depressants and six painkillers a day to keep the headaches away. I hoped that I might slowly reduce this consumption over time. My expectations of meditation were to learn techniques to manage stress better – though I'm not sure how I was going to do this! Well, I soon found out. Through some seemingly unremarkable techniques in which the teacher guided us, the extraordinary happened.

In the second week of the course, I experienced bliss. Five whole minutes of no headache without drugs! I had not been headache-free for months. Without meaning to, in reaching my meditative state, my headache had gone, merely as a "by-product" of my practicing – it was not something that I had deliberately focused on. So, after just two weeks, I was down to three painkillers *a week* and, after a few weeks of practice, I could fall asleep within an hour and, if I woke up again, slowly but surely get myself back to sleep within 20 minutes. Previously, it could have taken hours.

By just the sixth week of practice, I had reduced my antidepressants down to the minimum.

But, strangely enough for me, the effects of meditating were far more astonishing than just being able to sleep again. It has permeated throughout my life with completely unexpected results. I'm now just much calmer and nothing much bothers me anymore. Everyone has noticed this – I'm called the "Zen Woman" at work and in a deadline-driven corporate environment I can go home now completely relaxed. By just the act of meditating (and not deliberately trying to), the fundamental way I handle things has completely changed. No more conscious effort "to wind down" since I don't get "wound up" anymore in the first place.

In summary, I now *find meditation a seductive and strangely compelling place*. For the bliss and silence that sometimes I crave – forget chocolate and watching mindless TV – meditation is it for me! The health benefits of meditation for me have been incalculable.'

– Mary

Mary describes her story as 'mundane and ordinary' compared with others, yet she commenced her practice of meditation from a very dark place of suffering … and a body-overload of prescription drugs. I include Mary's story because it is quite astonishing in relating, not only the rapidity with which meditation began to 'go to work' on her health problems and general emotional state but, the extent of the effects that her practice had on her whole life. The great lesson to be taken is that she just did it! She dared to practice. In that 'seductive and strangely compelling place' lies the Path.

Chapter Nine

Mastering 'Right' Breathing

*'Right Breathing is, without question, the most important
"self-help" work you will ever do because it reaches into the very
life-force of your existence.'*

– Brahmasamhara

I said in the earlier introduction to Right Breathing that, when we were born, we knew how to breathe perfectly. I also said that, gradually, the anxieties and busyness of modern life have caused virtually the entire human population to forget how to draw whole-being nourishment from the precious *life-force* of breathing, so readily available to us every moment of our existence.

However, on your meditative Journey, Right Breathing (also called Rhythm Breathing or Natural Breathing) is vital because, unless you have a reasonable degree of mastery over this natural function … you will never be able to meditate effectively.

Now, if that is not sufficient reason to begin the practice of drawing nourishment from this most precious life-force, perhaps the thought of possibly living the rest of your life with greater health, energy and inner peace will encourage you to 'get into' this essential practice of Right Breathing.

The Benefits of Right Breathing

There are many books on the benefits of natural breathing, most of which are very short on true guidance of the 'how'. If you are interested, writings from the ancient Orient are particularly rich in 'knowledge', because the early practitioners of Right Breathing were not lost in 'techno-busyness' 18 hours a day and gave great emphasis to the welfare of their bodies, almost as a spiritual duty. They were deeply aware of the health benefits of Right Breathing.

Earlier, I mentioned the Shaolin monks' practice of *Wu Shu*. This also included the practice of *pa tuan tsin,* a series of breathing and lung-strengthening exercises based on 'quietness of being and relaxation' but which required much training to master. *It was believed that if you breathed as you were meant to, drank the right quantity of water (a lot!) and meditated, you would never become ill.* Now, that's something to reflect upon!

In today's global milieu, however, in which most people are hell-bent on poisoning themselves with just about everything they eat, breathe in, wash themselves with, live in and drink, I can't promise you lifelong wellness by just 'breathing right' but, I can assure you that your health will be vastly improved if you do practice Right Breathing. For the purpose of nurturing your meditation, this simply means being able to return to your original, natural way of breathing rather than 'learning' any difficult or 'extreme' yogic practices in which some of the monastic yogis delight.

As you will discover, just breathing naturally again is going to take some quite serious practice until it becomes habitual once more because the lovely ability you once had has probably long since been smothered under the flurry and clamour of meeting the expectations of your life. Nevertheless, it is only 'buried' not destroyed, so your task becomes one of 'renewing a lost art'. It is an enjoyable task though, not mission impossible!

* * *

To begin with, the deep calming effect induced by natural rhythmic breathing dramatically reduces and, indeed, can eliminate, the 'feeling of stress' (which is of particular benefit to anxiety sufferers). This calmness has the effect of 'settling' emotional swings and actually reducing negative emotions.

Fully energising your body with the oxygen of the *life-force*, automatically leads you to feeling far more positive, alert and alive. Almost immediately, you will find that you have more energy and a greater clarity of mind. Breathing fully and deeply lessens nose and throat congestion and will even improve the way you use your voice as you learn to breathe through your words *as you speak* rather than speaking in a higher, more nasal, staccato voice – an unpleasant way of speaking exacerbated by anxiety and stress.

When you begin to breathe naturally as a matter of habit, your internal organs automatically receive better nourishment and the additional oxygen purifies your bloodstream. You'll notice that the whites of your eyes become clearer and your skin will develop a healthier and more youthful appearance. Your lungs become more elastic and your chest and stomach muscles more supple. Breathing 'right' also helps to reduce blood pressure and, to top it all off, the taking in of all that *life-force* can strengthen your immune system and help to prevent or delay the onset of lung and other diseases.

All those benefits result from the *natural* art of breathing which the yogis call *pranayama* – the practice of providing your body with plentiful oxygen, exercising and extending your lungs more fully and so eliminating greater quantities of toxic waste. It is logical, then, that regenerating the body and boosting the whole system through 'Right Breathing' can be profoundly beneficial to your wellbeing as well as helping those already suffering from illness or disease.

The First Step – Awareness of Your Breathing

For most of you, breathing is a simple, automatic process of which you are essentially unaware. In fact, whole days may pass without you giving a single thought to this second-by-second miracle occurring within your body … until something 'goes wrong'.

I am not going to take up a lot of your time on the physiology of breathing but, very briefly, I want to discuss the mechanics (not as good a word as 'miracle' is it!) of the breathing process – simply because it helps understanding of the absolute 'need' for returning to Right Breathing.

Firstly, your lungs are bigger than you probably imagined. The lung sacs are like two large, elongated bags on either side of the chest, protected by your ribs. Healthy lungs extend from just above your collarbone to the lower part of the rib cage. The entire inner surface area of both lungs, if they were laid out like a patchwork quilt, would cover about half a tennis court.

The lungs are divided into lobes – three in the right lung and two in the left. Each lung has bronchial tubes leading from the trachea (windpipe), rather like the branches of a tree. These in turn, filter into a smaller network of 'pipes' called the bronchioles, at the end of which are little air sacs made up of alveoli. These are like tiny bunches of grapes. When you breathe in, your *life-force* is drawn all the way from your nostrils to these alveoli and then of course, you breathe out again, eliminating the stale air. Therein lies the miracle.

Breathing Two Ways – at the Same Time!

In the practice of *pa tuan tsin,* the drawing in of *chi* or *life-force* and then the expiration (breathing out) process is referred to as *external respiration.* But there is another process of breathing, of which master practitioners of yoga and *chi* breathing are also deeply aware, and that is 'tissue breathing' or *internal respiration.* This is an acute and mindful awareness, after taking a breath, of the vitality of the life-force, oxygen, being distributed by the bloodstream to the countless cells of the body, each of which has tiny mitochondria that are like little 'rods'. They contain enzymes whose job it is to break down and store sugar (like haystacks in a field but made of pure energy), waiting to be used. The oxygen you take in acts as a 'trigger' to release this energy just whenever you need it – which is virtually constantly.

Now ultimately, you don't need to know any of that. So why explain it?

Because of the fact that *99 per cent of people (probably including you), for the whole of their lives, use only about one-third to one-half of their lung capacity when taking in each breath* – thus inhibiting the dear little mitochondria from doing their job and automatically diminishing the release of energy into your body. You really run around with a couple of cylinders misfiring – just about the whole time. Now I don't want to bore you with numbers but I just want to underline the reality of 'right' and 'wrong' breathing.

The breathing cycle happens in the 'ordinary-breathing' person about 14 000 to 20 000 times a day depending on the level of exertion or stress. The meditative breather (when *not* meditating) will inhale and exhale between 5000 and 6000 breaths per day and the yogi master, while meditating, as little as 1500. The untrained breather will use about 170 000 litres of air per shallow-breathing day. But the practiced person will draw oxygen from nearly 300 000 litres ... with *less than half* the breaths of the 'normal' breather. So what does all that tell you, dear one. Perhaps that ... *the 'right' breather enjoys twice the energy for half the effort of the 'normal' breather.* What a good place to be!

The yogic 'awakeness' to internal respiration (and the nourishment derived from it) enables the meditative person to release this 'additional' energy at will and, thus, to enjoy the extraordinary benefits of the *chi* abundantly available as a gift from the universe. It is only a matter of being able to access it. The practice of Right Breathing, or *pranayama*, deep and conscious breathing, provides that access. It is *the* way to both nourish and benefit the body while preparing you further for the meditative Journey ahead. This is the natural wonderment we shall explore.

Awakening Breathing Awareness

I shall begin the Second Essence by guiding you in a series of little practices to awaken your awareness to the simple fact that ... *you breathe*. However, a couple of helpful hints first.

Through Nose or Mouth?

Hatha Yogis teach many ways of breathing for a range of health and mastery purposes. But, for the purpose of Authentic Meditation, just close your mouth and breathe both in and out through your nose. In some exercises later on, we shall use the mouth for exhaling, but please wait until we get there.

The reason for nose breathing is simple. Your nasal passages are beautifully designed with tiny threads or hairs called *cilia* that beat rhythmically to filter impurities from the air as you breathe in, reducing the amount of smoggy rubbish with which you would otherwise cake the linings of your lovely lungs. So, nose designed for inhaling – mouth designed for other things, and occasionally exhaling.

If you are a habitual mouth breather, even just switching to nose breathing will have a noticeable effect on your daily vibrancy and general health. I would like you to begin practicing breathing through your nose until it is a natural habit once more. This can become another Active Meditation (practices you can 'take with you') – starting now.

If you have difficulties breathing through the nose (head cold, blocked sinuses or congestion), then do breathe through your mouth on the basis that it is better to do that than not breathe at all!

Take It Gently

When you commence your breathing exercises, a whole new world may seem to open to you. It really can be quite exhilarating when you begin to breathe efficiently again. However, rediscovering this natural pleasure can lead to a tad of 'uber-enthusiasm'. If you are a little too zealous and begin to over–breathe (breathing too deeply and rapidly), without adequately 'training up' the lungs for such sudden additional activity, you may well experience some slightly unpleasant side effects. These can include feeling tingly in your body, light-headedness or dizziness and you may see 'floaty spots' before your eyes. Know that *none of these body responses are harmful* but experiencing any of them is the signal to immediately start drawing shallower and slower breaths. So, the message is take your early practice gently.

Exercise 9. *Breathing Awareness*

From now on, remember that whenever you commence a new meditative practice, as you are about to do, you will always prepare yourself with the Essences *first* – your starting point for *all* further exercises in your sanctuary.

> *So, in your sanctuary once more, sit in sukhasana, close your eyes and spend at least 10 minutes moving through the familiar phases of letting go tension ... now in one beautiful letting-go motion, gentling your body to deep physical calmness.*
>
> *When you are tension-free, take your mind-focus to your breathing and just become aware of your chest movement. When your mind is*

focused on the movement, start counting your 'in' breaths and 'out' breaths. After each breath in, count 'one' in your mind. Then after you breathe out, count 'two'. So, every in-breath is a 'one' and each out is a 'two'. Continue to do this for two or three minutes.

This first phase is quite beautiful because, when you are able to 'stay with the counting', it brings your awareness to the 'process' of your breathing. It *must do* because you are counting each one. So simple. After all that time of 'unawareness', it is wonderful to begin actually *awakening* to your lovely breathing. Work hard to keep your mind focused on the counting because, after a little while, the tendency is to think – 'too easy' – and, even *while you're still counting*, your mind floats off to … carry on thinking. Try and be awake to its wandering and guide it back to … just counting.

The next phase of the exercise is to do the same but … stop counting. Maintain your focus on the action of breathing in and out without the distracting mind-noise of counting. You will find your awareness of 'just breathing' will now become much clearer. Try and hold yourself 'within' this more pure awareness of your breathing for about five minutes or so.

When you are ready, complete the whole practice session in the usual way – *slowly*. I suggest that you add the breathing awareness exercises (counting – then letting go counting) to your tension-freeing regime for several days before moving to the next exercises.

Exercise 10. *Deepening Breathing Awareness*

When you feel ready to go on, practice through the First Essence until still of body (soon I shall assume that this has become habitual so I won't need to repeat it for every exercise). Move your awareness to your breathing – no counting now – your mind just focusing on the rise and fall of the chest and the air going in and out – still in your 'normal' breathing mode.

When you have settled into awareness of the rhythm of your breathing, take your mind-focus to just inside the tip of your nose. Become aware of the air moving past the tip of your nostrils as you inhale and feel it coming out as you exhale. Then listen to the sound of the air flowing as well as feeling it. Finally, become aware that the in-breath of air feels 'cool' and seconds later, the air being exhaled is 'warm'. How incredible that is! Maintain this awareness for a few minutes and then just focus back on the rise and fall of your chest.

In this same practice session, the next step is to become aware of your lungs themselves.

When you are ready, begin to imagine or 'visualise' the in-breath as a colour (I used to visualise the life-force as a rich golden colour). So when you breathe in now, visualise this coloured chi swirling into your lungs. Then 'see' the coloured air passing back out into the universe through your nostrils as you breathe out.

Do this about 10 to 20 times. It is not the most important exercise but you'll find it heightens your awareness of the fact that you do have lungs – part of the process of *awakening*. Then, gently let go the visualisation of the colour and return your awareness to normal breathing once more. Complete the practice session slowly, as usual.

Your Daily Practice

At the moment, your practice is Essence One (Letting Go Tension) followed by the several breathing awareness exercises you've just worked through. You are now practicing daily for about 15 minutes or so – longer if you so choose. If you are not practicing daily, or at least five times a week, you are seriously diminishing the chance to bring the benefits of tension-freedom and natural breathing back into your life. (That's a refined way of saying 'if you don't practice, you are wasting your time'!)

When your mind can steadily hold focus on an awareness of your breathing, you are ready to move on to breathing control, in which you consciously begin to 'direct' your inhaling and exhaling. It is from this moment that the practice of Right Breathing begins.

Mastering Your Breathing – the First Step

As you travel the meditative Journey, you gradually shed the little training-step exercises, leaving them behind on the side of the Path, their job having been done. Accordingly, once starting the practice of *breath control,* there is no need to continue using the stepping stones of the awareness exercises, because the new exercises intrinsically bring deep focus to your breathing anyway.

It is rather like my learning to ride a bicycle when I was about six, guided wisely by my dear grandfather. I would ride along happily knowing he was holding the seat – so I knew I was safe. Then gradually he would let go his hold for just a moment, petrifying me beforehand by telling me he was going to do it. I became used to these moments of 'riding free', which of course he gradually lengthened to a few seconds.

Then one day I was saying, 'don't let go for too long Pop', but there was no reply. Of course, on looking over my shoulder for him, I discovered with horror that he wasn't there but standing about 15 metres back chuckling to himself, whereupon I fell off … relevance of the story being we *let go* the holding on to little practices and techniques after mastering them, having used them as stepping-stones to enable us to journey freely onwards.

Exercise 11. *'Directing' your Breathing*

A new practice day in your Sanctuary!

> *Assume your posture and … you know what to do. Enjoy the feeling of being tension-free – the true joy of deep physical calmness – for about 10 minutes.*

(There's not much point in being on a journey if you don't stop and sightsee along the way from time to time!) Don't go any further into the breathing-awareness exercises – they're over.

> *Having reached body quietness, take your mind-focus to your breathing – but just being awake to the air going in and out of your lungs. Hold your awareness on 'just breathing' until your mind-focus is quite settled there. At that point, I want you to actually count the time it takes to breathe in and the same for your breathing out. So – breathing in now – 'one and two and three and' … so on. You will find that you are probably taking about a three or four count on both 'actions'.*

This exercise is to begin the important practice of *slowing the time taken for each breath* – just a little at the moment. This is the first step in consciously directing your breathing.

> *Now, deliberately set a count of about three more than you were taking. For example, if you were taking 'three' to breathe in and three out, breathe now to a count of 'six' both in and out. Continue counting to the slower pace until it is comfortable. Then, while maintaining that slightly slower rate of breathing … stop counting.*

Importantly, when you slow your breathing, *don't* swell your chest out to take in another 'three seconds worth' of *chi*. Just take in the same amount as before – only more slowly. Without the distraction of counting, your mind will now be more aware of just your even, slower breathing. Try and hold your awareness on *just breathing more slowly* for several minutes.

A 'Taste' of Meditation – the 'Little Pause'

Remaining in the same exercise, you are deeply focused on breathing without counting.

> *When you are ready and, after you have completed an out-breath, do not breathe in again for two or three seconds (don't count – just estimate). Then commence your slow inhaling once more. In effect, you are simply creating a 'little pause' between your breathing out and your next in-breath.*
>
> *Practice until you are pausing comfortably and, when you have this 'working', take your mind-focus to the pause itself. Become absorbed in the quietness that is 'just present' in the little pause for that two- or three-second period. Keep this exercise in practice for a few minutes, then return to your normal breathing (slower now of course) before completing the session.*

The little pause is another important step in your beginning to deliberately direct, or master, your breathing. Include it in your practice as a training exercise for just a week or two.

This exercise can be a quite profound experience (albeit very short) because you will have your first experience of a deep inner quietness when not actually breathing for a moment. Most importantly, you are *not thinking* either because, in that brief couple of seconds, *you don't have time to think.*

One day a student asked with concern 'what if I can't start breathing again?' I assured her that, if it weren't possible to start breathing again, I wouldn't be sitting before her right now! I would be enjoying the dusty trails of the hereafter. I told her not to worry as the body will do it automatically for you when it needs a new supply of oxygen … as it has since the year dot … and that 'I haven't lost a student yet'!

I tell dear freshlings that the experience of the whole-being quietness in that brief pause is 'like a little meditation' because being fully 'present' in such stillness is not unlike that which you enjoy in genuine meditation. In fact, a while ago, a famous actor (who had said she'd 'done meditation' for 12 years), was practicing and, after doing the 'little-pause' exercise, she came to me and, rather wide-eyed, said, 'for the very first time, I just found out what meditation really is'. You too, like her, are now on the Path to finding out 'what it really is'.

Your Daily Practice

Ideally, I suggest that you practice gradually slowing your breathing down to a 'six' to 'eight' count for about two weeks, or, until you feel ready to move on. You have now put your foot on the breathing Path that leads to 'twice the goodness with half the effort'.

The 'Technique' of Right Breathing

In your mind, I would like you to visualise your lungs divided into three segments: lower, middle and top. Most people only use the 'top' third of their lungs in what is called 'shallow' breathing, effectively leaving the remaining segments of the lungs 'out of action' unless the body is put under exertion … as for example, in running.

It's true of course that, thanks to the magnificent nature of your lungs, shallow breathing gives most of you enough oxygen to toddle along reasonably well most of the time. That's more or less fine until you *do* suddenly 'need more air' for strenuous activity. Then your poor unexercised lungs really struggle to take in more air ... because they have *forgotten how to breathe properly* ... and you become 'puffed out'. Now *that's* a problem.

Another drawback of shallow breathing is that it leaves the middle and lower segments of your lungs virtually unused. They become your personal garbage dump for accumulated, residual toxins because you are only breathing out from the top portion of your lung – leaving the rubbish behind.

Not expelling toxins has a negative effect on your whole wellbeing. Instead of experiencing oxygen-enriched vitality, the body spends much of its precious energy trying to eliminate toxicity; hence the modern maladies of general tiredness, easy exhaustion, lack of motivation and, significantly, increased susceptibility to sickness and disease.

You can easily find out whether *you* are a shallow breather. Firstly, listen to your speaking voice ... and your laughter. Is your voice rich, smooth and able to be projected (in other words, can it be heard on the other side of a room without raising your voice or shouting). Or, is it high in tone, staccato in speaking, nasal in sound and constricted in the throat. Is your laugh deep and mellow, or a shrill and breathless cackle like a hen that has just laid an egg? (Did you know that a yogi or Zen master can divine your life-long breathing habits, the very moment he hears you speak?)

Secondly, stand in front of a mirror and take a good deep breath. Watch your shoulders as you do it. In taking a really deep breath, almost everyone raises their shoulders quite noticeably, believing that they are taking in more air. Did you? The truth is, not a cubic millilitre more is squeezed in to your lungs by raising your shoulders. So, the very sound of your voice and the shoulders indicator tell you clearly whether you are a shallow breather.

If you *are* a shallow breather, you are about to practice letting go some very bad breathing habits.

The Secret to Right Breathing

The great secret to Right or Natural Breathing is so simple. It is the ability to relearn controlled, rhythmic, vibrant (but gentle) use of your entire lung capacity – *the whole time*, as a matter of habit, just as you did when you were a baby.

Knowing the secret is easy … but it's a little more difficult to achieve after a lifetime of shallow, breathing. However dear reader, be encouraged because I have seen countless students reap the benefits of Right Breathing (in accordance with their level of commitment and practice, of course) – so you can too. Not only that, people with extreme breathing problems may also enjoy significant improvement, just by reversing their bad breathing habits. One dear woman particularly comes to mind. She was (and is) suffering from emphysema, an eventually fatal lung disease. When she came to the Meditation Sanctuary, she had very limited lung capacity, wheezed when she breathed, could not utter a full sentence without needing 'more air' and had very poor skin colour. She began seriously practicing Right Breathing as well as doing extra lung cleansing and strengthening exercises (some of which I've included in Chapter 11).

Our objective together was not to try the impossible by restoring destroyed alveoli and damaged lung infrastructure but to develop the capacity and strength of the 'good' lung areas that remained. Very simply, after just three months, her medical specialist measured a seven per cent increase in her actual lung capacity, her voice modulated, she could speak without becoming so breathless and her colour began to develop a much more normal 'rosy' tinge. Today, she enjoys long, daily spells of discomfort-free living.

In this next segment, I shall guide you in the techniques of Right Breathing until gradually, they become absorbed into the 'naturalness' of your meditative practice.

Right Breathing

Exercise 12. *'Hara' Breathing – Using Your Lower Lungs*

Step 1

> *In today's practice, go to your sanctuary and simply lie down in the savasana position as in your very early exercises. Take a small book with you and just leave it beside you. Settled in the correct position, put your hand horizontally across your tummy and take a normal breath. Did your tummy push your hand up towards the ceiling a little?*

If it didn't, you can now confirm you are shallow breathing – just breathing in the top part of your lungs. If you did move your hand just by breathing, you are 'hara' or 'tummy breathing' … taking at least some air into your lower lungs.

Most Westerners are totally unfamiliar with 'tummy' breathing but in Zen meditation it has been a core principle for many centuries. The ancient Chinese masters called the specific area just below your belly button, *tan t'ien* (the field of heaven) because they believed this was the spiritual centre of their being. The general area of the mid/lower abdomen (that rises and falls with your tummy breathing), the Japanese masters called the *hara,* which they regarded as the source of energy.

They were right of course. What they had really identified was that breathing 'properly', using the whole lung capacity, provided you with a renewable force of energy … provided you with life itself. They had identified that, when you breathe as you are meant to, *chi* is taken deep into the lower lungs, thus pushing down the big muscle called the diaphragm (which rests across your belly under your lungs). This, in turn, expands the tummy area and, when you are lying down with your hand there, it will be pushed up towards the ceiling a little. If it didn't move, you are not 'immersing in the *tan t'ien*' – in today's language, you are not fully oxygenating your body. Don't worry if this describes you because you are not alone … 99 per cent of the population is rowing the same boat with you.

At least you have the opportunity now of getting out of that unhealthy boat by practicing *hara* breathing, just as the ancient masters did as the natural Way of breathing for wellbeing … as well as it being the core breathing preparation for meditation.

You are lying on your back, with a hand resting on your tummy and centred on your belly button. Now, slowly, deliberately, take in a larger, longer breath, endeavouring to take some air down into those lower lobes of your lungs that will then force your tummy to 'rise'. You may find it a little difficult at first – doesn't matter – just keep your hand on your tummy, trying to move it a little upwards with your in-breath (even just a tad to begin with) and feeling it fall.

Step 2

> *After a minute or two, place the book on your tummy and rest both hands back beside you in the correct savasana position. Now try to push the book up and down a little with your breathing. Most students find they can actually move the object, perhaps only a little to begin with. When you notice your 'field of heaven' moving, just take your mind-focus to that area and become aware of feeling the air going in and out of your lower lungs. You can do it – but remember don't over exert or you may get a little dizzy.*

Step 3

> *After this practice becomes comfortable, the next step is to put the book aside and, with your hands still face down beside you, just focus on your hara breathing – your full awareness on the rise and fall of your tummy. Remember, slowly and gently for a few minutes the first time or two.*

If the book keeps sliding off your tummy because it is of a 'certain shape' (the belly – not the book) then, unless you are pregnant, you are 'out of shape' and you need some physical exercise – starting today, dear one. It's not much use practicing the perfection of Right Breathing if the rest of your body is … well, needing a little tender love and care.

If you are pregnant, however, leave the book aside and just practice gentle breathing, endeavouring to get air into your lower lungs, but *without forcing* or worrying about pushing your tummy out any further. You will actually find your middle lung area expanding a little sideways, a natural practice we shall all move to shortly.

I am being kind to you at the moment! Many moons ago, my Zen Master, Suni, used to put two bricks on my stomach and make me move them 'very noticeably' up and down for at least half an hour (after which the *field of heaven* didn't feel so heavenly). For years, I had told students that little story thinking it was quite impressive until … along came a lovely man called Costa who said, 'that's nothing – *my* martial arts master used to *stand* on my stomach and make me move *him!*' These days, I have to tell both stories to students! But you don't need bricks (or your teacher) – just a light object to show you whether you are getting some air … where you should be getting some air.

Practice *hara* breathing for a week or, until it begins to feel more natural.

Exercise 13. *Right Breathing in Your Meditation Posture*

When your *hara* breathing is a 'happening thing' in *savasana*, you are ready to move on.

In your next sanctuary session, take sukhasana, your sitting posture, close your eyes and, after reaching tension-freedom, just become aware of your normal breathing for a minute, as you have practiced before. Then put your hand horizontally across you tummy with the centre of your hand resting over your belly button (Photo 10).

As you did when lying down, take a deeper in-breath (say, about a four or five count), trying to take the air into your lower lungs as before and so pushing your tummy out, which will move your hand out towards the opposite wall. Then just exhale slowly, allowing your hand to move back in towards your spine as the tummy 'deflates'.

10. Hand held in this position to check *hara* breathing.

Now, some folks can push their tummy out just using their abdominal muscles and not actually taking a breath at all. That's impressive but is 'cheating breathing'. If you automatically do this, that's fine but, after expanding your tummy with your muscles, *then* breathe into your lower lungs. Lo and behold, your tummy will go out further – and you are *hara* breathing.

> *After a few minutes, take your hands back to your mudra and just focus your mind on the gentle in and out movement of your 'field of heaven' as you did when you were lying down.*

Exercise 14. *'Plain' or 'Full-lung' Breathing*

Plain Breathing is effectively breathing as you have for most of your life, but just adding *hara* breathing onto your shallow breathing mode. This simply means that you begin to consciously use your entire lungs to breathe, not just the top part.

> *So, after having taken an in-breath through your nose and felt your lower lungs filling (tummy going out), then just take air, slowly and gently (perhaps a comfortable five or six rhythm in and out) into the rest of your lungs up to and including the top area – all at once. Try not to count consciously.*

You are simply breathing in and filling the whole lungs in one movement, but … 'kick-started' by taking air into your lower lung area first.

> *To breathe out, you can simply do what I call 'balloon breathing' – breathing out by collapsing your lungs slowly all at once – like letting the air out of a balloon. In this exercise, you can breathe out through your mouth and purse your lips (as if you are whistling) so you can hear the air gently leaving your lungs. The practice is to empty your lungs as much as possible so you can begin the cycle with your lower-lung breathing again – but breathing in through your nose.*
>
> *After becoming familiar with the 'sound' of emptying your lungs fully, then close your mouth and breathe out through your nose, just being 'aware' of your lungs emptying rather than listening to the breath being exhaled. The whole cycle becomes a 'smoothness' of action but now, always starting with taking air into the lower lungs … first.*

Practice your Plain Breathing until it begins to feel natural and when it does, slow the whole lovely action by adding another second or two to both your in- and out-breath. Don't take in lung-bursting amounts of air – in fact, it is best that you only fill your lungs to about half capacity.

Your Daily Practice – the Minimum Breathing Requirement

Each day in your sanctuary now, I would like you to continue commencing with Essence One (Letting Go Tension), which will automatically slow your breathing. When you are deeply tension-free, allow your mind to become aware of your breathing and begin to introduce your *hara* breathing and then naturally develop it to Plain Breathing.

It is *vitally important* that you practice the complete Plain Breathing exercise daily, as this is the *minimum breathing capability* required for Authentic Meditation.

* * *

Hara with Plain Breathing is Step One of your Right Breathing. However, if you never go further on your Journey than just this for the rest of your life, you will still find your general wellbeing gradually improving, simply because you will be inhaling at least some extra *life-force* as well as renewing the original ability of being able to eliminate toxins from your body more effectively and naturally.

Rhythm Breathing

Exercise 15. *Developing the Natural Breathing-in Skill*

Earlier, I also used the term 'Rhythm Breathing' as an alternative way of describing Right Breathing. It is sometimes called this because there is actually a beautiful, calming, natural rhythm to the way you once breathed – a rhythm buried by most folk in the bad habit of shallow breathing. I shall guide you now in beginning to restore this full rhythm to your breathing – the ideal way of breathing for Authentic Meditation and the perfect way to maximise the opportunity for true wellness of being.

Rhythm breathing is not dissimilar to Plain Breathing but, as the name indicates, it extends the breathing awareness and practice beyond the *hara* area to include deliberate, correct and effective use of the middle and upper parts of your lungs.

* * *

You have already been practicing expanding your lower lungs with your in-breath. The next step is to consciously expand the middle 'segment' of your lungs.

11. Hands held in this position to check starting point for 'mid-lung breathing'.

Put both hands horizontally on your lower rib cage (about one hand-width above where you had your hand for the start of tummy breathing) so the tips of the middle finger are touching (Photo 11).

The sequence now is to, firstly, hara breathe (taking air into the lower lungs and pushing your tummy out) as you have been doing. Then draw in more so the mid-section of your lungs automatically expands. When you do this effectively, you will notice that the tips of your fingers are forced to part as the air in the middle section of your lungs expands your chest sideways (see Photo 12). Then you will have the mid-section as well as the lower lobes of your lungs expanded by your in-breath.

Then just slowly breathe out using the 'balloon' method again, letting the lower and middle segments of your lungs gently subside. The tips of your middle

12. Hands held in this position to check effectiveness of 'mid-lung breathing'.

fingers will come back together again. Repeat this exercise several times, just trying to fill the lower and middle portions of your lungs (keeping the top of your chest still) before expelling. After a few practices, you can let go the 'ballooning out' through your mouth and exhale through your nose.

The third and final step to complete the in-breath sequence of Rhythm Breathing is to include filling the top third of your lungs.

13. Hands held in this position to check effectiveness of 'upper-lung breathing'.

Put your hands on either side of the top of your chest so the fingers are pointing towards your throat (Photo 13). Fill the lower lungs, followed by the mid-section then, breathe in more, expanding the top of your lungs. But, this time, be very aware of not raising your shoulders. Instead, feel your chest push your hands outwards (even if only a little), towards the wall opposite you.

Then, 'balloon-breathe' out as you let all three segments of your lungs just naturally subside together until you feel they are 'empty'.

You may find it helpful to say *'lower' – 'middle' – 'top'* in your mind as you breathe into each of the three areas one by one, gently filling them with *chi* and then, smoothly 'ballooning' out the residue.

When you feel the practice becoming comfortable, take your hands away and place them in your mudra. Then keep repeating the exercise with your mind deeply focused on the whole rhythmic sequence. Again, after a few minutes, let go the balloon out-breath, reverting to the more natural breathing out through your nose.

'Smoothing' the Breathing-in Action

Your breathing may be slightly jerky at the beginning as a result of filling one area distinctly before moving on to the next … as in, breathe a bit (lower lungs) – pause – breathe a bit (middle lungs) – pause, and so on. That is fine until you become accustomed to using your lungs in this unfamiliar way.

When you are managing this 'new' in-breathing quite comfortably, the endeavour is to *run together* the three actions of inhaling as one, smooth, fluid action – followed by the ballooning exhalation.

> *So, instead of saying 'lower', 'middle', 'top' as three distinctly separate words in your mind, you begin to say 'lowermiddletop' as one long word describing a single, smooth action of breathing in – still in the 'rhythm' sequence, followed by the gentle whole-lung breathing out through your nose.*
>
> *The final step in redeveloping your natural rhythm on the in-breath, is to let go using the words as reminders. Then, whenever you are ready, try and slow the whole process.*

Practice this exercise daily until the rhythmic inhaling begins to feel increasingly natural – because it is. Remember that your rhythm in-breath is a *gentle* action and that you do not need to fill your lungs to the brim. At this stage, I am just interested in your getting the rhythm right.

Breathing Out – Another Ancient 'Secret'

Believe it or not, there is a *right way to exhale* in Rhythm Breathing, a way which enables you to deeply rid yourself of stale, toxic air with *every* out-breath. Sounds fancy doesn't it … except that every baby can do it perfectly. We shall now work on this old skill to complete your Right Breathing repertoire.

Exercise 16. *Developing the Natural Breathing-out Skill*

The 'right', natural or yogic way to breathe out is practiced simply by reversing the new 'rhythm sequence' of your in-breath. You have been breathing in, 'lower' followed by 'middle' then 'top' (or hopefully now, 'lowermiddletop', as one smooth action) and that's exactly the same action for the out-breath. Let's try that.

After you take a full, rhythmic in-breath, commence your out-breath by expelling the air from the lower part of your lungs ... first. Pull your tummy in as far as you can (which is also pushing the diaphragm up). Then, in order, close your ribs inwards as air leaves your middle lungs and then collapse the air from the top part of your lungs to complete the movement. Now your lungs have been completely emptied of the 'stale air'.

Repeat the cycle again ... the in-cycle always commencing with the lower lungs filling first, followed by the out-cycle ... always with the lower lungs emptying first.

So, dear reader, away you go – start breathing!

To make it easier if need be, still follow your 'mind-instructions' of *lowermiddletop* but now, on both the in- and out-breath. This makes it virtually impossible to confuse the order of the rhythm. Stay with repeating the words in your mind until your body can 'remember the sequence' – then let go the mental chat so the words are not a distraction. Endeavour to breathe both in and out through your nose.

A 'Meditative Pace' of Breathing

The next step in mastering Right Breathing is to slow your breathing further – gradually taking longer and longer for each in- and out-breath. Although you have already been doing this by adding a few seconds here and there to your breathing action, *really* slowing or developing a 'meditative pace' of breathing is the maturing of your natural skill.

There are two reasons why we practice this. The first is that, as you increasingly master becoming tension-free of body, your whole metabolism begins to slow down, therefore requiring less and less energy – and less oxygen and so ... less breathing. Secondly, the slower the breathing, the calmer you become. The calmer you become, the less ... and so on, until it all becomes one beautiful natural cycle of 'quieting'.

Because your body's need for *chi* varies according to energy demand, you can actually 'learn' to modulate the pace of your breathing to meet that demand precisely. As the 'need' is lower when practicing the Essences or meditating, the pace of your breathing can be substantially reduced while still meeting all the body's *life-force* requirements with complete comfort. Animals hibernating over winter, for example, effectively go into very deep meditation and their breathing becomes almost imperceptible in its slowness, because they only need sufficient energy for breaking down their fat supply to keep their organs nourished and … to continue breathing.

My first Teacher, Bashayandeh, was a Master of *hathayoga* as well as *rajayoga* (meditation) and could so control his breathing that, during deep meditation, he would take up to two minutes to breathe in and the same out. As for my Zen Master, Suni, when I occasionally happened upon him while he was sneaking quiet time to himself in the meditation room, I sometimes thought he was dead he was so utterly still. I usually managed to resist grabbing for a pulse only by perceiving the faintest look of peacefulness on his face and the healthy colour in his cheeks. Even when I quietly sat and watched him, I couldn't detect actual chest movement as he happily journeyed around his inner being. He was practicing full Rhythm Breathing but virtually imperceptibly because his energy demand was effectively non-existent.

Your aspiration, however, is *not* to view your own breathing practice as some kind of Olympic event by carefully timing yourself each day, trying to emulate probably unattainable 'targets' (or keeling over in the effort). My Teachers started in their teens and dedicated much of their lives to meditation mastery through one Way or another but they too 'began at the beginning'. At this stage of your Journey, your training is just to slow your breathing comfortably to a pace commensurate with your body's need – and therein lies the beginning of mastery.

Exercise 17. *Slowing the Rhythm*

> *When tension-free, settle into your Rhythm Breathing. Begin counting in your mind again, but endeavour to slow your breathing to a definite eight or nine count. When you have imprinted the new count into your awareness, let go the counting as previously and settle into just being aware of your breathing in the slower rhythm.*

Very importantly, as I have said, realise that the practice is a slowing of your breathing, not using the extra few seconds to fill more of your lungs. You should still only be using about half of your total capacity but just taking longer to 'fill' to that level. You will probably find that adding just a few extra seconds is really quite comfortable. In so doing, the true achievement is that you will have slowed your breathing cycle, quite naturally, to about three or four per minute – a long way from the 'old' shallow breathing at 16 or so cycles a minute … and that, dear reader, is worthy of a little praise!

Realistically, for fruitful daily meditation, you need *not* extend the in- and out-counts beyond 15 seconds for each one – and less if that proves discomforting. If, on the other hand, you develop an aspiration to become more embedded in meditative pursuit, then each week or two, try adding a couple of seconds to the in- and out-count. Never however, add more than is comfortable by having to 'overfill the tanks'. Nor be tempted to 'get there faster', because you need to gently retrain your lungs for this unfamiliar practice. So just stay with the recommended exercises and pace at this stage.

Experiencing Difficulties

Because of a lifetime of bad breathing habits, some students do find practicing the full Rhythm Breathing cycle a little difficult. If this is also you, dear reader, do not become frustrated or think you are 'failing' (I said way back there somewhere, 'failure doesn't exist in meditation'). Your Path every day is to just sink into your practice, doing the best you can do. If you 'hit a brick wall' on Rhythm Breathing, just go back to *hara* or Plain Breathing for a while and gently try again when you feel comfortable.

Breathing – the 'Rhythm of Life'

Once you've practiced the 'rhythm' for a while, your entire breathing movement will begin to feel like a 'wave' motion – gentle and undulating – as if you are as standing chest deep in the ocean being softly moved by the rhythmic and soothing movement of the water. Continue practicing your wave movement … gently, gently like the ocean. It is this lovely wave rhythm that has led me to call this wonderful practice the 'Rhythm of Life Breathing' because you are learning to do exactly that – learning to renew the natural rhythm of your life while perfecting the Second Essence.

Your Daily Practice

After reaching your tension-freedom each day, direct all your attention to practicing breathing in the full rhythm sequence on both in- and out-breaths. Endeavour to stay with the breathing for 10 to 15 minutes *until you become absorbed in it*. Remember, you do not have to become a yoga master, just sufficiently practiced to be, as a minimum, using your lower lungs effectively. Gradually, you will find your mastery increasing until eventually, at least *hara* breathing becomes *habitual* and maybe even the full Rhythm Breathing … to the eternal benefit of your whole wellbeing.

Active Meditation

Remember, Active Meditation is weaving the skills you are 'redeveloping' into your daily life so that they gradually become both habitual and genuinely beneficial. You do not have to wait until you become a long-practiced meditator to experience the benefits of Right Breathing, as many of them can be virtually immediate.

So as you go about your daily 'busyness', as well as practicing Letting Go Tension whenever you think of it, I want you to add Plain Breathing to your Active Meditation 'to-do' list. Whenever it crosses your mind, take your mind-focus to your tummy and breathe slowly and gently into your lower lungs. That alone is a great little exercise until you are doing it quite regularly. Then, when you are ready, extend it to the more complete Rhythm Breathing – *always triggering the in-breath by hara breathing*.

It is a practice you can do anywhere, at any time – because you probably already have this funny little habit of actually breathing wherever you are!

Breathing Walks

A lovely way to 'take your practice with you' is to go for 'breathing walks' – short walks (say, around the block or half a kilometre or so to begin with) in which you *just walk* – but with your whole mind-focus on your Rhythm Breathing and the action of walking itself. It is not meant to be the usual little meander along, with your mind bogged down by the woes of thinking about anything and everything. It is just *breathing and walking – breathing and walking*. This contemplative practice of giving attention to each moment of walking and breathing becomes a delightful little practice of mindfulness.

Gradually on this wondrous Journey, you will discover that *every moment spent doing whatever you do* provides you with an opportunity to practice such mindfulness – the art of fully experiencing your life – as you live it – here and now.

* * *

The 'yogic method' of *complete* Rhythm Breathing has virtually never been written down being instead, passed from Master to Master, as it was to me, because it was considered one of the ancient secrets. I have been amused by this for years, because this 'ancient secret' is, in reality, the most purely natural way of breathing, known to every baby and forgotten by almost every adult. So let it be a 'secret' no longer – spread the 'words', '*natural breathing*'. (Just don't mind when babies in their cots and prams start pointing at you and giggling – tell them you're working on it!)

'Advanced' Yogic Breathing – The Illusion of Illusion!

Some seekers, in their reading or world wanderings, encounter yogis who may have spent much of their lives in 'retreat' in mountain monasteries or caves, practicing very advanced forms of *hatha* (physical) yoga and body control. Their practice often includes certain breathing exercises that can have a euphoric effect on the mind – often called 'transcendental experiences' – which some regard as 'mystical'.

Practitioners may speak of having visions such as talking with the great gurus or religious iconic beings, hearing enchanting music, seeing heavenly light, leaving their body to astrally travel, levitating and having ecstatic feelings of bliss and rapture. Their experiences are often compared with those of people who have experimented with so-called mind-altering drugs.

I need to discuss this briefly, as many students ask me about these 'wonderments' and indeed, if I will teach them how to have such experiences.

Long ago, a number of these practices were passed on to me and it is indeed true that one can have hallucinatory experiences as a result of employing certain breathing techniques. But, *such experiences have nothing at all to do with Authentic Meditation.* They are *not* 'mystical' or 'out-of-body' experiences but rather *inner-body* experiences: the physically tangible effects that result from engaging in various combinations of over- and under-oxygenating the body by taking breath 'control' to limits and extremes which are *not natural.*

Tricking the mind and fooling the body in this way is only a distraction from reality and has no part in Authentic Meditation. Engaging in such practices is not being kind to yourself and, further, it does not contribute in any way to reaching into your higher consciousness, enlightenment or wisdom. Believing and claiming that, for example, you can levitate half a metre off the ground while having an oxygen-deprived hallucination tends to indicate to me a seeking soul still looking in the wrong place for the true Path to inner illumination.

When beginning to enter into a meditative state of true stillness, however, various 'experiences' may indeed occur and they can be widely varied in their nature, from seeing colours to experiencing amazing joy … even a sense of pure blissfulness from time to time. But these are *natural experiences* that I call *by-products* of the meditative state that is reached when you later practice becoming still of mind and begin to enter into a 'place' I call the Serene Space. When you begin to dwell within this illuminating inner space, *all* such experiences naturally fade away. I'll expand on this in a while, when you are more likely to begin having some such 'experiences'.

Meditating authentically is completely opposite to the deliberate 'creating' of illusory experiences because, ultimately, meditation is the practice of experiencing, or unveiling, *the reality of being* – the reality of again becoming an enlightened expression of love, kindness and compassion. Such pure experiencing is *immeasurably beyond any created, hallucinatory experience.*

So, do not be tantalised or attracted by stories of 'amazing experiences' that are possible with extreme breathing practices. I can only say that practicing the authentic, natural meditative Path is *the* genuinely 'mind-bending' *Way of Life* which reduces illusory experiences, such as yogic breathing hallucinations, to the realm of amateurism – a long, long way from the wondrous depth of the true life voyage.

Chapter Ten

Refining the Practice of Two Essences

So far, you have been practicing the two key Essences, Letting Go Tension and Right Breathing, as relatively separate and distinct processes. The next step is to begin flowing one naturally into the other until, eventually, you're able to accomplish both at the same time. In effect, the two Essences become *integrated,* creating a natural, solid base for practicing, then also integrating, the third Essence – Stilling the Mind.

Exercise 18. *Flowing One Essence into Another*

> *On your mat again, take your sitting position, commencing your practice with the first Essence, Letting Go Tension. Close your eyes and smoothly run through the 'four phases' in a progressive, fluid manner until you become absorbed in tension-freedom.*

Now we begin the actual integration.

> *When you have naturally progressed to the Chocolate Melting phase, move your mind-focus to your breathing … at the same time as you are still letting go the remnants of tension.*
>
> *Fluidly, gracefully, begin hara breathing (as a minimum), then move to the full rhythm breathing if you can, remembering 'lowermiddletop' for both in- and out-breath. You are probably, quite naturally, taking a 'good' eight or nine counts to breathe in (or whatever time is comfortable for you) and spending the same time*

on your out-breath. As before, become absorbed in the undulating rhythm but ... endeavouring to be deeply aware of your body quietness as well.

Once settled, spend 10 to 15 minutes just being deeply present and absorbed in experiencing the deep calmness that seems to be radiating through your whole being before completing as usual.

Your Daily Practice

Persevere with this exercise until you begin to feel your Rhythm Breathing beginning to naturally 'overlap' your body calmness. Over the coming days or weeks, endeavour to build the time spent on 'mastering' this exercise to about 25 minutes daily. Don't force progress – just fall naturally into your own pace.

Exercise 19. *The Two Essences Becoming One*

Before we lift the practice to another level, there is one more exercise to begin to master and that is, practicing the first two Essences *together* from the very beginning of your session, not just 'flowing' consecutively or 'overlapping' as in your current work.

In your sanctuary again, take your posture but, just before you commence letting go body tension, take in a slow deep breath (of course starting with the lower lungs) and then release it gently while, at the same time, you begin letting go the tension around your eyes.

As you continue the slow out-breathing cycle, continue to let go tension throughout your body. You will find that tension is more readily let go when breathing out. Hold the calmness while you rhythm (or hara) breathe in again ... and repeat, gently letting go more tension until you are tension free while breathing deeply and slowly.

The effect of doing both deliberately at the same time can be remarkable as they have a compounding effect – they work synergistically. In other words, practicing Rhythm Breathing 'helps' the tension-freeing process which, in turn, automatically assists the slowing of your breathing.

Practice this exercise for as long as you need to until you find yourself slowly becoming absorbed in the experience of a beautiful, deep, quite inexplicable calmness rising from within.

Just Do It!

The aspiration of your practice now is to master the first two Essences so that they are genuinely a singular activity. 'Mastery', in this instance is not only being able to practice the integrated Essences with single-pointed absorption but also being able to just move into it naturally and increasingly quickly.

Now, any thought of 'quickly' may sound like a complete contradiction of everything I've said on *'taking your time'* and *'when you are ready'* and so on. It isn't. It is just that it *is* possible, with practice, to become highly skilled in letting go tension while overlaying full rhythmic breathing at the same time. This is relevant for those aspiring to the Great Journey because the practice of the Essences, although *intrinsically* beneficial, is really only a 'training stage' in preparing for full meditation. Once you can accomplish them at will, you no longer need to tarry in their practice, thus leaving the remainder of the 'allocated' time for … meditating.

As a little aside, the Essences (including Stilling the Mind) eventually can be attained virtually simultaneously, with complete body and mind stillness being reached in just a few seconds. I think I laughed and made some quite inappropriate comment like, 'yeh, right!' when Bashayandeh first told me of this next phase of my Journey, so he just … 'did it', right there and then! In seconds he was obviously deeply relaxed, his breathing virtually indiscernible and he was clearly in a meditative state – as he remained motionless for the next hour. When he completed, he just waved me away until next time. Lesson given! I'm sure it was the last time I expressed doubt or disbelief in *anything* he said.

On my next visit, he told me that it was simply a matter of 'mastering' each phase and *then*, fluidly, quickly and naturally melding them, without getting 'time-lost in techniques'. He made it sound easy – and it was. After a year or two of daily practice (yes, *that* easy), I too was able to sink into a *complete stillness of being*, including a deep quietness of mind, in just a few seconds.

Exercise 20. *'Quickening' the Letting Go*

Practice now 'just doing it' – just dropping gently, gently, into quietness of body while overlaying the lovely, slow rhythm of your breathing – one stage running fluidly, gracefully into the next with your mind focused attentively on just 'letting go' – letting go tension – letting go shallow, rapid breathing.

Your Daily Practice

Your daily practice now is to *maintain* your mind-focus on the 'feeling' of body stillness and the gentle, calming rhythm of your breathing.

In each practice for the next week or two, just endeavour to allow yourself to melt into quietness and the slow rhythm of your breathing a little more quickly each time – all without any forcing of pace. The initial aspiration is to reach a stage of just taking a few minutes to be deeply relaxed and breathing properly before giving your entire attention to 'dwelling in' the calmness. The effort now is to be present in the stillness *instead of* your mind-time being soaked up in practicing the 'techniques' of 'getting there'! This is another little time along the meditative Way to stop and smell the roses while becoming more deeply familiar with the unfamiliar.

Taking the 'Calmness' with You

At the end of the previous chapter, I said that practicing Right Breathing layered onto tension-freedom is like 'having two scoops of calmness instead of one'. As you practice integrating the two Essences, the budding experience of a 'double calmness' will indeed feel as though your whole being is getting a treat as it is lulled into a deep quietness, probably for the first time in your remembered life. You may well feel a rising sense of pleasure or even joy in your sanctuary practice simply because the early experiences of profound body stillness and restful rhythm breathing are in such stark contrast to the usual, often joyless, tension-filled busyness of your normal life.

In your very early training, however, such experiences of calmness, delightfully refreshing as they may be, are likely to pass when you finish each session. But, when you lengthen the time of your daily practice (say, from 10 to 25 minutes) and become increasingly proficient at becoming immersed in physical quietness, you will begin to notice that the feeling of calmness seems to stay with you, *beyond* your formal practice session. For a while, this lingering of calmness may only last for a few minutes but, as your practice becomes progressively more embedded as a natural habit in your life, the period of calmness will begin to become prolonged – because you just can't help it.

As your natural state of calmness is increasingly unveiled, it begins not just to be a one-off, happy experience you have and leave in your sanctuary, but an experience that starts to expand and settle increasingly naturally ('like stardust', as one student said) *across the activities of your day* and then, even begins to have effect on the way you approach, and respond behaviourally to, your daily endeavours. As Margo mentioned in her letter, she found this quiet hue of lingering calmness beginning to have *unexpected effects* on many aspects of her life.

You too, may find positive effects of your practicing stillness just … *happening*. But, as I have said, it is important that you have no expectation of 'things happening' – because they won't if you hang about waiting for the 'results' of your good work. *Just practice.*

Applying the Integrated Essences as Anti-stress Weapons

As well as experiencing positive effects that may begin to just 'sneak' into your life, it is important to continue, quite deliberately, taking elements of your sanctuary practice with you as Active Meditation so that you begin to *permanently transcend stress.*

From now on then, whenever you remember and wherever you are, each time you remember to let go tension, let that also be the trigger for *immediately* slowing, deepening and becoming rhythmical ('lowermiddletop' – in and out) with your breathing. It may take a while but, if you dare to include this among your daily 'habits' out there in the big world, the moments or minutes of deepening calmness in daily life will become an increasingly 'new normal' – and powerfully refreshing – 'way of being'.

A little story. I remember one hot day stealing forty winks on a friend's couch. When I awoke after a few minutes, she said, 'you *do* do it!' Upon my puzzled look, she explained that she had noticed my tummy rising and falling while I dozed. Right Breathing can again become *that* natural, dear reader and, very simply, if I can do it, so can you. That is one meditative practice that doesn't need years in a monastery to acquire. As I've said, just go watch a baby breathe … and copy same!

Targeted Practice – the Samurai Solution

The second aspect of this Active Meditation is to make it genuinely … well, *active*. Using the integrated Essences can be a powerful meditative weapon that may be triggered into play in your daily life on an 'as or when needed' basis. I call it the Samurai Solution. So many students come to the Sanctuary because of the bleakness of their days caused by constant 'stress'. So many speak of being almost continually anxious and even suffering regular anxiety or panic attacks. As you know, when you feel 'strung-out' by just living, even small, quite innocuous negative comments or events can lead to incongruous feelings of tension. These are the times of … 'as or when needed!'

Now, when life begins to fly out of control or when you find the head full of negative emotions just too overwhelming, you can now unpack the 'letting go-weapons' … and *apply them*.

At such times, the first step is to become truly aware of the negative 'feeling' – admitting to yourself that you are not doing too well right now – rather than succumbing to it or screening it with transient activity flurry (both, of course, which amplify the problem). You then put yourself into a situation of *choice*. You can *choose* to allow the tension to mount or … *choose* to apply some high-powered meditative tools to induce natural calmness.

The moment you begin to feel stressed is the precise moment to call on your yogic weaponry, just as a good Samurai warrior would to master a difficult situation. At that moment, immediately close your eyes and take your mind-focus to the muscles around them and begin letting go tension as you have practiced. Then, deliberately and consciously, introduce *hara* breathing and begin to slow the rhythm further. If possible, continue for a few moments or minutes to nurture *hara* into full rhythm breathing.

If, however, you have little time, just slipping quickly into tension-free mode around the eyes and deliberately slowing your breathing can offer almost instantaneous relief from stress and feelings of anxiety. The key to relief is becoming *absorbed in focusing* on both the letting go of tension and on your breathing rather than being overwhelmed by the terribly unpleasant feelings of tension and anxiety. This is not always easy to do but, with practice, can become increasingly natural – I assure you.

If you are in a place where it is a little too obvious to just 'chill out' with eyes closed, you can conduct this Active Meditation with your eyes open. If this is necessary, fix your gaze on an object in front of you or a spot on the wall before you begin the tension-freeing process. If you happen to be chatting to your managing director when the 'bad feelings' come, you can actually use his/her eyes as your point-of-gazing while 'letting go'. They will be delighted at how attentive you seem to be. But, don't forget to blink occasionally.

One student told me how she had targeted a high-stress situation with her 'new' yogic skills. She said she had been 'freaked out by the pressure' of having to make a major presentation to a board of directors of a major commercial enterprise. She thought (probably, more hoped and prayed) that her Active Meditation might be of value so decided to go sit in the boardroom 15 minutes before the presentation and just sink into her meditative relaxing and breathing. When it came time for the presentation, she told me that a 'deep calmness just seemed to stay with her' for the whole talk, which happily she described as a 'smash hit'. In just one day of meditative daring, she had faced and conquered her demon of public speaking.

She had recognised her rising panic and made a choice – to at least try and use her new meditative anti-stress weapons to 'let it all go' and, in so daring, succeeded.

Using Active Meditation as a weapon against the potential horrors of daily tensions in just this way can be quite literally 'life transforming'. Students sometimes say to me, 'it must be wonderful to be so calm all the time' and I reply quite simply, '*you* know how to be calm as well now – why aren't you?'

The message in my response is that you do not have to be a yogi or Zen master to experience life (yes, outside your safe sanctuary) with deep, abiding calmness. *Everyone can.* It is a matter of practicing your 'essential' skills and then daring to apply them when needed rather than submitting to difficulties with a 'woe is poor me' hand on the brow.

The good news is that, if you choose to employ your new yogic dexterity whenever necessary, there will come a time a little further down the Path when you find it 'happening' virtually automatically – 'kicking in' like a turbocharger on a racing car in *all* moments of stress, as your body begins to send out the *here-comes-some-stress* message as a plea for a little additional coping support. Then, a little 'further than further' down the track, *the anti-stress mode of response becomes habitual* to a point where you are virtually not able to be stressed at all.

However, all this 'meditative weaponry wonderment' relies on your practicing the Essences as a matter of daily habit in your sanctuary, as well as consciously committing to taking the little Active Meditation practices 'with you' into the outside world as often as you can remember.

If you do not practice, your meditative weaponry will be about as effective as a discarded old rusty sword. It is a matter of choice – *yours!*

Dynamic Breathing

Life doesn't give most people the luxury of time to sit around being deeply meditative for extended periods … as pleasantly stress-relieving from daily hassles as that may be. I'll assume then that, if you are reading this, you are not sitting in a cave on the side of a frozen mountain, for example, and that you are therefore leading something of a 'normally' active life that perhaps, from time to time, demands some more intense exertion. The low end of that additional physical effort might just be a slow walk to the letterbox at the bottom of the garden. At the other extreme, you might for example, exert yourself close to the limit by driving a racing car non-stop for an hour or two or be looking after young children all day … every day.

Most non-meditators, when exerting themselves physically, try to meet their additional energy needs by exaggerating already bad, shallow-breathing habits … and end up breathless or feeling faint. Even for practiced meditators, there is a tendency to let go Right Breathing under exertion and revert to rapid 'top-lung' breathing in the conditioned belief that it gives them more *chi*. It doesn't.

On the contrary, occasionally you can find 'breathing awareness' popping up in the least expected of places. I recently watched a nationally televised motor race in which the audience could 'listen in' to the various pit managers' instructions to their drivers while they were racing. I was deeply impressed to hear a single-word instruction shouted from a manager to his driver – *'breathe!'* Very wise manager.

If your daily exercise is really just a little stroll to the corner and back, firstly, *that is insufficient daily exercise for anyone* (unless you are an older person or recovering from illness). Secondly, the breathing modes already practiced in your Breathing Walks are quite sufficient for any limited additional energy needed, so at least remember to practice *them*.

During more vigorous exercise, however, there is a right way to breathe. I call that way Dynamic Breathing, which enhances endurance, performance and energy availability.

Dynamic Breathing is effectively Rhythm Breathing ... *without the rhythm* (a little like the way I dance ... much graceful movement of all the 'parts' but a sad lack of co-ordination into a *rhythmic* whole). Dynamic Breathing is simply the practice of deliberately breathing into the whole of your lungs (including your lower and middle lung areas) *simultaneously* and then expelling the air from the total lung area, also all at once. So, in effect, it is 'balloon breathing' on both the in- and out-breath.

In practicing Dynamic Breathing under real exertion, you will be drawing in up to four times your 'normal' volume of air at more than twice normal rate. Accordingly, you need to begin practicing this gently at first because ... you will pass out if you don't!

Exercise 21. *Right Breathing for Vigorous Exercise*

I suggest that, on one of your Breathing Walks, you decide to do a longer, faster walk that really requires some extra exertion. When you notice that you are beginning to 'puff' a little to get more air for the increased energy needed, begin consciously expanding the whole of your lungs at the same time (breathing in through your nose if you can). Be deeply aware of including the hara area.

On breathing out, expel the air from your full lungs all at once, making sure that you 'squeeze in' your tummy to create the space for then taking in extra, truly fresh air.

Breathing in this way will gradually ease the need to 'puff' as you will be taking in plenty of *chi* – even for vigorous activity. As the final part of your practice, I suggest you watch one of the leading marathon runners and be transfixed by the beautifully graceful and seemingly effortless naturalness of their whole-lung breathing.

Then, for further inspiration, I shall lend you a 'mental image' of one of the many lovely people *I* find inspirational.

Eva is ninety. Her frail old body is so bent over that she really only sees what's on the ground in front of her feet. But Eva walks (or rather, shuffles) by my house every single day, propped up by a walking frame to stop her falling. She is so slow taking each step that, every time she totters past, I pray to the universe she makes it home.

But about every fourth step or so, Eva stops, visibly takes a long, deep breath and moves on. I initially thought she was doing it because she was puffed out with effort – until I noticed her having a little smile to herself after each deep breath. Her 'shift' on earth will probably soon be finished. But, in the meantime, she is determined to really live and enjoy every eternal precious moment, including a *clear and conscious pleasure in – just breathing.*

Reaching into Effortless Practice – Concluding the Second Essence

If you have practiced your way through this chapter (not just read it), firstly, I admire your endurance (gold stamp applied to middle of forehead – if that helps). Secondly, although it may not seem to be the most exciting aspect of your meditative Journey, as I have said, *Right Breathing is, without question, the most important 'self-help' work you will ever do* because it reaches into the very core of your existence – your *life-force!*

Continue to practice all the breathing exercises, both in your sanctuary and out there in the big people's world until the continuity of your practicing really does bring a sense of each exercise becoming effortless – when you feel it is a natural part of you. It is at that point you know you are *possessing* it … and that is the signpost indicating your readiness to move on.

* * *

A Little Story of Encouragement

Depression and Meditation – A Doctor's Story

'In 1998, at the age of 46, I was king-hit by depression and an obsessive-compulsive disorder.

It was at a time of my life when I was busy, had a lot of responsibility and was under a fair bit of stress. I could talk for a long time about what the reasons may or may not have been but the more I think about it, the more I reckon it is not all that important. Sure, one needs to identify the things that may need to change and, if possible, change them. But, I like to keep things simple. I was like a fox with its leg caught in a trap and there was really only one question; what do I do?

I was lucky in that, being in the medical profession, I could access good treatment quickly. Drugs and psychiatry were invaluable and got me back on my feet and able to get on with life. But they only got me so far – and when I went off the antidepressant, eventually I would relapse.

I don't know when I started thinking of meditation but a fork in the road was definitely when it was said to me, "we don't own our thoughts". It was worth "thinking" about!

Whatever one may think of that statement, I now believe we can control both our thoughts and our emotions. For me, meditation has opened that door. Meditation has enabled me to increase my familiarity with my mind; it has reopened what I would describe as my basic nature – realities from when I was very young.

One very helpful exercise for me was when the teacher at the Meditation Sanctuary asked us to go back to a past memory and its associated emotion and guided us in the meditative practice of separating the emotion from the thought and then practice letting the emotion go. It can be done. The memory is there and, being the past, is immutable. The emotion was there *then* – but we *can* let it go – if we know "how".

For me meditation is part of the "how". I believe it is many other things as well.'

– Dr Y (name withheld for professional reasons)

* * *

Dr Y arrived at the Sanctuary about a year ago. I didn't know he was a doctor and, for a few weeks, didn't even know his name. But I remember him so clearly from the first moment. He seemed such a withdrawn and preoccupied man. He had the appearance of being 'haggard' and lined of face beyond what I 'guessed' his age to be. When sitting in class and listening, he simply stared at the floor. When spoken to, he was polite but brief and avoided eye contact. There was no smile on greeting. I could tangibly feel his depression and suffering and dearly hoped that he would 'stick the course', knowing that if he had the courage to practice, meditation may well give some relief from whatever was 'ailing' him.

A few months ago, I received the following note from Dr Y:

'I woke this morning. Beautiful day. It was comfy in bed. A surf would be good. I felt the need to meditate and I had to iron my work clothes for the week. I missed out on the surf. Meditation was good – it can take a while to settle my mind. As you know, it improves with practice. For me, I prefer what you have been guiding us through lately – the letting go and clearing the mind. As I was doing the ironing I looked out at the day and thought, yes, a surf would have been nice.'

Cheers
'Y'

When I received this note, I knew then that Y had returned to his wellbeing. I knew this because of the 'mindfulness' that was clearly shining through the wording of his note like a beacon. He was deeply 'present' – he was 'aware' of the surf, the comfort of the bed, the ironing. He was not 'lost in thought' and negativity. In just the two words – 'beautiful day' – he really wrote a textbook on mindfulness! How often we don't notice!

Chapter Eleven

Breathing Exercises for the Unwell

Long ago, my life was probably saved, both literally and metaphorically, by being fortunate in finding those masterful people I mentioned earlier who guided me in the practice of effective breathing techniques to overcome my then-chronic asthma.

I've included some additional yogic breathing practices below for people who may have lung problems or disease or who suffer breathing difficulties caused by asthma or various allergic reactions. They are exercises essentially designed to gradually increase lung capacity, better eliminate toxins and develop strength in the lungs as well as in the chest and stomach muscles. I can't promise they will 'cure' all breathing difficulties and lung illnesses but, adding them to your Right Breathing will provide some further relief and benefit … as a very minimum.

Please commence them slowly, increasing the repetitions gradually. *Do not extend yourself physically beyond feeling comfortable at any time.*

Keep a record of your daily practice, starting each exercise with one repetition on the first day and only moving to 'two' after three days and 'three' repetitions after another three days, and so on. The aspiration is to build your strength slowly until you are doing these exercises for about 10 minutes, preferably twice a day. Note that if you are unable to stand, you can practice most of these exercises sitting on a chair or even in bed.

I emphasise that all these exercises are *additional* to your daily practice of Right Breathing.

Deep Breathing – 'Opening' Your Lungs

- *Stand straight with your legs together and hands by your side. Close your eyes if you wish and just let go some tension – without falling over. Introduce gentle, hara breathing for two or three minutes, to bring your mind-focus onto your breathing.*

- *Breathe in to a five-count while slowly lifting your arms straight out sideways away from your body until they are horizontal to your shoulders – remembering, as a minimum, to breathe air into your lower lungs. Hold your breath for three seconds with your arms extended before slowly returning them to your side, again counting to five while breathing out – 'ballooning' if you like, but preferably through your nose.*

Start with doing it just once and increasing the repetitions over the weeks ahead as I suggested above. When you are comfortable with the exercise and able to do it several times, you can also increase the count to slow the activity.

- *The same as above, but continue to raise your arms so they are held vertically above your head with your fingers touching and pointing towards the sky. Again, use a five-count in and out for your breathing and pause at the top while holding your breath.*

Increase repetitions and time count as above.

Cleansing Your Lungs

- *While standing, put your hands on your hips and take a good, deep breath, filling your whole lungs, starting with your lower lungs first. Do this on a slow five-count in. Then expel all the air as suddenly and forcefully as you comfortably can … through pursed lips – like a 'fish mouth'. Bend forward a little as you expel the air, emptying your lungs as completely as you can – pushing your tummy in at the end to get rid of that last little bit of used air.*

Again, start with only one the first day and now you know what to do from then on.

- *Breathe in as for the last exercise but, this time, expel all the air in three separate, forceful puffs (instead of one big out-breath) through a tight 'fish-mouth' so your lungs have to work hard to force air out. Stop momentarily, but completely, between each puff. Make the last of the three 'puffs' a longer, complete emptying breath, again pushing your tummy right in.*

Repetition developed as before. (I still do this early each morning as it both cleanses the lungs and keeps them 'toned'.)

- *Standing with legs apart now, breathe in deeply while stretching your arms above your head as in the exercise above – and then lean slightly backwards. Hold your breath for a moment. Suddenly bend forward and downwards towards the floor (your arms held straight so they prescribe a large arc as they come down).*

- *At the same time, breathe out forcefully with a loud yell through your opened mouth (like Haaaaaaa!!! – but, don't frighten the horses or the neighbours!). Let your arms and head just hang down loosely for a moment. Then slowly breathe in as you 'arc your arms' back up to the starting position again (arms above your head).*

Once only the first time and develop slowly from there.

Strengthening Lungs and Increasing Capacity

- *Breathe in deeply through your nose, hold your breath for as long as you can comfortably and then force it out as slowly as possible through a very tight 'fish-mouth' (your cheeks will 'puff out' while you do this one).*

This is called the 'Victorious Breath' in yoga and is great for the tummy muscles.

- *Breathe in and out quite forcefully and quickly through your nose by pushing the whole abdomen in and out – slowly at first or you will pass out! Ever so gradually you need to develop the pace to about 60 per minute (yes, one 'in and out' every second or so). Then, when you want to conclude, make the last inhalation a forceful, deep breath and hold it – for as long as you can and slowly exhale.*

Practice this only for about five seconds the first day, building up to about 30 seconds. Always make your last exhalation a long, slow, 'relaxing' one. This one is called 'Bellow Breathing' and is a great practice for helping 'everything' including nasal disorders. You will automatically feel your chest and abdomen muscles getting a good workout.

Having Fun in the Process!

This is a fun way to begin to strengthen your lungs and chest and tummy muscles. You need a candle and a lighter.

- *On the first day, place the lit candle close to your mouth and blow it out with one forceful breath using your 'fish mouth'. Just do it once on the first day and slowly increase the number of times you do so in the way I've indicated. Then each day move the candle progressively a little further and further away before blowing it out. Later, when it is too far to actually blow out, continue moving it further to see if you can just flicker the flame with your breath.*

You will feel the effort required from your chest and tummy muscles to blow it out and eventually you will be able to move the flame … all the way across a room. This is a wonderful, exercise for children with breathing problems (as long as *you* supervise the candle-lighting part).

Cooling Breath

One very hot day a few years ago, I sat with a friend and watched the great tennis player, Pete Sampras, playing in a Grand Slam match. At one point, my friend said, 'what's the matter with this guy – he spends half his time with his tongue hanging out. He looks a bit goofy!' I said, 'He might look a little strange, but look who seems to be the cooler of the two'. By this stage, Pete's opponent was literally bedraggled from the heat and sweating profusely but the champion's clothes were clearly much dryer and he had beads of perspiration on his brow rather than rivulets of water running off him.

I explained that Sampras was doing a yoga breathing exercise called *sitali* or 'Cooling Breath'.

- *Stick your tongue out between your teeth, half open your mouth and breathe in quite deeply and forcefully. Then breathe out through your mouth. Now, the important part of the exercise. Take your mind-focus attentively to the 'cool' feeling on your tongue when breathing in. Soon, your whole body will begin to feel cooler – as a result of genuinely cooling the surface of your tongue with sitali.*

Try a Cooling Breath on a hot day – it works! You might look a little 'goofy' or like a dog panting on a desert-hot day, but you'll be cooler than all of *them!*

Right Breathing – Again

- *Back to your sukhasana posture. Complete each breathing exercise programme with a few minutes of full, slow Rhythm Breathing.*

- *If at all possible, make your Breathing Walks a daily habit, endeavouring to increase the distance regularly, if only by a few metres each time. Practice Right Breathing while walking … mindfully.*

Up to you now. Keep sweet old Eva in mind. Breathe and enjoy every breath – consciously.

Chapter Twelve

Knowing the Unquiet Mind

In the introduction to the Three Essences earlier, I discussed how having a mind that struggles uncontrollably like a 'wombat in a wheat bag' is *the* barrier, greater than the Great Wall of China, to your *awakening* – or renewing the true clarity of consciousness experienced by a child. I said that most people spend most of their time *thinking their life away* wastefully, their minds clogged with the babble of busyness, worries and woes. I suggested that a mind saturated and burdened with the onerous muddle of unmastered thinking is a consciousness so cluttered that it prevents the 'self' truly *experiencing* its existence – let alone being *enthralled by the living of it.*

You may well think that surely you and others are not really like that – or at least, not like that all the time. Well, dear reader, I meet many hundreds of people every year and truth is, only rarely does one come along genuinely gleaming with the *lightness of being* – an occasional soul just allowing themselves *to be,* in this very moment … no matter what the moment brings.

This 'lightness of being' I speak of comes from being able to *unveil* the naturally pure consciousness – to unfold once more the natural mind which is not muddied by the self-absorbed struggle of wall-to-wall thinking. It was the guru, Jesus of Nazareth, who said, 'unless you see as a little child, you will not enter the kingdom of heaven' and later added that 'the kingdom of heaven is *within* you'. So I think the little child sitting on the rug watching the willy wagtail had a far more profound 'inner knowingness' of this wisdom than most adults ever reach. His mind was pure, free and uncluttered to the extent that he *experienced* the kingdom within.

I want to tell you that it is possible for everyone to re-enter that 'enlightened kingdom' – to regain your innately pure and free mind and once more, *repossess* profound *awakeness* to existence ... right here, right now. It is possible for all to transcend the self-created muddle of the mind and, as the Buddha said, 'see what *really* is'. The mind of the child on the rug was so pure and uncluttered that he 'saw what really was' ... he was *at one with* the magnificent 'isness' of his existence ... *at one with* the kingdom within.

But, dear one, I do not want you to believe me. *I want you to find out for yourself!*

Allow me to mix up some metaphors. I want *you* to let the wombat out of the wheat bag. I want *you* to sit on a rug transfixed by a willy wagtail or, for that matter, transfixed by anything at all! I want *your* mad monkeys to stop leaping about your mental branches. I want *you* to experience a permanent lightness of being – the reflection of a truly healthy, mature mind. I want *you* to discover for yourself that practicing the Essences and then practicing Authentic Meditation is *the* Way to truly illuminate the innate magnificence of *your* 'being'!

Getting to Know Your Mind

The process of thinking itself is not a negative quality. Quite conversely, it is a great gift 'evolved' upon us from the universe. It is just that most people use the gift unwisely which, I say to my students, is 'like spilling your beautiful mind all over the floor'. So the journey in this chapter is firstly, to see just *how* we think, then, in final preparation for meditation, begin practicing *The Peaceful Stillness of the Silent Mind* (as the Tibetan lama, Yeshe, titled one of his lovely books). Later, after you have practiced the 'peaceful stillness', we shall have a look at 'mastered thinking' ... just how to using our gift of thinking in a yogic, mindful way.

In order to meditate effectively and authentically, we need to be still of being and this includes being 'quiet of mind'. To do that effectively, however, you need to become consciously aware of your mental processes and the intensity of the erratic activity that is happening in the 'brain part' of your body.

You need to know what you are letting go.

The initial aspiration then, is 'getting to know your mind' so that it can be gradually *nurtured back into a reawakened naturalness*, just as you have been guiding the reawakening of your tension-freedom and natural breathing.

Exercise 22. *Just Sitting Still!*

I tell students that the very first exercise I give them is the easiest they will ever do on the meditative Path – and, being the easiest, it is also the hardest. I simply ask them to sit still on their mats for 15 minutes and do … *absolutely nothing!* I give them no explanation of the purpose of the exercise but lay out a few 'ground rules', such as 'you can sit however you wish, wriggle, move, look about you, count the number of boards on the floor, but … do not lie down, don't close your eyes, do not pretend to meditate and … please don't talk to other students'. Then I say to the now-baffled group, 'remember, everything we do has purpose and meaning'.

What a crazy array of responses students have to this simple, but almost impossible, exercise. At first they stare at me to see if I am serious. (I am.) Then, there can be a little curling of the lip as a few think, 'I'm not here for this nonsense, I'm here to learn meditation'. (They are.) There are the ones who almost immediately look at the clock to see how long it is before they can escape this obviously strange teacher. Then, after a little while, they seem to become resigned to the task and settle in, usually becoming quite still … for perhaps a whole minute or two.

Then … the wriggling, shuffling, looking around and general disquiet starts. (Amuses me – but then, I am easily amused!) Some just become plain bored … I can tell by the 'I'm-so-bored-and-displeased' look on some of their faces. One dear student, on the other hand, told me that she found it 'wonderful having 15 minutes to do nothing' until she began 'feeling guilty that she *should be doing something'. There* was a woman ready, but ready, for meditation.

> *OK then. You've just read the ground rules for yourself so I would like you to go to your sanctuary and just sit and do … nothing. You can put your watch in front of you or set the digital alarm – but no cheating: the full 15 minutes please. Go!*

Now that you have completed the exercise, be honest. How did you feel? A little rattled? Did your mood change in some way while you were 'just sitting'? Also bored witless perhaps?

When the 15 minutes have concluded, my Sanctuary students are usually not too happy either – even less so when I ask, 'why did you *not* do what I asked of you?' Confused faces. 'I asked you to just sit and do nothing – but you didn't do nothing. What did you do?' Increasingly baffled faces. Each looks around at the others, hoping someone knows what this goose in front of them is talking about.

'*Thinking!*', I yell. 'You were *thinking!* Not only were you thinking flat out but you were becoming agitated, angry and just plain bored – right?' Guilty smirks, nods and a little laughter.

Then I say with a grin, 'Of course, it is OK for you to have been thinking – that's what you've been doing every waking moment of your lives since you were about 18 months old! So sitting and being lost in thought is perfectly normal … at the moment.'

'Being bored is fairly normal too,' I add. 'But know that "being bored" is a sign as clear as a tattoo of *I love Mum* right across people's foreheads, that they are not truly engaged with their lives.' I tell them that a truly meditative person can *just sit* – not even meditating – for any length of time without becoming bored because they are constantly immersed in reality and fully awake to, even mesmerised by, the wonderment of their existence. *How could they possibly be bored?*

Then I ask them, 'in all of that busy thinking you were doing while just sitting for 15 minutes, do you actually know what you were thinking about?' After a little ponder, most admit that they can only remember thinking of a couple of major things. Can *you* remember all the things you thought about when you were 'just sitting'? Bet you can't.

The Process of 'Thinking'

The reality is, dear reader, that *all* (non-meditative) humans think *all* the time and very rapidly, processing approximately one billion neurological activities each second – depending on which latest scientific count you listen to. Also, it is virtually impossible to stay singularly focused on the *content* of our thoughts because we think by 'association of ideas' (thinking about one thing rapidly 'reminds' us of another thing and then another, until we are on a 'train of thought', with the initial thought rapidly becoming buried in the association process).

To compound the erratic nature of thinking, as you will discover shortly, the mind also literally flits from the past to the future, and back again, with surprisingly little attention paid to the present moment. All this brain flurry happens in a mad mix of both mind-talk and mind-images, mostly at the same time. Then further, as the mind scurries about like monkeys jumping from tree to tree, it carries our emotions rather helplessly along the same erratic course.

So, the *real* problem with our thinking is twofold. Firstly, it is the fact that our mind is 'full of babble' without any 'still time' whatsoever and, secondly, that most people are completely unaware of this relentless, mental agitation *as it is actually happening*. (The phrase, 'lost in thought', was created by a very wise person.)

The first and most important task then is to wake up and 'see' for yourself just what is going on in the old brain department so you really understand why it is imperative to still that unquiet mind.

Exercise 23. *What Your Thoughts Reveal*

For the next few exercises, you will need a writing book and a pen. Store them in your sanctuary as you will gradually discover that writing is one of the most valuable of meditative tools. The first exercise is to help you begin to be aware that you *are* thinking and then to become *aware of the content* of your thoughts. Do not be surprised that you are likely to be ... utterly surprised.

Sit comfortably in your sanctuary so that you can write in your book. Just close your eyes for a short while and take your mind-focus to your thoughts.

Begin by trying to be aware of exactly what you are thinking about. For example, if you are thinking about having a cup of coffee, 'know' that you are thinking about a cup of coffee! If you find it difficult to 'capture' your thoughts, you can ask yourself, 'what was I just thinking about?' Usually that will bring your attention to just what was going on 'up there.' Let your thoughts just meander along but with you trying to hold real awareness of each, actual thought – not getting lost in them.

Once you have 'tuned in' to your mind, start 'capturing' your thoughts and scribble them down in your book as they happen, no matter what the thought. Just grab each one and translate them into a word or words – uncensored (only you get to read your writing).

Don't try and compose a learned, flowing essay or a creative and logical piece of writing. Just identify whatever thought you are having, trying to be 'awake' to even tiny, flitting thoughts and put them on paper. Do this for perhaps 15 to 20 minutes after which you will have at least two or three pages of 'mind-notes'. Now, have a close look at what you have scribbled down. Your thought recording might have been something like this sample one of mine …

'Seagull. How lovely its flight. Free-flying across the beach. Guess it flies over lots of beaches – last holiday was near the beach – she was a nice person who ran the motel – her gardener was a bit tough – he didn't like me – well, I didn't know I parked on his silly garden – three stones and a geranium – how can you call that a garden – the whole thing was about as big as a frying pan – fried eggs, bacon, hot buttered toast she brought for breakfast was lovely – toast – I burned the toast this morning – late for work – hate that – work was so dreary today – project not finished – has to be finished tomorrow – can't finish it on time – what can I say to the boss – he will not be a happy chappy – I'm for the "high-jump" – could just leave town – sounds good – can't though … hate this tense feeling!'

Now comes the interesting part. *What we write is profoundly and deeply revealing* about how we humans 'think'. Have a look at my little thought-story again. See how, in about 20 seconds of thinking, my thoughts have 'taken' me from smiling at a bird flying free to thinking worriedly about an unfinished project. How did that happen? How can one just mentally meander away like that?

Look at the first thought you wrote in your book and then at the very last thought. They also have nothing to do with each other either – they are on completely different subjects. Right? If it is any consolation, you are not the only mental wanderer – 99.9 per cent of all students in class have exactly the same result.

If you read over your whole thought-story, you will be astonished at just how many subjects you managed to cover, most seemingly unrelated … and all you did was grab your thoughts as they 'innocently happened'. In your first reading, it will seem as if your mind 'has a mind of its own', indiscriminately jumping from one thought to another without apparent direction or purpose. But pop back now and have another peep at my story with its seemingly indiscriminate grab-bag of rubbishy thoughts.

If you read closely, you can pick up definite links between the thoughts because many of our memories are 'filed by association'. Seeing a seagull over the beach, for example, 'reminded' me of a holiday at the beach, which 'reminded' me of the motel at the beach, which 'reminded' me of the nice lady who ran the motel … and so on. You see how thinking of one thing brought out the file with a similar thought and then off I zoomed on a theoretical 'train of thought' until I just … got lost … ending up 'crashing' the train with feelings of tension. Have a look at yours again – probably very similar to mine, with clear links or 'associations' between the thoughts.

The disturbing aspect of this little exercise is that most minds operate exactly like that … *the whole time.*

The tremendous power of the little links or associations between the thoughts drags 'you', quite unknowingly, from one to the other, making it extremely difficult to think cohesively, continuously or with single-pointed focus on just about anything at all. For most of your life, your mind is rather like being a helpless passenger on a 'train of thoughts' – with the train mostly bouncing wildly along off the rails. And thinking by association of thoughts is only the beginning of the little secrets your 'thought-writing' will reveal to you.

> *With pen in hand now, please read your thought-story again from the beginning but, as you do, draw a line under any thought that is not about the present moment (that being the actual moment when you were writing).*

So you are underlining thoughts that are obviously about the past or clearly about the future. For example, in my thought-story, I would put a line under 'last holiday was near the beach' – 'she was a nice person' … 'I burned the toast this morning', and so on (because they are thoughts about the past), and also under such thoughts as 'has to be finished tomorrow' – 'he will not be a happy chappy' (clearly, thoughts about the future). Do that all the way through your writing until the end.

> *Now, go back to the beginning again. Look at all the thoughts that are not underlined, which really should be thoughts relating specifically to the present – thoughts that are likely to have been triggered by an immediate stimulus (for example, while you were writing, you heard a train in the distance or smelled the coffee being brewed downstairs and noted that down). Draw a circle around such 'present' thoughts.*

So, in my little mind-wander, I would have put a circle around thoughts such as 'Seagull. How lovely its flight' (clearly in the present, because I am happily admiring its flight while watching it), 'project not finished' (stating a fact as of this moment) and 'Hate this tense feeling' (expressing the stress I am experiencing *right now* in response to a possible future event).

So your whole writing is now full of underlined or circled thoughts. Let's see exactly what profound revelations just a few lines and circles can reveal.

Firstly, you will notice that none of the pages feature only underlined sentences without any circles. Right? Conversely, none of your pages has just circles without any underlinings. So your underlinings are interspersed with circles at various intervals. How do I know? Because, again, virtually all students who do this exercise in the Sanctuary have exactly that result.

If you look closely at the underlinings and circles, you will see that your thoughts have been marked in a seemingly random way – perhaps something like this; *past, past, past, present, future, past, past, future, future, future, past, future, present, past* – or variations on that theme … thoughts about the past interspersed quite randomly with thoughts of the present and future. Importantly, you will also see that the underlined thoughts are far more represented than the circled thoughts.

What you have in front of you is empirical evidence that your mind chatters and flits quite haphazardly and frequently between the past, the future and the present … *even while you are just sitting there in your sanctuary!* Most importantly, the fewer number of circles show that you spend relatively less time 'being in', or experiencing, the present than you do thinking about the past (which has actually gone forever and only exists as 'memories') or the future (which hasn't even come along yet).

While you have pen in hand, go back to the beginning of your writing and once more look at the first thought you have jotted down. This time, try and *reflect on how the writing of that thought 'made' you feel.* Would you say it was an unhappy thought or a happy thought? Go back to my little exercise for a moment. For example, my first thought was 'Seagull' – neither negative nor positive really – just a neutral observation. But, the next thought was, 'how lovely its flight' – an obviously happy and positive thought.

> *So, in reading your first thought/s, when you get to a positive one (such as, 'I love my relaxation exercises'), I want you to put a plus sign (+) above that thought. When you read along to a negative or 'unhappy-making' thought ('work was so dreary today'), mark it above with a minus (–) sign. If it is a thought devoid of emotion – just factual (as in my first thought, 'Seagull') just leave it unmarked. Continue through to the end, marking your thoughts, where relevant, as positive or negative.*

Once done, have a look at the pluses and minuses (positive and negative thoughts). Almost certainly, you don't have all your 'thought-story' covered with *just* plus signs or *just* minus signs. You have a mixed bag of both and again, they will be intermingled. Your pages probably look something like this … + + + + − + + − + − + − − − − − − − − + + + + − + − +, and so on.

Believe it or not, these simple little markings reveal one of the great secrets, and one of the great truths about, not only our thinking but of our whole lives.

* * *

After I ask my students to do this exercise, I make the comment that 'nobody came and gave you 'good' or 'bad' news while you were putting down pluses and minuses. You were just sitting quietly here in the Sanctuary, but yet, over the space of just 10 minutes or so, you experienced changes in your feelings ranging from 'happy' to 'unhappy'. How can that be?' The answer is very simply that you *create your own happiness and unhappiness* by having conditioned emotional responses to stimuli – and, in this instance, the stimuli were only your own thoughts!

The great secret – the great yogic wisdom you have uncovered for yourself, is that, *it is your mind alone that causes your joys and your woes.*

By just looking at your 'story', you can see how easily and frequently you slipped from one emotional response to another. These variations in your emotions are, in fact, happening *constantly* in your 'real' life … hardly a recipe for a steady, balanced calmness. Now, they may not often be immense swings of emotion but, certainly, the majority of people live on a very 'wandery' path, constantly bouncing from 'positive to negative', like bouncing off the walls of an emotional 'life-corridor' rather than walking poised and steady down its centre. Mostly, you are not really aware of this emotional swaying until the variation is quite large (such as experiencing grief, anger or joy) because *you are conditioned to being like this* – you are conditioned to living in this 'outer' daily consciousness of rapidly changing 'feelings' as your 'normal' way of being.

I, too, was 'put through' this exercise by Suni Kaisan. While I was sitting in a quiet place of meditation, trying to grapple my trampolining mind onto a page, he was also writing on a sheet of hand-made paper – but with a little calligraphy brush. When I had finished, I was asked to hold up my work and show him. He didn't explain the revealed 'secrets' in detail as I have above. He just looked at it slightly disdainfully and said 'busy mind – dog's mess – no good'.

I got the message – well, some sort of message. Then I had the youthful temerity to ask him what *he* had been writing. He smiled and showed me an ink drawing … rough, but beautiful … of an *ichi enso*, a brushed circle which, in Zen, is the motif of the purity of 'now' – the state of *satori* or conscious enlightenment. In just one drawing of a circle (like the circles you drew around your 'thoughts in the present'), he was teaching me that, '*I am perfectly present the whole time and supremely conscious of my existence now without the burden of conditioned thought of past or future*'.

He needed to say no more. It was yet another important awakening on my pothole-strewn Path.

Visual Flooding – Thinking in Pictures

So far, we have given attention to our thoughts being represented as 'words' or 'verbal thinking'. However, in addition to words, our brain is also alive with images – with pictures. Visual imagery, or thinking in pictures, is a far more subtle form of our thought processes and actually takes three forms – 'responsive', 'reflective' and 'imaginative'.

Responsive imagery is when we *respond* to the sound or idea of a particular stimulus with a mental image of that stimulus. For example, when we hear a bird singing or a train in the distance, we will often 'see' the bird or the train either as a fleeting snapshot or as a moving image in our 'mind'.

Reflective imagery comes to our mind when we are triggered to recall memories. For example, glancing at a photograph of our parents on the mantelpiece may bring a 'vision' to mind of the farm on which we once lived. These visual images may then unfold as a *reverie* as we *reflect* on the memory of past events – as if playing part of an old video we saw long ago.

Imaginative imagery occurs as we mentally project ourselves into the future or creatively contemplate possibilities. It is like creating a little 'theatre of the mind' in which we are the central character playing out a fantasy. This form of thinking can be deeply seated in our desire for happiness expressed as 'wouldn't life be great if …' or 'won't my life be wonderful when …' whereupon, we disappear into a 'daydream' or a fantasy of wishful thinking. Conversely, it may arise from a sense of dread or fear (based on previous experience) relating to a future 'unpleasant' event such as visiting the dentist tomorrow. Some people can 'use' their 'imaginative imagery' creatively and, for example, 'see' the colours for a painting not yet started or 'glimpse' the plot of a novel not yet written.

However, just as our 'word thoughts' are largely unmastered, so too is our visual thinking because the three mental 'picturing patterns' I've described don't just happen in neat little packages which you experience with focused attention. They ripple and merge, one into the other, to provide a constant, flowing, silent, mostly present backdrop to the 'noise' of your word thinking.

I have likened your verbal thinking to chattering monkeys or a wombat in a wheat bag – ceaseless, strident and lumpy. I describe visual thinking as 'mind flooding' because it reminds me of floods I experienced as a boy in the Australian outback – shallow and dark, flowing slowly and silently as far as I could see with pieces of debris being carried along in the muddied waters until they became caught in the occasional old fence, eventually clogging it, until it sagged under the gathering weight and fell over.

These metaphors are beautifully appropriate for the way people think *before* beginning their journey into meditation. The silent visual imagery is the floodwaters carrying the debris of the chattering words along until, eventually, minds become cluttered and clogged with the relentless flow of ever-burdening mental rubble … until they 'fall over' into unwellness or unhappiness.

Mirages of the Mind

When you have completed those little exercises, have a look at your written pages as a whole. There before you is an accurate 'physical' representation, a 'snapshot', of the way your (and most people's) 'outer or ordinary' consciousness usually functions. A rather jumbled mess indeed but, ... it is much more than just an untidy page of scribble.

In reality, of course, thoughts don't 'just happen'. The brain is triggered into action by an internal or external stimulus of some kind. It can be a 'memory' popping up or seeing something which triggers thinking (as in my 'seeing' a seagull) or a 'senses experience' (such as hunger pangs) or the melody of a bird singing in the tree outside the window. Having been triggered, the thought-process gains momentum until it is producing an unstoppable train of unmastered thought.

I said back in Chapter Four that 'our unmastered thinking alone' quite literally creates a mental cage, a prison of mind conditioning from which it becomes very difficult to escape – because not only are we unaware that it has a door that can be opened – *we are mostly unaware that we are even locked in!*

I shall borrow Suni's words about *my* thought processes and 'lend' them to you for a moment. If you have a last look at your writings, you too may see 'busy mind – dog's mess – no good'. Our simple mind-stories vividly show that we spend much time thinking our lives away rather than being 'awake' and experiencing each precious moment of the *here* and *now*, which, given that the past is gone and the future is not here, is *all we actually have.*

Portraying our busy mind in 'physical' form on a page can be the Realisation that there *is* a cage – but that it *does* have a door ... represented by the 'present moments' of your 'circles'. One student described the sudden Realisation of what he was 'looking at' as 'mind-blowingly uplifting'. When *you* have the awakening that your unmastered thoughts (and attached erratic emotions) are rather like miscellaneous debris scattered along the morning shore, you also have become ready to cease being distracted by these *mirages of the mind.* You have become ready to let go the illusions created by 'wrong' thinking so that *your clarity of consciousness of the 'present' can be renewed.*

On the wall in the Meditation Sanctuary, we have a framed ink and brush drawing of bamboo given to one of our students by a Vietnamese Buddhist monk. On it is written the words, *Living in the Present. How Lovely This Very Moment Is.* Oh indeed!

* * *

On this next leg of your Journey, it is time to commence readjusting a lifetime of 'wrong thinking' by practicing the third Essence, Stilling the Mind. It is the practice of letting go the clogging and cluttering effect of overwhelming and haphazard 'trains of thought' that lead nowhere. It is the practice through which one can be released from the emotional driftwood that floats through the inner being from the past. It is the practice of letting go a way of thinking that offers only the hollow emptiness of wishful thinking or dread of a future that hasn't arrived yet.

Superimposed on the first two Essences, Stilling the Mind is the practice of creating a place of clarity, a serene space, *a truly uncluttered consciousness of the present,* within which the wonderment of Authentic Meditation can be nurtured, grown and matured.

Becoming Aware of Your Thinking

When you 'captured' your thoughts in your book, you were essentially unaware of the 'secret story' they told you about just how your mind 'works' (and, ultimately, about the state of your being). But now you have taken an important step in *seeing for yourself* (which is the 'process' of the Journey, as all great teachers have said), the muddled way the mind thinks and the erratic minute-to-minute effect it has on emotions.

The next step then is to practice *becoming aware of what you are thinking while you are thinking.*

In effect, the practice is to awaken to the 'train of thought' … *as it is happening* so you begin to know 'where your mind is'. Practicing to become aware of your thoughts, rather than lost in them, is the first meditative stepping stone towards *mastering the mind* – the precious ability to be able to focus, calm and then … still it.

The Essential Stillness

For all exercises from here, you will need to commence each practice taking 10 or so minutes to become tension-free of body while breathing slowly and deeply as practiced. From now on, I shall use a phrase, *sink (or move, reach, flow etc) into your Essential Stillness* to indicate spending time on the first two Essences rather than detailing this necessity each time. Later, when you move more deeply into meditation itself, reaching your Essential Stillness will also include the third Essence, Focusing the Mind.

Moving to your Essential Stillness at the commencement of each practice is now crucial because it provides the beautifully calm, undistracted 'inner space' in which to focus more clearly on your 'mind-work'. In fact, stilling the mind is really not possible if you are not quiet of body and breathing.

See that little lizard on the rock over there – just drinking in the sunshine and not moving a muscle, as peaceful as … well … as peaceful as a lizard on a rock. Message is folks … that's *exactly* how I want you to be in preparation for all your new, mind-awareness and mind-focusing practices.

Exercise 24. *Observing Your Thoughts*

Sit now in your posture with your hands gentled in the *mudra*.

> *After reaching your Essential Stillness, take your focused attention to your 'mind' and begin to allow yourself to just think. Let the thoughts occur as 'they' wish and as they pop in, just begin to focus on them – exactly as you did when capturing and writing them in your book earlier. Just stay with them for a while, observing them, being conscious of them, almost as if they are separate from 'you'.*

The aspiration is to begin to 'know' what you are thinking. The first few times you try this exercise, your mind may wander away from the 'conscious watching' of your thoughts as you grab a passing train and get 'lost in thought' for a while. That is fine at the beginning because, soon enough, you will remember why you are just sitting there and again direct *conscious attention to your thoughts.*

After having 'gone for the ride' as an observant passenger on the 'train' several times, you may begin to experience fleeting but distinct feelings that there are two of 'you' – one, the quiet and silent observer watching the 'other' who is the 'chatterer' having all the wandering thoughts. Be happily assured that there is only one of you and the silent observer is simply the 'inner self' (or the 'reality' of you) beginning its awakening and getting its first little glimpse of the conditioned way your 'ordinary' or 'outer' thinking mind has peppered you like sparrow-shot for most of your life.

Becoming aware of your thinking in this way is the very beginning of mastering the mind.

Exercise 25. *Deliberately Directing Your Thoughts*

After practicing thought awareness, the next exercise is to begin 'taking control' of them, which we can liken to at least 'steering the train', before perhaps slowing it and hopefully bringing it to a halt. (I've just had an 'association of thoughts' on the 'steering' word. When I was about six, my uncle decided that it was time for me to learn to drive. He allowed me to sit on his knee and 'steer' the tractor as we were heading back to the farmhouse for lunch. Big mistake. *Very* big mistake. Missed the gate, went through the fence.) In practicing steering your 'train of thoughts', you will do some big-time 'fence busting' – but that's fine. The best-of-the-best have a trail of broken meditative fences behind them. Mine stretch back over the horizon.

In this next exercise, I would like you to set yourself a 'thought-task' that will involve memory and perhaps some 'imagination'.

For the purpose of the activity, let's say that your thought exercise is imagining a drive into the city. The key to the exercise is *not* getting 'lost in thought' – not just being a passenger watching the thought-scenery unfolding miscellaneously. Try and be aware of 'where you are' in your mind – be aware if you drift into the past, for example, or when you start meandering into wishful thinking or fantasising about the future. Above all, be awake to the moments of thinking in the present – which is the 'story'. Try also and be aware of any feelings or emotions that may seem to arise.

So reach into your Essential Stillness and then start the thought-awareness exercise, focusing on what you are actually thinking. Begin to 'steer the train'. It might go something like this:

... getting into the car – find the key, gotta be in one of the pockets – (in the present, annoyed), saying 'goodbyes', starting the motor, saying 'good morning' to the neighbour (all in the present, happy), quietly cursing his dog for being on the lawn again (present, annoyed), reminder to self once more to mow it on the weekend (future, unhappy) and pulling out of the driveway (present) … weekend – must remember to ask Madelaine and whatsisname to the barbie on Sunday (future) … maybe not, he drank too much at the last one (past, unhappy). Turn the corner … traffic … again (present, unhappy) … kids used all the hot water this morning (past, unhappy) … must finish that report today (future, apprehensive). Red lights – a quick look in the rear vision mirror to check out the make-up or the tie (or both!) (present) – look older than last week (past, unhappy) … green light, cars right and left, drive again (present) … 'HEY YOU! – what the *^%&*^# do you think you're doing' (present, angry) …

Of course, there are millions more mental 'doings' (not all at the forefront of conscious thought) activated by endless, peripheral visual stimuli – shop fronts, advertising signs, hoardings, bedraggled trees, people on the median strip, radio, music, announcers' commentaries, another red light – all the way to town.

Did you notice that, in addition to the mainstream imaginary 'story line' (driving to work), which I was endeavouring to deliberately steer (and managed to stay on the rails, reasonably well I thought – for about five seconds), I was nevertheless 'distracted' by the power of the association of ideas. I let go control and wandered into the past and the future, *despite* trying to stay in the present.

As I have said, dear reader, that is how *your* mind works the whole time – perhaps trying to 'do the right thing by you' (getting you to work) but getting continually distracted. I have no doubt that your process was similar – trying to stay 'mainstream' but getting 'distracted'. Fact is, you will have dredged up hundreds of fleeting little snippets of thought from your past and certainly crowded in hundreds more fragments from notions you are harbouring about the future, from the beer after work to the new house for which you're saving.

But, back to the point of the exercise … were you awake to what was happening in your mind – to your actual flow of thoughts, even when you 'went off the rails'?

Practice the Steering the Train exercise for a few days or until you find it increasingly easy to stay on your mainstream story. As the distractions become less, you will be beginning to take control of your thinking, which is perfect preparation for the next practice, *slowing your thinking*.

* * *

Having observed the out-of-control nature of their thoughts in their 'mind-revealing' exercises, most students doubt that the 'mind' can be slowed even a little, let alone completely stilled. They tend to hold onto their reservation until we do some simple exercises to help the doubters discover for themselves that *everyone* can not only slow their thinking but also experience a pure clarity of mind – if they so choose.

Over the first two weeks of the Introductory Course at the Meditation Sanctuary, we do a four-part exercise, but I don't explain the purpose of it until all segments are completed. The first part you have already done. That was the exercise of 'just sitting and doing nothing'. Of course, this 'boring' little non-activity was designed to show you that your 'normal mind' is a cacophony of babble that makes Stravinsky's music sound like the single sweet note of a Tibetan bowl being brushed.

The second part of the exercise you have also done ... writing down your thoughts. Yes, we looked at the 'secrets' in your writing but, what I didn't say then was that *the very act of writing down your thoughts slows your thinking by about half.* It must do, because you 'thought a thought' then actually paused in your thinking to focus on writing it down.

A little digression here if I may. Long ago, when studying English literature at university, I had a wonderful professor called Harry Heseltine. He always used to *read* his lectures very rapidly, as if he were late for an important meeting – no looking up at his students, no discussion – just vast amounts of good data in which we students marinated for a whole, urgent hour. For that entire period, all you could hear was the scratching of busy pens like cockroaches having party-time! There was *no time for miscellaneous thinking, because of the intensity of focus required ...* (and therein lies the secret for the beginning of meditation).

In one of the early introductory practice sessions, students at the Sanctuary are all given a tennis ball. They are asked to draw a design on it, which personalises it as 'their property'. (They are later asked to swap 'their' personalised ball with another student, keep the one they are given ... and contemplate the 'lesson'.) The ball is then used in the practice of the third segment of the four-part exercise. You can get a tennis ball and do it too if you wish or just 'see the lesson' in the practice I describe now.

I ask the students to simply start throwing the ball from one hand to the other. They sit and grin and do exactly that until I yell, *but you must not drop it* ... whereupon tennis balls soon start escaping everywhere.

Then I ask them to move their hands farther apart and to start throwing the ball faster ... lots more balls bouncing all over the place ... embarrassed laughter fills the hall as balls are retrieved and the scene before me begins to resemble a fairground with kids scurrying all over the place to find the next thrill.

Then I say, 'now, we shall do it all again, but this time, *close your eyes and focus deeply on not dropping it.*' I add that they may repeat the words, 'don't drop the ball' to themselves if they wish. What happens? You've guessed it. Rarely does anyone drop the ball. All you can hear is the *throp, throp, throp* of 30 or so tennis balls being whacked into the palms of mindful hands.

Of course, they don't drop the ball because, firstly, all external distractions they can see (like all the other people throwing a ball) have been eliminated and, secondly, while repeating 'don't drop the ball' to themselves, they are in effect beginning the practice of saying a *mantra*. This, as I said earlier, is the repetition of a word or phrase for the specific purpose of quieting the mind *to a single point of focus*. So, in just closing their eyes and concentrating on throwing a ball while focusing on just one word or phrase, they have entered an inner quiet place, free of miscellaneous chatter, in which they can 'see' or visualise the ball with greater clarity. But the main point is, with their mind now so singularly focused, they have, in fact, *slowed their thinking by about 95 per cent.*

So, what of the remaining five per cent you may ask? The answer lies in the final part of the exercise. I ask all students to put their ball down. I have already mentally 'selected' one student, whose name I suddenly shout out followed immediately by my yelling, '*Catch!*' Shocked by hearing his name roared at him, he looks at me, startled ... by which time, a tennis ball I have thrown quite vigorously is almost upon him. Although he has only a split second to become aware of the missile about to hit him, invariably he catches it neatly.

In fact, 99 per cent of students catch the ball perfectly and gracefully, even though a number of students at whom I've thrown the ball breathlessly tell me later that they were stunned to have caught it because they've 'never been able to catch anything'. Why have they suddenly developed a 'new skill'?

The student catching the ball, for just a tiny moment, experiences a pure state of consciousness and awakeness without *any* overlay of conditioned thought (such as 'I can't catch anything!'). He ceases thinking the moment he hears his shouted name and, when seeing the ball almost upon him, instantly achieves the perfect, single-pointed mind-focus required to respond, in less than half a second, to catch it. He, in fact, experiences a moment of *satori* (the word used by the Zen masters to describe the state of No Mind or, perfect clarity of consciousness … without thought).

To Zen practitioners, this 'state of being' is the 'summit' – the highest form of *awakening*. That, even if only for a second, is the very 'super-conscious' state the student experiences in catching the ball.

The point of the final part of the exercise is simple – to demonstrate that it is utterly possible to go way beyond just slowing the mind to single-pointed focus. It shows that any randomly selected student can experience perfect clarity of consciousness – being purely *awake* for a brief moment. It follows that, if it is possible for just this brief moment, then with training and practice it is possible to experience it for longer. The reality is that, with an intensity of practice, *satori* can be experienced by *all* who so choose, firstly, *at will* and finally, as a *permanent* 'state of being'.

Now that *you* have become aware of the real possibility of mastering thought, it is time to move on a step or two by commencing the practice of *slowing down* that babbling mind.

Exercise 26. *Slowing Your Thoughts*

In practicing the previous exercise, when you feel able to direct your thoughts without 'wandering away' too frequently, you can now commence using these embryonic 'mind-mastering' skills to begin slowing mental activity.

Spend 10 minutes reaching your Essential Stillness. Then take your focus to your thoughts, allowing them to meander where they will, while you again play the observer. Now, as they tumble along, begin

> *to put a 'mental voice' to your thoughts so you hear them with your*
> *'inner listening' at normal speaking pace. Or, putting it more simply,*
> *'talk to yourself' without anyone else's being able to hear.*

You will then have your equivalent of something like this happening in your 'upstairs department':

'I can hear a bird. Is it the same cuckoo shrike that was in the vege patch yester ... forgot to go to the bank ... seriously dumb, man ... rent due today ... there's that bird again ... its voice is so sweet ... like the magpie ... why does the magpie have such a lovely ... better than that opera singer on the car radio yesterday ... she was soooo ... radio needs fixing too ... spent too much at the garage this month ...' – and so on.

The thoughts will flit quickly and still move by association of ideas but ... limiting the unmastered chattering to speaking pace *immediately slows brain activity* by at least half. The effect is the same as earlier capturing your thoughts and writing them down except that now you are achieving the same effect through 'mind mastery', without the assistance of a task such as writing (which slows the thinking mind by focusing it – by giving it 'something to do').

Speaking your thoughts to slow them is a little like being chased by a bull (only safer). If you haven't been chased by a bull and don't know what I'm talking about ... you can either go taunt a bull and find out for yourself or, accept my telling you (from personal experience) that, in such a delicate situation, one thinks in a rather focused, single-pointed way ... as in, 'that %&# fence is too far away ... oh god, he's gaining on me ... how far is that %&# fence away now ... oh god, he's still gaining on me'.

See how the thinking became more 'controlled' and *slow* ... because it had 'something' single-pointed to focus on ... like a fence ... and some sharp horns. Oh, you want to know what happened? My situation analysis was gifted in its accuracy. The fence *was* just a metre too far away and the bull *did* gain on me. The bull's thinking also then became quite 'single-pointed'. He threw me over the fence (I landed relatively unscathed), whereupon my thinking became as erratic and rapid as my heart rate (but, of course, only for a moment).

In your session each day (tension-free and breathing 'right'), continue to become aware of your thoughts and then speaking them with your 'mental voice' thus slowing them (without a bull!). Then, listen to the voice to be increasingly aware of exactly what you are saying/thinking.

When ready, complete the exercise in the usual way.

Exercise 27. *Focusing Your Mind to a 'Single Point'*

Having slowed your thoughts by consciously speaking them in your mind, you are ready to begin bringing your train of thoughts to a virtual standstill – to a 'single point' at which you begin taking control of the seemingly uncontrollable.

> *In one of the practices in which you have reached your Essential Stillness, become aware of your thoughts and voice them in your mind for a while, as before. Then suddenly 'grab' one of the thoughts you have just spoken (for example, 'I can hear a bird singing') and repeat it … and keep repeating it over and over, making sure that you are giving full attention to that one word, phrase or sentence you have chosen. Having settled on a word or phrase, keep repeating it for a minute or two before completing your session.*

A little hint! Wait for a positive and pleasant word or phrase to grab, rather than jumping on a negative one such as, 'I hate my job', because repeating a negative thought will surely drag some negative emotion into your practice.

In grabbing a word or phrase and repeating it with due focus, you are in fact preventing the next thought (for example, 'how lovely that bird's song really is …') and the next one – and the next – from automatically following the first. In holding focus *single-pointedly*, all you have left 'in mind' is the repeated word or phrase that is taking up the 'mind-space' previously saturated with other miscellaneous mental chatter … (bit like single-mindedly running from a bull – not a lot of mental space available for planning what to have for lunch).

Your mind is not yet perfectly still, but you have reduced the standard babble to a single point of focus. In this instance, you have 'used your thoughts' to begin creating that classic *technique* for stilling the mind – the *mantra*. We shall travel on now to explore more deeply, both this and other and classic techniques of stilling the mind.

* * *

A Little Story of Encouragement

Little Creatures and Dewdrops

'A friend suggested I try meditation and I was persuaded at the time because I was having trouble sleeping. Simple. I sat on my cushion, the full sceptic, looking out for signs of a cult as I listened to my teacher's dulcet tones. I decided to "cherry pick" and remain as much at a distance as I could. In my job I am trained to be critical and questioning … and that I was.

I did find comfort in sitting each day and decided that practicing relaxing, breathing and stilling my mind was not a bad way to start my day. I began to look forward to my lessons and to be among a group of people held together by a common "interest", for want of a better word. Being mindful (or aware of the present moment) brought an unexpected feeling of joy to me. I decided to do the Intermediate course and now enjoy the love and kindness of the Meditation Sanctuary.

Looking back, my mere 18-month Journey has culminated in a series of changes, some quite noticeable and some hardly detectable at the time. I don't know whether I can attribute all of the following to my practice but I would like to share some of them with you.

- My first observation was that I laughed instead of cursed – particularly if the toast landed butter-side down.
- Morning walks in my garden became compelling … I paid attention to the little creatures and dewdrops.
- I used to smoke 25 to 30 cigarettes a day. My sleep was punctuated every two hours with a couple of gaspers. Now I am free from all that.
- I have lost 11 kilos and now exercise daily. Junk food was always on the menu – now it doesn't enter my head, let alone my mouth.
- I listen to people instead of being preoccupied with what I'm going to say next.
- I've taken up yoga and love it.
- I move more slowly.
- I sing.

I could go on and on … the list is growing every enjoyable day.

There is, however, a more profound change that I have noticed. From the age of 20 (I am now 48) my life has been severely disrupted nearly every year for a number of months. I have a chemical imbalance known these days as bipolar disorder. If left without intervention, I can become extremely "high" and psychotic for a number of months, then plummet to the deep black depths of suicidal thought for what seems like forever. I have had many hospitalisations, high levels of drugs and many courses of electro-therapy.

As the years have passed, I have managed to find a combination of drugs that have enabled me to study and hold down a job. The drugs are not without their side effects. When I'm about to "go high", I have to take a particular drug. If taken in high concentrations it lowers my epileptic threshold and I fit violently and often. As a consequence, I developed a high level of anxiety and terrifying panic attacks.

I have noticed that since I have been meditating, things have changed. I am calmer and more self-contained. I have become aware of my episodes many weeks earlier, which means I can intervene with appropriate medication at a much lower dose and the episode is much less disruptive. Instead of six weeks off work, I have had a couple of days off and I've forgotten what it's like to have a fit and the fear of hard surfaces that went with epilepsy is non-existent – no more anxiety or panic attacks.

I can't say that following my meditative path has been the sole reason for these changes. I think a good dose of wisdom has helped as well.

I know I have found something so simple and yet so resonating and feel blessed.

Did I mention I sleep through the night now …!'

– Liz (name withheld for personal reasons)

* * *

I was aware of a student in class who seemed 'different' to the others. I knew she was 'considering' every word, every exercise … carefully … 'finding out for herself'. Liz, who is a scientist, 'tested' meditation for herself – and accordingly, has uncovered its wonderment and beneficial effects.

Chapter Thirteen

Classic Techniques for Stilling the Mind

'While I was waiting for something to happen … something happened! I realised I was waiting for something to happen.'

– *Beckie Waples, Sanctuary Student*

There are many 'techniques' that you can practice to accomplish the art of Stilling the Mind. In this next segment, I shall guide you in some of the most classic, authentic, beautiful and, above all, *effective* techniques. Initially, I would like you to practice each of them as we go along. In due course, you will find that one or two may seem easier or 'do the job' for you better than others. It is then absolutely fine to retain just those and let go the others.

Many teachers labour under a gross misapprehension that the use of a technique alone (such as using a *mantra*) over a period of time, is actually meditating. This is not so. As I have said, a technique to quieten the mind to single-pointed focus is *only* a natural prelude to, or 'right' preparation for, Authentic Meditation. In reality, all the techniques are ancient, wonderful practices devised by old masters specifically to be used as 'tools' to help clear the mind of miscellaneous chatter so you can *then* journey on to the 'real stuff'.

Further along your Path, and having practiced using various techniques to achieve single-pointed focus of mind, you will then also *practice letting go the techniques themselves* so that pure meditation may be experienced in the beautiful inner 'space' you are able to access when free of *all* distractions – including the techniques of single-pointed focus.

In the final analysis, all possible 'techniques' – from repeating a *mantra* or gazing at a candle to wild dancing in circles – are effectively the same because the true purpose of them all is their singular use to ease the mind away from chatter and into the relative quietness of being occupied instead with just one thing on which to focus. So know that whatever way or technique you finally choose as 'yours', is as valid as any other way.

I have chosen to include in this chapter yogic techniques which are gentle and natural rather than more extreme practices such as the aforementioned frenzied dancing in circles like the famed Whirling Dervishes. Although, of course, if you *would* like to try that …

Letting Go the Training Steps

In practicing each of the mind-stilling techniques from now on, you let go all the 'training steps'. So, for example, you now 'skip' the practices of thought awareness, talking your thoughts, grabbing a phrase, and so on. They again have been valuable little stepping- stones that you have crossed and can leave by the wayside, their job done.

Only the reaching of your Essential Stillness precedes each new exercise, as always.

Some Typical 'Experiences' During Mind Quieting

Do you remember back there in the book I talked about the 'experiences' of so-called 'advanced' breathing techniques? I said that later you might indeed have some 'amazing natural experiences' materialising in your practice. Well, dear reader, practicing techniques of Stilling the Mind can be the *beginning* of the 'later' I mentioned because layering these techniques onto the first two Essences may well produce some 'by-product' experiences. Best I outline some of the typical ones now, so there are no surprises awaiting you. Note though, that the experiences of *your* practice may not be the same as, or even similar to, those I mention below … and that is absolutely fine.

In the early phases of quieting the mind, any experiences are likely to be quite mild, but they may seem to become more obvious as you begin to 'win the mind-wrestle' with your thoughts. In other words, as thoughts recede, little experiences may 'pop in' to fill in the emptying thought-space, until your mind becomes familiar with the highly novel 'idea' of its being still.

Note, too, that little experiences may seem to vary according to whether you are practicing 'audio' techniques or 'visual' techniques, but conversely, just to be contrary, may seem quite disparate and unrelated to anything at all. You may indeed have none, which is totally immaterial to the effectiveness of your practice. Importantly, don't 'hang in there' waiting for bells and whistles – let go any expectation of 'things happening' – just sink into your practice as usual.

* * *

In an 'audio' technique, such as silent or vocalised repetition of a *mantra*, after you have become absorbed for a while, your first awareness of a 'happening' is that your thoughts may seem to 'separate' from you and just seem to be floating about 'out there' rather than 'in here'. As one student, Hannah, described it delightfully, 'I was aware of my thoughts, but they seemed to be in another room'. Exactly.

Thoughts will seem to become 'distanced' until you are holding focus for longer periods without being distracted at all by miscellaneous mind activity. Gradually, thoughts simply quieten as your *mantra*, for example, takes centre stage. You then may find that the word/s of a *mantra* gradually loses any sense or meaning and just 'morphs' into an ongoing, lulling background sound or 'white noise' that seems to encompass you and may seem to be just 'happening' by itself without effort from you. Now that's a lovely place to stop and rest awhile.

In quieting techniques that involve 'visualising' an object as a point of focus, instead of background sound, you may occasionally 'witness', for example, vivid colours or nebulous colour-shapes that move formlessly before you or bright, beautiful light. One student completed an early-stage meditation and felt that her 'vision' of purple planets was so real and astonishing to her that she looked up suddenly and asked the rest of the class whether they had seen them too!

As you move closer towards a state of true 'thoughtlessness' (in the nice sense of the word), experiences may occur that are sufficiently vivid to stir up your quietening mind into thought again – like, 'whoa, where did that come from?' In the settling, singularly focused mind, some people do have 'visions' (startling unfamiliar colours, morphing faces, beautiful ethereal light shows, iconic figures appearing, and so on) or hear 'sounds' (voices, music or chanting).

You may also lose immediate perception of your body and feel quite disembodied, as if you are not 'here' or you are rising from the ground or floating in space. Any such experiences in your practice are perfectly harmless and normal.

In fact, *any experience you may have in quieting the mind is an utterly natural inner-body experience* because all your practice exercises are completely natural so … just 'go for the ride'. Such experiences arise simply because the non-meditator's brain is not familiar with 'stillness' and makes a rather fumbling effort to 'fill the empty space' from its infinitely large and jumbled library of words, sounds and pictures.

Note that I called them 'utterly natural *inner-body experiences*'. I did this because there are no such 'things or events' as out-of-body experiences that some claim their vivid experiences to be … although in deep stillness, it may 'seem' that you are not aware of your body at all. Watch out, dear one, for those of the 'spiritual-fringe persuasion' wanting to take some of the weight out of your purse or wallet while trying to fill your head with notions that truly normal and natural experiences of Authentic Meditation are something 'other world'. They're not.

Importantly, do not become distracted or seduced by experiences. It is possible to get 'lost' in them because they can be very pleasant and, accordingly, some people may actually seek them out or develop desire for them. You will soon realise that flamboyant or vivid experiences are really only transient by-products of settling the mind.

When you move into a true meditative state later in your practice, such experiences become increasingly muted until they just disappear and, eventually, they do not occur in this way at all. There *are* experiences of meditation proper but they are not of the vivid kind – they tend to be increasingly profound, insightful awakenings and realisations.

Quieting Technique of the Mind Mantra

The use of a *mantra* to quieten the mind is an ancient and classic technique practiced across many cultures and in different formats, from the repetition of a single word to the chanting of elaborate verses that usually have religious connotation. It is known traditionally that *mantras* were composed as Vedic* hymns and used as a quieting practice long, long ago (as in millennia) by sages called Rishees.

These wise old ones had felt that, when deeply meditating, they perceived fine sound vibrations which they then endeavoured to translate into a sound that could be repeated because, to them, that sound represented their meditative experience of the Divine. In the classic way, a *mantra* (the repetition of which is also known as *japayoga*) is most often spoken, chanted or hummed aloud. A little later, I shall introduce you to this soothing vocalised technique that has the wonderful meditative effect of settling the whole being. In the meantime, we shall continue where we left off in the last exercise and practice using the *silent repetition of a mind mantra* to now refine the hushing of the busy mind.

There are some who, within a religious context, feel that a *mantra* is 'sacred' and that you should have your 'own' *mantra*, given to you by a master. From my point of view, this is just fine, and indeed quite beautiful, if the *mantra* is being practiced as an act of worshipful devotion to, say, a guru such as the Buddha. But, a little word of warning. There are some people at the outer fringes of non-authentic 'meditative practices' who ask to be paid to provide you with a 'personal' *mantra* which is said to have special or sacred power that enhances your individual practice. Be wary, dear reader, as such 'profferings' are devised purely as yet another way of taking money from the innocent and unwary seeker. *Mantras do* have a sacred power all right – the wonderful 'power' of being able to bring the mind to single-pointed focus. Now that's *real* power and is *freely available to all*.

So, in Authentic Meditation, any word or phrase can be used as a *mantra*, even 'wheelbarrow', because it is not the word or phrase itself that is important,

---

* The *Vedas* (which means 'knowledge' in Sanskrit) are the oldest sacred texts in Hinduism and are said to have been 'revealed' to the ancients (rather than composed).

it is the effort and effect of repeating it with focused attentiveness. My initial *mantra*, for example, was simply, 'I love rainbows'.

For this next exercise, I would like you to have chosen a word or phrase that you find soothing or lulling in its repetition. This will be the *mantra* you can use for a while, although you can change it if or whenever you wish.

Exercise 28. *Practicing a Mind Mantra*

Back to your sanctuary once more.

Spend some 15 minutes building your 'base of calm' and rest deeply within it for several minutes. Then move directly from focusing on your Rhythm Breathing to introducing your chosen mantra (such as 'I love rainbows' – whatever) and begin repeating it over and over so that you can 'hear' it in your mind.

Now endeavour to become deeply absorbed in the 'sound' of your word or phrase and try to hold pure focus on it for about 10 minutes or, for as long as you wish. When you want to finish the practice, you let go the mantra by taking your mind-focus back to your breathing and completing as usual ... slowly.

Losing Focus

Sometimes, while repeating your *mantra*, you will find your attention lapsing. Your words may become like running a tape on a 'background loop' in your mind ... '*I love rainbows ... I love rainbows*' ... while other thoughts wander in and are playing like another track over your *mantra* ... '*I love rainbows ... wish that helicopter would go away ... I love rainbows ... that sweet bird is back, oh good ... I love rainbows*' ... you get the picture. This is to be expected in early practice so do not chastise yourself or become impatient.

As soon as you become aware of thoughts 'visiting', awaken to their happening, acknowledge them and just gently guide your full attention back to 'listening' to the full sound of your *mantra* until you become embedded in it without the interruption of thoughts. Soon you will find yourself experiencing a whole new level of calmness as you cease to be disturbed or distracted by thoughts and their associated emotions.

If you find focusing on a *mantra* a little difficult at first, either continue to practice until it becomes easier (it will) or simply move to another technique. Remember the wise monk who said, 'if you need to start 1000 times …!

Completing a Practice with the Third Essence

In all your exercises to date, you have practiced the 'right' way to complete each one. But now that you are quieting your mind, you have another dimension, the Third Essence, to consider in completing practices effectively.

Firstly, as before, become aware that you wish to complete. Then, gradually let go the focus of your mind-absorption (the sound of your *mantra* for example) *by slowly shifting attention back to your breathing.* Remain absorbed in your deep, rhythmic breathing for a minute or two before completing slowly, slowly, in your usual way.

This is even more important now because the very practice of the Third Essence will have taken you into a much deeper calmness – the lingering 'effect' of which you do not want to shatter with a 'bumpy' landing. *Remember, the longer the practice, the longer the completion.* That simple. Permission to suddenly 'get up and go' is granted only in the event of an extraordinary occurrence during your practice … such as an earthquake … and even then …!

Moving to a New Technique

You only move to the practice of a new 'technique' of mind-quieting, after you have accomplished the previous exercise and have become really comfortable with it. Don't succumb to the 'I want it now' syndrome. Learn from the mistakes of others – like that Brahmasamhara guy who, a long time ago, was invited to leave his master's *ashram* for a two-month 'reflective holiday'.

Quieting Technique of the Vocalised Mantra

Thousands of years ago, the Rishees understood that the whole universe is comprised of energy that vibrates (just a whisker before the 'discoveries' of modern scientists reached the same conclusion). This vibration supposedly makes a sound which the Rishees are said to have experienced in their meditation. It is this sound that these 'yoga-men' reproduced as the 'word' *aum* (say *aahh – ooo – mmm*) which, in many popular practices today, has become *om*.

When *vocalised* and repeated as a *mantra, aum* becomes a very beautiful way of integrating the second and third Essences because, to practice vocalising it effectively as the original yogis did, you *need* to use your Rhythm Breathing while single-pointedly focusing your mind on the tangibly physical vibration you will feel. It is another classic technique for stilling the mind. Let's look at how it works in principle, before putting it into practice.

In Rhythm Breathing, you breathe out in the order of 'lower, middle, top'. In this exercise, you do exactly the same except that, with your voice, you are creating a beautiful sound on which to focus. The *mantra* is vocalised as you exhale and lasts for the duration of each long out-breath.

Aum is a perfect word for extended slow *mantra* expression because the three letters can be drawn out for as long as your out-breath lasts. You can divide the three sounds into three equal parts as you breathe out rhythmically or give greater emphasis to the '*mmm*' segment resonating by holding that part of the *mantra* longest. It doesn't really matter.

Exercise 29. *Humming with Rhythm Breathing*

To become familiar with vocalising while Rhythm Breathing, I suggest that you start practicing with humming.

> *Off to your sanctuary, shut out the world and sink into your Essential Stillness. Give serious attention now to slowing your breathing (at least 10 in and out if possible) and then focus particularly on the lovely rhythm of your out-breath. When you are ready, begin to quietly hum aloud while you breathe out.*

Now, dear reader, note that a meditative *hum* is the holding of a single, quietish, lowish note for as long as you comfortably can, not a virtuoso performance of 'Ave Maria'! But hum loudly enough so you can hear with your ears – not your 'inner listening'.

When you are underway, take your mind to your throat and let the tension seep from it (while maintaining your hum). You will find your voice deepening and becoming more resonant, maybe a little like the exquisite chanting voices of the famous Gyuto monks from Tibet. As you settle into the practice, begin to take your mind-focus to the lovely vibration you will be feeling throughout your body. Remember to practice the 'lower, middle, top' rhythm each time while breathing in again as well.

I suggest that you practice humming on your out-breath for several sessions until you can hold a long, steady note through each out-breath. Do *not* be like the enthusiastic student who, in wanting to be doubly effective, asked, 'why don't we do it on our in-breath as well?'

Exercise 30. *The Vocalised Mantra – Japayoga*

When you are humming consistently and slowly, you can begin to replace the hum with the *mantra, aum.*

So, while breathing out, the first part of the aum mantra, 'a', (pronounced 'aahh') begins in your hara area with tummy breathing. The 'u' (pronounced 'ooo' as in 'wool') seems then to emanate from the 'middle' of your lungs because, as you continue to breathe out, you are closing your mouth slowly in preparation for making the 'm' sound. Then, when the sound of the 'm' follows, it is held with your mouth closed so the vibration ('mmm') resonates in the head and then beautifully, through your whole body.

Spend time (perhaps several or many sessions) giving attention to developing a lovely evenness of breathing and sound until you feel the whole practice is coming to you naturally.

Exercise 31. *Quieting Thoughts with a Vocalised Mantra*

When you have developed 'evenness', you are ready to begin using the practice as a technique to quieten the mind.

Take your mind-focus specifically to the vibrations that you are creating throughout your body when you are voicing 'mmm' and become absorbed

> *in the 'sense' of the vibration. Maintain single-pointed focus on it and, as usual, if thoughts come in, just let them go by becoming reabsorbed in the vibration.*

Gradually, you will find yourself 'sinking' into the lulling beauty of the sound and the sweet calming of the vibration. You will just become aware that your thoughts have either faded or become like fleeting visitors who pop in but leave immediately when they see that you are busy (well, *some* visitors are like that, aren't they).

Some practitioners feel that, in repeating a *mantra* in this way, we align our vibration with the natural vibration of the universe and that we create positive energy in the 'doing'. Whether that lovely old mythology has any truth matters not, but I do know that *a vocalised mantra feels as though you are massaging every cell of your body.* You certainly experience an inner sense of great harmony and peacefulness (and you are practicing your Rhythm Breathing into the bargain). Perhaps, that is exactly what the ancients meant.

I have always found the vocalised *mantra* quite delightfully soothing and its practice is most valuable for rapid alleviation of the symptoms of anxiety and depression. Oh, and it is brilliant as a technique for quieting the mind – which is where I think we started this exercise.

In our Meditation Sanctuary, we often create a soft, calming and harmonious environment in which to meditate by playing the lovely background sound of monks chanting *mantras.* Perhaps try it in your sanctuary.

Chanting with Others

An astonishingly lovely little extra exercise is to practice your voiced *mantra* with another or others. If practiced with a group, take your mind-focus to both the vibrations *you* are feeling and the sound of the whole group. Again, it is a deeply soothing exercise and you almost feel as though you are sitting with those ancient Rishees listening to the divine sound of the vibrating universe.

If practiced with *one* other, endeavour to gradually shift *your mantra* to the same note and tone as the other practicer, particularly when you are humming the 'mmm' sound at the end of *aum.* After a while, you will find 'harmony' with the other voice and it can seem as though there is only one voice. The experience is quite beautiful.

As an aside, when my children were babies, I could inevitably lull them to sleep by placing their head on my chest and just humming the *aum*. Try it you mums and dads – you may thank me!

Completing an *Aum Mantra*

To complete the *aum mantra* technique, gently quieten and then 'let go' voicing the sound. Take your focus back to your deep breathing and then you know what to do.

Enjoy this beautiful exercise and practice until you can effectively quieten your thoughts. It is a practice you can take with you for a very long time, just for the sheer meditative enjoyment in the doing of it.

Quieting Technique of a Visualised Object

This next technique in attaining single-pointed focus of mind may be a little more difficult for a short time because we introduce another element, *deliberate visualisation*.

Visualisation is quite different to the usually random visual imagery (mind pictures or imagination) that mostly accompanies your equally random thinking. Deliberate visualisation is a practiced meditative faculty and can become a highly disciplined and valuable member of your mental faculties. It involves the harnessing of your normally 'loose' imagination so that it develops into 'focused imagination' or ... visualisation. You can, with practice, 'learn' to direct your imaginative thoughts with a high degree of precision – in effect, developing another valuable technique (a kind of visual *mantra* this time) to help you reach into single-pointed, mental composure.

Exercise 32. *Quieting Thoughts using a Visualised Object*

Before you commence this practice, think of, or imagine, a small, simple object that, if placed before you, you would find attractive to gaze at comfortably for some time. For example, it might be a small flower or an autumn leaf, a blue cube or just a red dot of paint. It doesn't matter, as long as it is not complex in appearance. When I practiced this exercise, my chosen 'personal object' was a white flower of the daisy kind that featured a small orange centre.

> *Again, settle in your sanctuary and spend 10 minutes or so reaching into your Essential Stillness but, this time, do not introduce your mantra.*
>
> *After bringing yourself to calmness of body and breathing, move your focus to your 'mind'. As soon as possible, endeavour to visualise your chosen object as clearly as you can in your 'mind's eye'. You will either 'see' or visualise it as an object external to yourself (as if it is 'out there' in front of you) or 'imagine' it as if it is 'in' your mind. It matters not.*
>
> *Once you can 'see' it, slowly endeavour to direct your full awareness to the object and just hold your mind-focus on it for as long as you can. Look at it, concentrate on it, examine it, appreciate it and keep your mind attending it.*

In the early stages, thoughts may well run happily through your mind (as in … 'I can see it, I can see it, aren't I clever'). Such flitting thoughts may often be quite strong and seem to mingle and mess with, or even supplant or drown out, the image of the object. This is quite usual in the early stages. When you become aware of this happening, just gradually bring your visualised object back into focus. With practice, you will find you can hold your object before your inner vision for longer and longer until you can just gaze at it without any thoughts surreptitiously trying to 'sneak in'.

Just sink into the experience of being still of mind again until you are ready to complete this exercise exactly as you did the previous one.

Exercise 33. *The Visualised Mantra Technique*

I was originally guided in this next technique by Bashayandeh. He told me that if I could master it it would prove to be one of the most effective techniques in quieting my jabbering thoughts. He was right! In effect, this mind-quieting technique combines the two you have already practiced, the mind-*mantra* and visualising a simple object.

Another lovely day in your sanctuary for settling into your now familiar Essential Stillness, this time going as far as adopting your mantra to quieten the disquieted mind.

After you have held mind-focus on your mantra for a minute or two, begin to envisage a blank space in front of you, such as a whiteboard or a neutral coloured wall. Visualise it clearly before you – while the mantra is still 'ticking over'. Then 'grab' the word or phrase you are using as your mantra and visualise it as 'words' before you on your blank 'space' (board, wall – whatever). So if you have been mentally voicing 'I love rainbows', for example, they are the words that you mentally 'write' on your board. Now you are 'looking at' your mantra.

Look at the letters with your 'inner eyes'; see them clearly – note the style of writing and the colour of the print. Examine the words and keep reading them over and over from beginning to end, saying them very, very slowly in your mind.

Then begin to just look at the phrase and start trying to let go your 'mind mouthing' of the words until you slowly bring the inner voicing to a halt. So instead of reading the words aloud in your mind, you will gradually begin to see them as a 'picture' before you – a picture made of words.

When this happens, even fleetingly at first, you are actually visualising a thought. You are 'seeing' your thinking (or a little part of it) with an inner clarity.

Dealing with the 'Spoil-sport' Thoughts

While you hold your visualised *mantra* on your 'clear-space', inevitably other thoughts will pop in to your mind and you may experience the dual effect of holding a word picture quite clearly, while your mind happily wanders off through the front gate and gets itself 'lost in thought'. There are two ways to drill your mind back to focused attention.

As soon as you realise that your mind is not fully focused in the right space, the first practice is to just consciously direct your focus back to the repeating of your initial mantra, giving it an intensity of concentration that restrains, then stifles, the 'outside' thoughts.

Then, all over again, create the written visual of your mantra until you can simply hold relatively thoughtless attention upon it. Do this mental manoeuvre as often as is necessary to quieten the old mind.

The second approach is to become aware of the intervening thought, ('how lovely that bird's song is', for example), 'grab' it and turn that very thought into words you can 'read' in your space in place of the original visualised mantra. Then, each time your stillness is interrupted, grab the subsequent thought and visualise it, supplanting the previous pictured thought with the new one.

Soon, you will find yourself just holding one, uninterrupted visual thought on your space. When you are able to concentrate on it with minimal interruption, maintain your inner gaze on it for up to several minutes if you can and then complete your practice by taking your mind-focus back to your breathing – and so on, to completion.

I must tell you that, although I found the accomplishment of this technique difficult in the beginning, once I'd 'cottoned on', it soon became the easiest and most effective way of getting my thoughts to single-pointed focus. I adopted it as 'mine' until the time came to practice letting go *all* techniques.

At this stage of your Journey, by the time you deeply relax, settle your breathing and reach into a mind-quieting technique, you are probably spending about half an hour per session in your sanctuary ... *every day*.

Mind Quieting Technique of Rhythm Breathing

One of the most popular of the classic techniques practiced to reach deep mental composure is focusing your awareness single-pointedly on your breathing and simply staying there, rather than moving on to another technique. This is one of the main meditative practices used for countless centuries by the Buddhist people as well as other meditative groups.

However, I have heard of so many teachers directing their students to 'slow your breathing' and just concentrate on the 'in', and 'out' breaths'.

This level of breathing is great for a light relaxation *but* just focusing on 'in' and 'out' *without* training in *hara* and then full Rhythm Breathing means that you could spend a long time becoming genuinely still of mind. Indeed, most such practitioners take a *very, very long time* (as in years) to 'learn' to reach a true level of mental stillness without deeper understanding of the profoundly calming yoga breathing techniques. Quite simply, most students usually retain their 'shallow' method in the common simplified practice and, accordingly, are virtually unable to reach the depth of whole-being stillness required for Authentic Meditation.

Already you have taken the second Essence to a point further than most meditation practitioners will ever get to even hear of, let alone discover through practice. However, as you know, what *you* have practiced so far is *renewing* your wonderful, *original* breathing skills so that you might enjoy a profound calmness of being – way beyond just being aware of breathing in and out.

When you practiced your Rhythm Breathing earlier, your thinking would certainly have become quieter than the normal babble because you were singularly directing your focused effort on the moment (as in, for example, repeating 'lower', 'middle', 'top'). But, nevertheless, in so doing, you were still experiencing *some* mental activity rather than a pervading stillness of a silent mind.

In this exercise, the practice is to *use your Right Breathing as the quieting technique – as the actual point of focus* to still the mind.

Exercise 34. *Breathing as the Point of Focus*

So reach your Essential Stillness, settling into the rhythm of the breathing 'wave' without mentally saying 'lower, middle, top'. But do not introduce your mantra or a visualised object.

Take your mind to the 'wholeness' of the breathing activity, which means being aware of the breath coming in and out through your nose and the beautiful full rhythm of your slow, gentle Right Breathing – moment by moment. Your whole mind rests in the awareness of the rhythm of ... just breathing.

The aspiration is to keep your mind on that awareness – focusing single-pointedly on sinking into the harmony you will 'feel' being created in your body by the gentility of the rhythm. When those little thoughts feel they are missing you and wander back 'home', just accept them as the signal or trigger to take your mind-focus back to … just sinking into the rhythm. If you let them distract, they will distract … that's their job.

Gradually, you will find that focusing on the rhythm creates an increasing intermission between individual thoughts. (It is often said that 'meditation is the space between thoughts'.) You will also discover that absorption in the rhythm is extremely mentally lulling – and then quieting. You will become increasingly immersed in the gentle sound and movement of your breathing, just as you were singularly aware of your *mantra* being repeated in your mind.

As with all your exercises, layer this practice across the first two Essences for about 10 or 15 minutes. Continue practicing this technique until it is effective in quieting thoughts and then move on to the next when you are ready.

Completing the Breathing Technique

You complete the breathing technique exercises by commencing with a conscious, lung-filling deep breath and then finish as you know how.

Quieting Technique of 'Whole-body' Breathing

When you are ready, you can extend the effectiveness of the breathing technique with a very lovely practice.

Earlier, you practiced a 'lung-awareness' exercise in which you 'imagined' that the *chi* or *life-force* was a colour (say, golden) and I asked you to visualise it swirling around your lungs as you breathed in. The next exercise is similar to that practice but now taken further.

Exercise 35. *'Whole-body' Breathing*

> Upon settling into your Rhythm Breathing, begin to visualise 'coloured'
> *chi* swirling around and filling your lungs.
>
> This time, on your in-breath, try and visualise the coloured air going
> 'beyond' your lungs – as though it is spilling over from them – and

flowing gently into your whole body, as if you are not just breathing into your lungs but into all of you, from the top of your head to the tips of your toes. On your out-breath, visualise the coloured air being 'drawn back' from throughout your body, then out via your nose and into the universe from whence it came.

For a little while, you may have difficulty in visualising the air being drawn into your whole body at once and your mind may dance about while trying to 'see' the coloured air filtering all through you. Soon though, the visualisation will become more natural and you will seem to feel the coloured air 'permeating' you and, just as naturally, being 'emptied' of it with your out-breath.

Continue this practice until you have an instinctive awareness of the coloured air being breathed naturally into your whole body. You are then likely to find that the level of focus required 'blots out' most thoughts quite automatically. Your mind will seem to just merge into a kind of golden-coloured rhythm (or whatever your chosen colour is). If you have thoughts sneaking about, you know what to do. Bring your attention back to the practice in hand, as always.

Now the big step!

While drawing air into your 'whole body', let go visualising the colour. That was just a temporary 'tool' to help you train up for the real practice. So the visualisation now becomes one of deep focus on taking in life-force with each in-breath and being aware of its nourishing every cell in your body. The out-breath then takes the spent 'force' back out into the universe.

You now deliberately focus on this deep sense of 'whole-body' breathing as your point of focus to keep your thoughts at bay.

Again, you add this practice to the first two Essences for 10 or 15 minutes before completing.

Visualising *Chi* as Vitality

If you so choose, you can extend the last powerful technique even further by visualising the in-breath of *chi* as a *vitality of wellbeing* seeping through and nourishing your whole body. Endeavour to visualise a feeling of 'wellness' pervading your body with each breath. You can also visualise the *chi* as a *sense of joy* that you happily attract with your in-breath.

Quieting Technique of 'Eyes-open' Gazing

If one practices meditation in the *Soto Schu* tradition of Zen as I have done, many monks of that 'school' meditate with their eyes open or, at least, 'half-lidded' or half-open. In class, I call this classic way of quietening the mind, 'Zen Practice', which is not, strictly speaking, accurate. However, in doing so I simply mean practicing with eyes open like a Zen master.

I am reminded of a lovely traditional story about Bodhidharma, the Indian monk who introduced Buddhism to China. It is related that he sat before a wall gazing single-pointedly at it for seven years (some say nine; I say, 'for a longish time') in his effort to seek inwards for his enlightenment.

For some of you, practicing mind-quieting exercises with your eyes open may initially prove harder than with closed eyes because your vision initially 'floods' with the countless distracting images you see before you. For others, who find babbling thoughts intensifying into a raucous clatter the moment you close your eyes, you may find practicing with opened eyes 'a revelation', (as one student said to me).

Before you go off to your sanctuary again, select a small, simple object to take with you: a lovely flower, a leaf, a coloured glass sphere, a little river stone – anything that is of a pleasant nature to you and with a restful colour. Sometimes I used a clear, glass marble (which I have to this day – albeit showing the chips, scars and scratches reflecting its long and faithful duty of just sitting and doing nothing!). At other times, I used a flower that I had dipped into water, creating little crystal-like droplets that clung to it. When we practice in our Sanctuary, there are invariably beautiful flowers lovingly placed around the Meditation Hall which, apart from being soothingly decorative, create perfect 'objects' for open-eye meditation.

Exercise 36. *'Zen' Practice One – Opening Eyes onto an Object*

> *Place your chosen object on the mat before you so that it is in clear focus (I shall use a flower for the purpose of the exercise). Then, close your eyes to commence the practice and proceed to your Essential*

Stillness. Hold the stillness at Rhythm Breathing for five or so minutes …
meaning that you do not proceed to any previous technique of stilling
the mind.

Once settled into your hara (as a minimum) or Rhythm Breathing,
open your eyes, immediately fixing your gaze upon your chosen object.
Continue to hold your gaze on the object. If thoughts want to dance
in and enjoy the fun, just gradually 'bring your mind back' by
intensifying your mental focus on the object.

After being within the deep quiet of your Essential Stillness, when you first open your eyes onto your object you will feel a flooding of startling visual awareness – very different to the 'inner awareness' you have been experiencing. You will see the colour of your object with vivid intensity – it may seem to 'hit you between the eyes' like a little shock. For just a moment, you will see with pure 'thoughtless' clarity of consciousness – exactly as experienced by the child on the rug.

Almost instantly, however, your old conditioning will kick in to interrupt this pure experience with thoughts such as 'wow, look at that!' as you react to the sudden, visual stimuli hurtling into your mind-quietness. The response will be exaggerated simply because of the contrast between 'where you have been' (within the Essential Stillness) and 'where you now are' (surrounded by visual stimuli).

Such an intruding response is 'normal' but, as the open-eyes technique is to be used to still the mind, not to excite it, the object now becomes the point of focus to 'occupy' your mind. Gradually, your response will settle as your thoughts begin to diminish and wilt under the 'mastery' of your singular gazing. In other words, as one of Suni's assistant monks once eloquently said to me, 'just stare at the thing until your mind gets bored and shuts up!'

As you know from practicing other techniques, the 'space between the thoughts' will just seem to lengthen as your awareness of the object increases and deepens to 'fill' the mind – leaving less and less space for flurry. In effect, the object at which you are gazing plays exactly the same role as the *mantra* or as visualising an object with your eyes closed: they are *all* objects or subjects for single-pointed focus. They are all your 'temporary assistants' in the task of bringing the mind's burdensome chatter to a standstill.

Initial Experiences of a 'Zen' Practice

Just as there may be little meditative experiences with your 'eyes-closed' practice, there are certainly some natural experiences that will occur in just staring. As you melt into the exercise, the colour of your object (even if, in reality, it is dull) may gradually seem to be so brilliant that it 'shines' or 'luminesces'. Then you may begin to 'see' your object's shape, colour, texture and lines – the intricacy of its 'being' *in a way you have never seen before*. In my own initial gazing on a flower, I experienced a powerfully heightened sense of its delicate perfect petal shapes and folds, and the rainbow lights in the water drops upon it, *all of which were actually there the whole time* but which I hadn't been able to see because my mind had been so preoccupied – with thinking.

As you settle further into thoughtlessness while gazing upon an object, you may have deeper experiences, such as the 'vortex sensation' in which the environment, in your general peripheral vision around the flower, becomes a kind of swirling, undefined, neutral or single-coloured blur or a 'vortex' at the centre of which the flower is in crystal-perfect focus.

As your thoughts succumb to the power of your gazing, you are likely to have a gradual, perhaps even overwhelming, sense of the beauty of your object – no matter how plain and mundane to your 'ordinary' perception.

Earlier I mentioned a talk given by Ajahn Brahm, from the Bodhinyana Monastery. At one point in that same talk, he was about to take a sip of water, but suddenly stopped and stared at the glass, as if transfixed. He simply said, 'isn't it beautiful' … smiled, and then drank. Such a sense of beauty welling from within may also be accompanied by a rising feeling of wonderment, even joy, all over-layered with an increasingly heightened sense of calmness.

Seeing 'Visions'

You too may have 'visions' such as seeing 'auras' of different colours around the object. It is 'believed' by some that auras are coloured 'fields of energy' emanating from objects, including our bodies. Some 'spiritually-tuned' folks claim they can see these radiating colours and can 'read' them for signs of illness in the body – different colours for different illnesses. One of my dear students, Zoe, after listening intently to my guidance on an exercise, suddenly exclaimed, 'do you know that you have an aura? I can see it – it is gold!' After another class, during which I had noticed her 'single-pointed gaze', I smilingly asked, 'what colour was it tonight?', to which she replied matter-of-factly, 'purple'. Back to Zoe in a moment.

Some time ago I read of an extraordinarily revealing experiment conducted to discover the 'reality' or otherwise of auras and to explore the genuineness of aura readers. For the experiment, six people were seated on a stage behind a screen, over which only the backs of their shoulders and heads were visible. Six 'professional' aura-readers were invited, one by one, to go along the stage at their own pace, writing down the colour of the 'auras' they perceived and from that, note down any illness or physical dysfunction they diagnosed in the subjects behind the screen. Their results were collected, collated and analysed. *Each reader saw different colours in each of the subjects.* The ailments 'diagnosed' for each of the subjects also varied widely from 'reader' to 'reader'.

Then … the aura readers were given two pieces of data. Firstly, all the subjects had been selected deliberately for their excellent physical health. *None* suffered from any of the diagnosed 'ailments' the aura readers said they could 'see'. Then the researchers turned around the 'subject' on the far right of the stage to face the aura readers.

It was a wooden dummy. Enough said.

Zoe *did*, however, see an aura around my head. But … *it was an optical illusion,* such as we can all create by staring with single-minded focus for a few minutes at any object placed against a background of a different colour. Our eyes will 'see' a third colour 'between' the two objects – *an aura.* So, if you stare at your object now, a by-product experience of the exercise may well be a 'vision', an optical illusion, an 'aura'.

To the authentic meditative practicer, gradually *unveiling the reality of the true beauty of everything* – to see just as a little child sees – as the monk, Ajahn did, is far more breathtakingly enthralling than *any* make-believe 'visions'.

The Initial Experience of 'Oneness'- Seeing from 'Within'

As you hold your gaze, there will come a 'moment' for some of you (or a 'gradual awareness' for others) when you seem to lose your sense of 'separateness' from your object. In other words, you might lose the sense that you are 'here' and the object is 'there' – you will seem unable to distinguish between the self of 'you' and the object. You are then experiencing what can be called, *becoming one with the object*.

In your experiencing a sense of 'oneness', you have not, of course, become a flower. You are gazing *at* a flower but looking at it without imposing any thoughts upon it. You are not having your usual conditioned response of, for example, 'oh, isn't that a pretty flower, isn't it a lovely colour', which is exactly what happens to you virtually every second of your 'normal' waking existence as you 'thoughtfully' interpret absolutely everything you experience. You are simply just aware of the flower with a clarity of 'inner seeing' that can be awakened when you gaze while experiencing single-pointed quietness of mind.

You are seeing it as you would have as a little child, before you were clogged up with words, concepts, automatic interpretations and judgements which gradually have become your outer life – your daily 'outer shell' of conditioned reactions and responses. You are now, in effect, 'opening to' the flower with your whole being or, as I say, *seeing it from within* – which means being truly or wholly aware of it *just as it really is*, not the way you have thought, or *think* it is.

Not bad for just opening your eyes.

The experience of the loss of 'duality' (me here – it there) and the consequent perception of 'at-oneness' is, in fact, a hint of, or the prelude to, the crystal-clear consciousness and wisdom of the enlightened who perceive, experience and live their understanding of 'interconnectedness' – the oneness of, and with, everything … the whole time. More on that a little later.

'What if I Blink?'

Some students complain after the open-eyes exercise that they have 'sore eyes' – which happens in their trying to hold a powerful stare on an object and not allowing themselves to blink, as if they were trying to hypnotise a rhinoceros!

Best to blink, dear reader, particularly during a full, open-eyes meditation, because blinking prevents your eyes from drying and becoming irritated.

However, when you *do* blink in the early stages, you'll find that some of the effects you are experiencing, such as the vortex sensation, will disappear and you will see the object as 'normal' again. When this happens, simply continue your gaze until your focus becomes 'pure' once more. As you proceed deeper into your practice, you will find that you become totally unaware of your blinking and that your concentration and focus will be uninterrupted by it.

Completing the Preliminary 'Eyes-open' Practice

This is a simple completion. When you are ready, just close your eyes.

For a short while, you will be aware of an 'after-image' – a picture of your object seemingly printed on the inside of your eyelids with the same clarity as if your eyes were open. This will soon fade and, as it does, gradually take your mind-focus to your breathing and complete in the usual way.

Practice this exercise daily, layered onto the first two Essences, until you find that your attention to the object is leading you naturally to a still mind and you are perhaps enjoying some of the natural experiences I outlined above – not for the sake of 'having lovely experiences', but because the very fact of experiencing them means that you *are* becoming still of mind.

Exercise 37. *'Zen' Practice Two – Commencing with Open Eyes*

This next exercise is similar to the previous one, but increases the 'degree of difficulty' because it entails reaching all Essences (profound tension-freedom, rhythm breathing and stillness of mind) *with your eyes open … from the beginning of the practice*. It is one of the most important of the meditative exercises because it can be used, when you have mastered it, as a quite miraculous Active Meditation to ease stress, tension and anxiety as well as extending the early practice of mindfulness.

> *Once more to your sanctuary and set your object before you as you did last time and take up your meditative posture before it. You begin this practice by focusing your attention on the centre of your object.*

Here comes the harder part. You now gaze intently at the flower for the purpose of *minimising external distraction while taking your mind-focus inwards* so you can reach the first two Essences … all with your eyes open.

So, when your eyes have settled into 'staring' at the flower, begin to focus your mind 'inwards' on letting go tension from your body. Then, fluidly shift your mind-focus to your Right Breathing until you have fully layered that on to the state of being tension-free.

Now, the third 'step' takes your mind-focus 'outwards' as you redirect attention to the object on which you have been keeping eye-vigilance – but probably largely unaware of its being there as your mind 'bedded down' the first two Essences.

As you cement your awareness on the object to let go your thoughts, gradually they will fade until the purity of your attention becomes a 'substitute' for your thinking. Continue to immerse yourself in *just gazing* until you again begin to experience 'seeping' into a oneness with the external object while being quiet of mind.

Exercise 38. *'Zen' Practice Three – Wall Gazing*

I earlier mentioned the revered monk, Bodhidharma, and his seeking enlightenment by staring at a wall ... for years. It is, in fact, a wonderful meditative practice except that, in my humble opinion, spending years at the wall 'waiting' for enlightenment is rather missing the spiritual boat. Perhaps try it my way first.

First, *select your wall* ... best find one free of graffiti or any such distraction. (That reminds me of a most ironic recipe I once stumbled across. It was in a cookbook dated 1854 and was for 'Hare Stew'. The very first instruction in the recipe for the erstwhile chef was, *'First, catch your hare.'*). Ah, yes ... so first ...

As in the previous exercise, you commence with your eyes open, generally just gazing at the wall or a particular little part of it if you wish. When settled, again take your mind-focus inwards, relaxing to tension-free status then slowing and deepening your breathing.

On reaching into these two Essences, take your mind-focus outwards to the wall and simply ... gaze at it (there really being little else to do while sitting in front of a wall!).

For a while, you *will* have thoughts wandering into the old brain – like one or two I remember such as, 'what on earth am I doing here … Suni (who guided me on this practice) must be crazy'. Soon, however, in experiencing the meditative power of the exercise, I was, for the 100 and umpteenth time, reminded of my good Master's superior wisdom.

The practice is of course, *quieting the mind without having a specific point of reference* (such as a flower) upon which to focus attentively. The most effective way of now dealing with little interloping thoughts is as before – simply grab them as soon as you become aware of them and visualise them as words before you on the wall itself. This can be very difficult, but the very effort to 'see' them is usually sufficient to quieten the mind quite quickly. The second way is to go back 'inside' and focus deeply on your breathing until you are quieter of mind, and then resume gazing.

Ideally, I would like you to practice this Bodhidharma exercise for several weeks on a daily basis, until you are really comfortable in readily quieting the chatterbox.

Possible Experiences 'at the Wall'

In this exercise, you have no physical distractions such as your flower – just the wall – so your by-product experiences can be quite different to the more vivid responses you may have felt when gazing at an object.

In the early stages, there can be a sense of 'colour flooding' in which the colour of the wall (even if a neutral colour or white) can seem to be a massive sea as big as the universe in which you are *just floating*. One of my own experiences, for example, was that thoughts gradually seemed to 'get lost' in the 'overwhelmingness' of this neutral sea of colour, enabling the full experience of *just gazing* to arise.

You may feel the sense of oneness with the colour or you may feel as though you *are* the colour. At a more advanced stage (but not necessarily requiring practice over a great length of time), there can also be a sense of 'nothingness' arising, perhaps accompanied by a sense of peaceful bliss.

Don't chase any anticipated response – just gaze and see what happens. Remember, any experience is normal because, after all, you are just sitting and gazing at a wall … as one does!

Completing a 'Zen' Practice with Eyes Open

The early part of completing a totally open-eyes practice is different to your usual way because, this time, you *complete the exercise with open eyes as well.*

> *When you feel ready to complete but, still gazing, 'bring your mind back' to your breathing and focus on that for a while. From there, you have a choice of completion techniques.*
>
> *The first is when you are ready, ever so gently, look away from the object or wall and allow your sight to dwell on another object, and then another, while beginning to slowly move your hands and then the rest of your body as usual. If you complete slowly, your calmness will remain with you for a while.*

The other option is, while still gazing at your object or the wall,

> *just 'allow' a word or a simple thought to drift into your awareness. If you are gazing upon an orange flower, for example, you may allow the words 'orange' or 'it's so beautiful' to hazily waft through your mind. When a thought does arise, become aware of its presence and begin to allow your inner attention to drift from gazing at the object to the early thoughts.*
>
> *As soon as you find yourself conscious of a word/thought arising (and then other thoughts that will naturally expand from it), the sense of oneness will seem to fade and the object, or wall, will gradually appear to become increasingly 'normal'. Soon you will find yourself consciously 'looking' rather than 'gazing'. You can then shift your gaze from your point-of-attention while beginning to move slowly towards gentle completion.*

The Little Disappointment

I need to mention that, for the first few times after you do an 'eyes-open completion', you may become acutely aware of the 'reality' of objects at which you then 'look'. For a little while, that which seemed colourful and bright when 'seeing' with your *inner sight,* may now appear to be dull in colour, simple and lifeless – in other words, in deep contrast to the visual vividness you experienced in the exercise. Some meditators speak of a feeling of 'disappointment' that the vibrancy appears to have gone from their 'outer' world after a Zen exercise.

Two points of comfort. Firstly, in your *early* eyes-open completions, the outer world will soon return to its usual appearance because you will automatically return to 'seeing' it in your old conditioned way. In other words, as the mental chatter resumes, it 'takes over' or refills the mind that you had opened to 'superconscious' experiences (such as perceptions of profound clarity and beauty) in your meditative stillness. As 'old normal' returns, any sense of disappointment or let-down will subside.

Secondly, however, as you go further into your eyes-open practice, the clarity of your developing 'inner sight' (insight) and the 'normal' appearance of your outer world will, ever so gradually, begin to meld as you let go your conditioned way of seeing things (even when you are not engaged in formal practice). You will retain a heightened awareness and a greater purity of mindfulness so your deeper inner sight, rather than just conditioned thinking, will once more become the natural way you view your life environment – and all that is within it.

For that, dear reader, I can assure you, it is worth practicing ... and practicing.

The Experience of Rising 'Emotions'

I have related some of the typical experiences you might come across as you submerge into mind-quietness. In your practicing any of the techniques of single-pointed focus, you may also have some unexpected experiences ... this time of 'feeling emotions' or even 'feeling emotional'.

In an earlier exercise, you saw very tangibly (the plus and minus signs on your writing) that your emotions are attached to, or indeed, are *generated by*, your ... thinking. However, as you will have discovered over the time of your practice, when you are giving pure, single-pointed focus to a subject (such as a *mantra*) or an object (say, a flower), *feelings of emotions cannot be triggered by thought,* because you are no longer thinking! 'Just plain logic', as my wise old father would say.

But, even so, emotions *can* arise, although usually more muted and diffuse than 'normal'. Students never say to me, for example, 'I just suddenly felt angry at John'; they are more likely to say, 'I slowly became aware of a feeling *like* anger and I don't know why.' So, the paradoxical question has to be … how might emotions become present without apparent stimulus?

I shall endeavour to briefly explain why this may occur and then look at what to do if unhelpful emotions pop up in this phase of your practice.

In the freedom-space of relative mental stillness, where babble ceases because of your focused attention on a subject or object, you are still conscious, awake and aware – in fact, more deeply so than while thinking in the 'normal' unmastered way (which clouds the experiencing of true consciousness). What can happen in this quieting space, devoid of the distraction of the usual thought-mess, is that *we begin to 'expose' the 'self' of who we think we are.* It happens like this.

In our daily life, many of our memories of deeper emotions, particularly nasty negative ones, such as anger and guilt, may in fact be *suppressed* (filed in the far-reaches of our memory) or *disguised* with some compensating behaviour (excessive shopping, drinking … just about any form of exaggerated behaviour). This happens because feeling horrible old emotions is often painful, and confronting them is even more so. Over time, we then develop very clever ways to 'hide' from them, or filter them into acceptable comfort zones (for example, deluding ourselves that any adopted, excessive compensating behaviour is 'really not too bad – everyone does it'). Sometimes we create barriers (such as denial), so high and strong, that the naughty hurtful feelings can't climb over them.

However … in *just sitting* with quieting mind, stored emotions of a negative kind can just pop out for a bit of a run because, while you are still of being, there is no longer any busy, self-occupying 'behaviour' in process to cover them over. *While meditating, of course, there is no behaviour at all.*

Also, while just sitting quiet of mind, the normal barrier of babble between a conscious thought in this moment and all those memories banished to the never-never, is gradually eliminated. *While meditating, there is no thinking at all.*

In other words, dear reader, while being meditatively, single-pointedly focused, we *let go* our usual tools – our familiar defence mechanisms that we usually skilfully employ to dampen, placate or hide negative emotions. But, still being 'stored' within our memory bank (because we haven't yet used meditation to see them, understand them and let them go) and unimpeded by our created barriers, they can just float into the quiet space of our awareness as … the 'feeling of an emotion'.

We can, in fact, experience emotion of one kind or another during *any* letting-go-thought technique, even just staring at a wall. However, as I said, with the actual thinking-gear disengaged, the emotion is likely to be quite non-specific … just a 'feeling'.

As with all by-product experiences, emotional responses will vary from person to person and may be mild, transient and occasional or, quite the reverse, relatively strong and more frequent. The most important aspect to share with you is that any experience of emotions will only occur while you are either just thinking 'normally' (so not practicing at all) or in the actual process of using a technique to quieten the mind. *They only occur in the transition phase* – the phase of focusing the mind that falls *between* unmastered babble and the purity of the Zen No Mind – uncluttered consciousness.

Such experiences, 'events' or emotions *never occur in pure meditation* because we sink into a pure, silent superconsciousness devoid of thought, response, behaviour, technique or subject-of-focus. In this clear space, the meditative experience transcends or, is beyond reference to, ordinary 'conditioned' emotions. It is in this meditative space that we begin to reach into the Self of *who we really are*, not the 'self' we are conditioned to 'think' we are.

At a later stage of the meditative Journey, we can also use meditation as a tool or 'weapon' to see and understand our emotions and behaviour with great clarity and, in so unveiling this profound 'inner sight', be enabled to truly let go all that inhibits our experiencing life as it is meant to be experienced … wondrously, enthrallingly free of all negativity. At that stage, *one becomes the purity of meditation*, or transcends to becoming what I call a Being of Graciousness or returning to be an *awakened being* … as you were when a little child … where emotional negativity has dissipated into its rightful place of meaninglessness.

That more advanced exploration is beyond the ambit of this book, which focuses rather on guiding you to create those 'tools' and 'weaponry' (the mastery of pure meditation) so you can travel on when you are ready, perfectly equipped with the strongest possible climbing staff for the higher reaches of the Journey.

In the meantime, that leaves the real question of 'what to do' if, or when, emotions arise while quieting your thoughts with one of the single-minded focus techniques.

Firstly, it is important to inform and reassure yourself that the arising of any emotion while quieting the mind is natural, harmless and temporary, although you may feel a little discomforted. Secondly, *at this stage of your Journey*, I advise against some teachers' practice of telling you to just sit and 'feel the emotions' until they go away. If they are deep, negative emotions, just dwelling in them (and getting lost in them) *without the practiced meditative equipment to see and understand them with profound clarity and then, meaningfully and wisely, let them go*, can be distressing.

There *is* a way of dealing with distracting emotions that may arise, particularly negative ones, a way with which you are already familiar. You treat emotions that arise in an exercise (I repeat, *at this stage of your progress*), exactly as you have been dealing with your thoughts … *you let them go* in the gradual, gentle, natural way you have practiced 'letting go' throughout the three Essences.

Exercise 39. *Letting Go Diffuse Emotions*

If an interruptive emotion arises when practicing mind quieting, firstly, just acknowledge that it is 'there'. Don't fight it – even if it is beginning to seemingly 'well up' from within you, as, for example, anxiety does. But, before the emotion intensifies, endeavour to take your attention back to either the first Essence, Letting Go Tension, or to your slow Rhythm Breathing. Give either of those calming practices absolute focus – become absorbed in their doing – so that you are really there, fully experiencing them.

In making this calmness the core of your focus, you will find yourself gradually letting go miscellaneous emotions because they cannot be present if your entire mind-focus is directed with a purity of attention to 'something' else. The key is in 'focusing' and not allowing yourself to wallow in any negative feeling.

> *After becoming calm again, resume the mind-focusing technique on*
> *which you were engaged when emotions began to wander in. Remain*
> *deeply aware of maintaining your body in tension-free mode and be*
> *particularly mindful of your slow, deep, rhythmic breathing.*

As I said, when you sink deeply into what I call the Serene Space without
a point of focus, you will begin to experience a level of meditation at which
negative emotions will not arise.

Ah, the Critics – is Meditation Just Avoiding Reality?

Some practitioners (of the non-meditative kind) at this point say that the
'letting go' I have just described is 'avoidance' of the 'reality' of emotions.
The reverse is true.

I once attended a talk on meditation by a beaming and rotund (most
Buddha-like) Tibetan monk. Later, he asked for questions … and sure
enough, received the (then) classic one, 'isn't meditation just a nice little
escape from reality?' He smiled, was quiet while he looked at the questioner
for a few seconds, and then asked her if she had practiced meditation. When
she said she hadn't, he quietly suggested that she perhaps should … and
find out the answer for herself.

He was hinting, of course, that on practicing meditation, she would
discover it to be *the most profound Path to a deep clarity of understanding the*
Self … a long, long way from using it as an 'escape from reality'.

Interestingly, the question of using meditation as an 'avoidance tactic' is
being asked less and less now, as the observably unique value of meditation,
in enabling people to return to their wholeness of wellbeing, is increasingly
being studied scientifically in leading tertiary institutions worldwide. There
is a widening understanding of the quite extraordinary benefits of meditation
and, for example, I now rarely have a class that doesn't include a member
or two of one of the myriad branches of the medical and related professions.
One student, a doctor, recently commented to me that 'mindfulness is now
becoming mainstream in medical practice'. I let out a small 'wahoo!'

Used as the Masters understood it (as a *way of living*), meditation can be
'applied' in the gentlest, most self-caring, gradual and enlightening way so
that *all* negative emotions (and consequent negative behavioural modes)
can be insightfully let go. Metaphorically, all that 'emptied space' is then

available for inner profound peacefulness and positive, illumined life-purpose to well up naturally from within.

Daily Mastery of the Three Essences

If you are still with me at this point, dear reader, you have already been committing yourself to umpteen weeks or months of practicing the three Essences. You are now quieting the body, 'righting' your breathing and hushing all those chattering monkeys down to a single point of non-thought focus.

With practice of the third Essence now completing your core Essential Stillness repertoire, you will begin to experience a seeming 'expansion' or deepening of your whole-being calmness. Quite simply, as you practice the three Essences you will begin to glimpse, to experience, a little taste of your awakening consciousness, a glimpse that will now intensify into gradual revelation of the 'inner' being as your Journey progresses.

It is the lovely glimpse of 'what may be.'

Now you need to cement the habit of immersing daily in the practice of the three Essences – practicing gracefully and fluidly, so that the time in your sanctuary is spent more and more in the Stillness rather than in the effort to reach it. When you feel you are able to hold a singularly focused mind for a few minutes or more, you are ready to journey further up the mountain.

Chapter Fourteen

Mastery – Letting Go the Stilling Techniques

'A friend said to me yesterday, 'you don't talk about doing meditation anymore. Why?' My response was, 'I don't talk about breathing either, do I?'

– Suzie Price, Sanctuary Student

In my earlier endeavour to explain what meditation *is*, I said that the meditative Journey, from the very first steps to as far as you want to go, is not a matter of learning more stuff but rather 'unlearning' – it is the practice of *letting go*. All the exercises you have diligently practiced so far have been based on this concept of 'letting go' that pervades Authentic Meditation. Most meditation tuition stops at the point of leaving the novitiate holding onto a mind-stilling 'technique', such as focusing on breathing or repeating a *mantra* (remember the woman I met at the guitar festival who spent 17 years just repeating a *mantra* and believing she was meditating).

However, *it is only in the actual letting go of the mind-stilling techniques as well that Authentic Meditation becomes possible.* It is only then that you can truly begin unveiling the 'serene space of the purely silent mind' – that space free of all mental clutter, *including* the one surviving distraction … the techniques themselves.

You then take the Journey into a realm of meditation mastery that few experience.

* * *

The mind-focus techniques have fulfilled their task so it is time for you to let them go, thus enabling the Serene Space to just 'well up from within'. Now this rather fancy place of the Serene Space will be mentioned at the end of each of the 'letting go' exercises and I shall later discuss the 'experiencing' of it at some length. For the moment, though, understand the Serene Space to mean the supreme stillness that you can begin to experience when the mind is *completely free* of all mental debris and distraction of any kind. It is the common end point to letting go any of the mind-focusing techniques.

The Mind Mantra

The first technique you practiced was the repetition of a mind-*mantra*, the silent repetition in your mind of a resonant word or phrase that helped you quieten your thoughts as the *mantra* gradually 'took the space' of your thinking.

Your aspiration now is to maintain the 'effect' of the three Essences but without the distraction of a *mantra* ticking over in the background of your mind. I start with this one as I found it the easiest when attempting my first letting go of mind-focusing techniques.

Exercise 40. *Letting Go the Mind-mantra Technique*

> As before, progress through the three Essences, bringing your mind to
> single-pointed focus with your mantra. Give very particular attention
> to it, until you are aware that your thoughts have largely disappeared
> into the soporific lulling of your repeated words.
>
> Now, imagine that your mantra is being 'played' to you on a
> distant radio. As you listen, I want you to begin to turn the sound
> down in your mind, just as if you might turn down the sound on a
> radio. Importantly, do the 'turning down' ever so slowly, almost
> imperceptibly, but keep listening to the sound of your voice saying

the mantra, even as it becomes progressively quieter and recedes 'into the distance'. Gradually, the effect is to feel yourself almost straining your ears to 'hear' the sound as it ever-so-gradually fades into – no sound.

At some point of the 'turning down' process, you will find yourself fully focused on sound that isn't there. You will then be tension-free to the point of being unaware of your body, unaware of your now-natural, slow rhythm breathing and your mind will be focused on … nothing.

What do you think happens then … in that first exquisite moment of experiencing a purely silent mind? Bells, whistles … enlightenment? No, not quite, dear one … *you will probably begin to think!* That first experience of the *Pure Stillness* can be so profound that your mind will almost certainly go 'wow – I've done it' (or your equivalent thereof). Then you'll think, 'oh no, I've just blown it!' as you become 'aware' that thoughts just started to wander into the stillness.

But know that having a few thoughts in that first awesome moment is perfectly fine – the best of the best meditators triggered off thinking with their first experience of the Pure Stillness. Bashayandeh told me that his first mind-opening dabble into the Serene Space made him so excited he couldn't get back to meditation for a week. For me, it was more a sense of splendid wonderment – that *did* lead to some 'wow' thoughts.

The excitement is natural, dear reader – it follows the brilliant delight in feeling that you really have journeyed to an extraordinary place. That first breathtaking glimpse of it seems to open the whole secret vista of the true Journey. It is like being starving hungry and peeping over a ridge to see the most perfect fruit-laden valley stretching infinitely before you.

So back to where you were. You have faded the *mantra* to a complete hush and found yourself just 'listening' to silence – until your inner quietness was almost certainly interrupted by thought. What to do then?

Simply 'switch on' and 'turn up' the volume on your mantra again. Then, you just repeat the leisurely 'turning down' to silence. Every time a thought comes in from then on, that is the process … focusing on the mantra to 'drown out' thoughts and again, fading it gently away to nothing.

The key is continuing to *keep straining to hear the mantra – even though it is not there.* That keeps your attention mindfully on, and within, the serene silence. It may take days or weeks to practice reaching into the purity of this silence. It doesn't matter. Rely on the practice I have just described … just keep 'turning the sound up and down' and one lovely day you will find that the time of quietness between actual thoughts begins to be noticeable and will progressively lengthen until you are quite able to hold your attention on the silence.

When there is simply no thought at all, you will just seem to experience the silence as a more dominant awareness than any interruptive thoughts until you find yourself just present within the stillness. You will find yourself gently sinking into the Serene Space of the Silent Mind, although you remain awake and profoundly aware.

When you can, introduce your *mantra* for increasingly less time each session until you are only repeating it for a few seconds before beginning to soften it away to nothing.

Completing a Practice from within the Serene Stillness

As you become increasingly proficient at the letting go of techniques and begin to dwell in the Pure Stillness, the important issue then becomes how to complete such a 'meditation' – how to *let go* being present within such an appealing tranquillity to 'return' to your day-to-day existence?

The process of completion is as previously. Firstly, your inner being will just become aware that you are to complete. It may take a little while to be ready but when you are, bring your mind-focus to the rhythm of your breathing and then complete in the usual way.

Remember always – *the longer the meditation, the longer the completion.*

In your early 'letting-go-technique' practices, you may want to set a digital clock for, say, half an hour so that, at the appointed time, soft music (for example) begins playing. As your practice of these exercises grows though, you will uncover an inner understanding of what is loosely called 'time' – an understanding that enables you to complete simply when you know that you are ready – or that 'time is up'.

What if I Can't Start Thinking Again?

If I had a dollar for every time I was asked that question, I would have enough for an annual holiday in, well …would you believe West Beelbangera (nah, go look it up!). Seriously though, I am asked that question quite often and I can, with electrifying clarity, remember my first minute or so of sinking into a consciousness without thought.

For a mere moment there was a 'feeling' of wanting to 'go back', as I seemed to have entered a very different, startling and 'unfamiliar' place – a vastness with no training wheels for the first ride and, indeed, nothing to hold onto. But this was quickly overcome by a kind of awe and I felt as if I were being overwhelmingly attracted and drawn to this 'seductive and strangely compelling place', as Mary earlier so perfectly described meditation. There was a profound, unfathomable 'knowingness' that whatever was happening was 'right' and secure.

Anyway, my answer to students is that 'if you couldn't start up the old mind again, I wouldn't be sitting here before you'. The reality is that no matter how intense your meditation, the naturalness of the practice and the 'need' to use thinking for adequate existence always generates 'start up' just whenever the need is realised.

The Vocalised Mantra Technique

The next technique in taking your mind to single-pointed focus was the classic *mantra, japayoga* – the actual voicing or chanting of a *mantra* so you could hear it with your 'outer' ears. The letting go of this technique is a very beautiful practice and, in the Meditation Sanctuary, we actually have requests to practice it together from time to time.

Exercise 41. *Letting Go the Vocalised Mantra Technique*

So, as before, into your sanctuary and reach your Essential Stillness but, for the first few practices, start quieting the mind by using the simple version of japayoga – just the hum.

Hold your mind-focus on the lovely vibration of your humming – which is loud enough to physically hear it – until you are aware that you are quiet of thought, just absorbed in the humming. Then, just as you did in the last exercise, begin to turn the sound down.

Over several minutes, slowly, gently, soften and recede the sound until it becomes almost inaudible and then allow it to just disappear into your breathing, quietening it to … nothing.

If thoughts start getting themselves all excited again, simply bring your humming up in volume to drown them out and then repeat the turning down.

The key to this practice is fading the voice gradually, reducing the sound in little increments so you don't seem to consciously notice your voice becoming quieter. Eventually, there is simply an awareness that you are again (just as in letting go the mind *mantra*) … 'listening' to silence. It is a very effective exercise because a 'presence' or 'memory' of your voice seems to remain for a while, blanketing any thought that may want to arise. Sometimes, when thoughts are completely hushed, the silence in the Serene Space can feel extremely tangible, almost tactile – so physical and 'real' that it seems to soak up any attempt at thought.

The endeavour then is to hold your awareness fully present in the 'superconscious' stillness that follows the quieting of your voice to silence – lovely silence.

The Same with '*Aum*'

When you wish to let go the technique of the fully-voiced mantra, aum, you practice exactly as you did with the voiced hum. You soften and recede your voice on the 'mmm' … the sound that resonates so beautifully in your head. Again, quieten your voice to silence and keep your attention focused on the lovely quiet space into which you reach.

Keep your 'mental' hand on the 'volume switch' so that if thoughts want to crash the party, you simply resume your lovely chant of aum and then gradually fade it away to silence once more.

Soon you will find yourself sinking into the Serene Space increasingly without interruption and for as long as you choose to meditate within it.

The Visualised Object Technique

This was the technique of stilling the mind to single-pointed attention by introducing the 'art of visualisation'. Remember, you quietened your mind with your imagining or visualising an object on which you concentrated your focus. The aspiration was to develop such an intensity of focus on it that it would be the dominant presence, gradually subjugating thoughts meekly to a single point.

The aspiration now is to let go the visualising of the object so again, in the very letting go, you are able to submerge fully into the serene and silent space.

Exercise 42. *Letting Go the Visualised Object Technique*

There are several ways of letting go the visualisation technique.

Into your sanctuary again, this time quieting your thoughts with the technique of focusing on your object. When you reach the phase of being deeply aware of the object to the point that your thoughts are 'out there' somewhere – not 'in here' – begin then to fade it from your 'inner view'. Imagine it losing colour and brightness, as if you had left it out of water too long. Keep fading the image until it seems to become cloudy and without real definition.

Keep just letting it go through fading and then it will just ... not be there. You will simply be gazing into a space once filled by the object.

Of course, just as the first successful turning down the sound of your *mantra* probably created an exuberant reaction ('aren't I great'), so the complete fading of your object may trigger off a quick mental 'I've done it!' That's just fine. Simply visualise the image again whenever thoughts come along and apply singular focus to it once more before doing your 'fading trick' all over again ... and again ... until you find that thoughts finally succumb, leaving you 'just gazing' without thoughts interfering.

Alternative Ways of Letting Go the Visualised Object Technique

Another way of 'eliminating' the image (thus letting go the focusing technique) is to visualise the image becoming smaller and smaller until it becomes a tiny pinpoint that then just disappears altogether into the ether. Yet another is to 'dissolve' the image, like soluble aspirin in a glass of water. You just 'disintegrate the image' so there is nothing on which to focus attention.

One dear student used to visualise wrapping the image in paper and throwing the lot into a river and then watch it float away. (Too many additional images for me but, if it works …) My own favourite was 'watching' the image being pushed out into space (as in universe), knowing that if it went 'out there', it couldn't come back.

You can probably divine that it doesn't matter a hoot what 'method' you employ to rid your mind of this visual focus-point. The essence of the practice is to 'diminish' the image, *in whatever way*, until you are gazing into a space of … *no thought, no image*. As before, if thoughts arise – repeat the whole 'action' as often as necessary.

The Visualised Mantra Technique

Remember the Bashayandeh specialty – repeating your *mantra*, freezing it, grabbing it, visualising it as a word or words in front of you and then 'staring' at it until you had quietened the chattering mind. We then also looked at the 'grabbing of miscellaneous thoughts' if they dared to wander onto your patch and replacing the visualised *mantra* with the intruder thoughts 'writ large' on the space before you – eventually leaving you effectively still of mind but gazing at a frozen 'word-thought'.

In effect, this exercise was a combination of the previous two – chanting a *mantra* and visualising an object. I said it was one of the harder ones but that its accomplishment was eminently satisfying. Now to practice letting it go as well … equally edifying!

Exercise 43. *Letting Go the Visualised Mantra Technique*

Once more to your sanctuary. Move through your 'routine' until you have reached your mantra visualisation. Again hold a word picture, focusing on it fully for a minute or two.

When you are focused deeply on the word image, mentally try to 'push' it or 'slide' it sideways from the space before you so that it disappears from view. You can also try fading it slowly (as in the previous exercise) until it disappears into nothing.

It is not easy, but very achievable, so persist gently without forcing. Then, in one of your practices along the way, it will just happen. You will push the word away or fade it, leaving you just gazing into a quiet blankness.

As no surprise, of course, a sneaky thought will almost inevitably be lurking in the background, wanting to rush in and take the place of your previously 'written' *mantra* or thought words. So, as it lurks, capture it, mentally write *it* too before you and focus intently on it, thus preventing other thoughts bumbling in. Then you push or fade the new word-thought away as well. You will reach a point where this process is just naturally repeating itself.

As you become practiced at dismissing each thought, you will very gradually begin to be aware of the next thought actually germinating. You will 'see it coming' or feel it 'out there' before it becomes a fully fledged, meaningful thought. The art of the exercise now is to hoodwink the arising thought into not reaching maturity.

So, as the thought just begins to appear, grab the first one or two words of the rising phrase, 'write' them before you and 'terminate' them. Then repeat with just the beginning of the next thought … and the next, until gradually they will cease to appear with any real strength at all.

Finally, at some point in repeating the previous exercise, you will just begin to 'feel' a nebulous hint of a thought coming. *Before* it actually materialises into meaningfulness, you'll find yourself able to prevent it from even getting to the surface of your clear consciousness just by maintaining your gaze. It is as if you have the 'idea of a thought' but the very stillness you are developing in your mind becomes a natural barrier to the thought becoming a reality – you let it go before it actually arises.

Then, one day, you will become aware that you are gazing at your blank space with your inner mind, completely, alertly conscious – but without any word-thought at all wanting to thrust itself forward. With practice, you will be able to hold your gaze at the 'blankness' for a little longer each time until you find yourself just gently gazing into the presence of stillness for as long as you choose.

The Breathing Techniques

There were several specific breathing techniques you practiced as points of focus (just like a *mantra*) to assist in the quelling of thoughts. Letting go the breathing techniques you had used to quieten thoughts is quite interesting as we can't really let go the principle activity of the technique ... breathing! So the aspiration for this 'letting go' is, in effect, *to let go conscious awareness of the act of breathing* until you are dwelling in the Serene Space, and for that we have a lovely exercise.

Exercise 44. *Letting Go the Breathing Techniques*

Begin reaching your Essential Stillness in the usual way although, this time of course, you remain focused on your breathing. Progress through your Rhythm Breathing phase to visualising coloured chi coursing through your whole body. Then let go the 'colouring' and just move to awareness of your body being saturated with life-force on each whole-body breath and 'stay with it' until you are still of mind.

The masterful practice now is to visualise breathing the life-force both in and out 'through' the whole of your 'outer' body – as if each breath is being drawn in from the entire universe, by osmosis, through every pore of your skin – and breathed out in the same way. Become absorbed in this practice, breathing very slowly, almost imperceptibly now, just 'feeling' the life-force entering your whole body and 'taking out the garbage' when it leaves.

During this exercise, gradually you will lose awareness of the 'boundary' or 'border' of your body – you begin to feel as though life is just 'coming into you' from a vast space. *You will begin to have a sense, not of 'breathing' but, being 'breathed'* … until eventually, you will not be able to tell the difference between what you think is 'you' and what you think is 'not you'. You may then have a lovely sense of being 'at one' with your breathing. You become so deeply absorbed in the exercise that you lose all sense of self and all sense of breathing. They 'become', in effect, one and the same!

Over time, many students have mentioned to me that this very practice alone, and the sense of 'being at one' with their breathing, seemed to help in alleviating some of the heaviness of health and emotional difficulties. One student felt that this practice alone was so powerful that it, more than any other, began to open her to her enlightenment – she began to experience and understand the concept of 'non-duality', the connectedness of all there is. That is a genuine meditative possibility with this delightful exercise.

I want you to practice 'through-the-body' breathing until you *lose consciousness of the breathing effort* (yes, do read that carefully dear one – I don't want to lose *you* just yet!). Gently sink into the harmony that you will inevitably be unveiling between 'you' and the Serene Space until you have a feeling – an awareness – that you *are* your breathing.

At that point, the 'letting go' mission for this technique will have been accomplished.

Open-eyes Technique

One of the more advanced practices of quieting thoughts with single-pointed focus was the series of exercises requiring practice with your eyes open. In the first one, you opened your eyes onto an object and throughout the remainder you conducted each exercise with open eyes, as do many of the Zen masters.

The practice now is to use the object at which you stared to … let go needing the object.

Exercise 45. *Letting Go the 'Open-eyes' Technique*

You have no doubt heard that some yogis and miscellaneous gurus have the mystical ability to 'make things disappear' or make them 'invisible'. Well, dear student, you are about to find out how they do it and, as all beings are equal and none have any greater 'power' than any other, you may be able to practice the 'great secret' yourself.

> *In your sanctuary, commence an open-eyes practice with your chosen object placed before you. As previously, hold deep focus on your object until you reach your Essential Stillness.*

The aspiration now is to move from 'staring' intently at the object to the 'act of gazing' or 'awareness without seeing'.

> *To do this, you gradually shift your focal point to another point ... on the other side of the object so you begin 'gazing through' your object. That point can be a metre past it or somewhere on the other side of the universe – it doesn't matter.*
>
> *Another way is to hold your finger at arm's length in front of you, between you and the object, gaze at the 'spot' of air where your finger is and then remove your hand back to your mudra – leaving you gazing at a 'nothing place' between you and your object but, in line with it.*

Some Further Experiences

In this exercise, prior to actually experiencing deep stillness, you may well have some further visual experiences simply because, before you draw your mind into a deep 'unseeing' quietness, it will be temporarily distracted by that which the eyes are still 'seeing'.

Firstly, you may see that your object is 'out of focus' and, accordingly, an array of visual effects and optical illusions may occur – all harmless and natural. The object may seem to 'multiply' so you see two or three of them. It may become opaque, multi-dimensional or appear to float, move, fly or rotate. It may change colour or be surrounded by a beautiful light or other equally lovely 'illusions'.

Gradually, however, if you practice maintaining this intensity of gaze *through* the object, it will just 'disappear'. I have done this on my own meditation mat that I told you about earlier. It has a quite complex design on it and one of the experiences that frequently occurred in my practice was that the object (a large marble in this instance) indeed 'disappeared' but, more impressively … for a while, I was deeply aware of the complex design of the carpet *under where the object 'had' been!*

However dear reader, the aspiration is not to ride around on a magic carpet (now you know where all that started!), but to reach into a pure stillness of being. Continue gazing and, gradually, these optical illusions will cease completely. After a period of time, *you lose all awareness of the external … it all disappears!* You find yourself gazing within … gazing into the Serene Space, exactly as if you were practicing an eyes-closed meditation. In letting go, you lose the sense of separateness between 'you' and the external into which you are gazing. You experience the *actuality* of 'oneness'.

And … gazing through the wall?

Similarly, if you have been practicing gazing at the wall to quieten your thoughts, letting go this technique is effectively the same as the last exercise.

Exercise 46. *Letting Go … the Wall*

> *Simply take your focus to an imaginary point a metre or two on the other side of the wall or to a point at about arm's length between you and the wall and conduct the whole exercise just as you did previously.*

Just Gazing

Having reached the stage of being able to let go all thought as well as the mind-stilling techniques themselves, the aspiration then is to continue *just gazing* upon and into the Serene Space which is the beginning of Authentic Meditation – the practice of *being deeply awake and aware without holding on to anything.* As one wise master said, '*it is the act of gazing which is important,* rather than any "object" of the gaze'.

Gradually, these letting-go practices lead you to a place where the external 'is not' – where you may allow yourself to gradually sink into an *illuminating* stillness, or the Great Stillness, for as long as you choose.

Completing a 'Just-gazing' Exercise Started with Open Eyes

As before, you will become aware of your aspiration to complete without needing to 'think' about it. When you are ready, slowly bring your focus back onto the physical object (or wall) in front of you. In effect, you cease gazing in order to resume 'staring' … with awareness of that at which you *are* staring. Then return your focus to your breathing and settle there awhile, before completing in the usual way. Take ample time on the completion so that the stillness you experienced begins to rest with you into your day.

A Little Story of Encouragement

'I'm Glad to Be Alive!'

'For almost 30 years, I had carried around a seemingly immovable burden of guilt from the past, which was crippling, debilitating and coloured my world grey, sometimes black. My unbalanced and distorted thinking combined with unbearable anxiety, distress and tension led me to alcohol dependence and suicidal thoughts.

I didn't live – I barely existed.

One of the many professionals I consulted along the way (including hypnotherapists, cognitive behavioural therapists, psychiatrists and general practitioners) highlighted my plight one day when he told me, "life is to be enjoyed, not just endured".

For a long time, I really did try to find the key to unlock the door to this other colourful world where people laughed, loved and threw themselves into their lives with abandonment, but I could only see it all through a dull pane of glass. It seemed that I was destined to be a spectator forever. During an episode of depression a couple of years ago, my doctor gave me a choice. He said I could either try a new antidepressant drug or perhaps begin to learn meditation. I'm very glad to say I decided on the latter.

The improvements in my life didn't occur overnight or without many hiccups along the way, but I was able to learn how to banish that long-held guilt by practicing meditative techniques I learned in classes at the Sanctuary. To me, that's a miracle.

The "letting go" process seemed never-ending and was punctuated by many tears but I'm so glad that I persevered. The relief I experienced when I was finally able to let go that past scourge was overwhelming and it has enabled me to remove the pane of glass through which I used to observe life.

When a decision has to be made these days, I no longer fiddle-faddle around, seek others' opinions and then doubt my conclusion. The added benefit is that I am able to communicate more effectively with others as I can explain myself and listen to them in a less self-centred, emotional way. The other thing I have noticed is that people who used to be able to "press my buttons" have lost their power. Not only do I not join in but I am quite unable to be negative at all in any response. I share this with you as I believe it is the culmination of all that I have encountered so far on my Path.

Today I embrace life wholeheartedly. There is a depth of peace and joy in my life which is very precious. I'm glad to be alive and to be able to participate in my own life and the lives of others in a positive way. I live in the "now" not in the past.'

— Ashia (name withheld for personal reasons)

Chapter Fifteen

The Serene Space of the Silent Mind

*'I've sat and watched the giant tree in the drive shed its leaves
in showers of confetti on the wind. Perhaps more importantly,
I've just sat ...'*

– Wendy Limond, Sanctuary Student

By the conclusion of the 'Letting Go Techniques' exercises you practiced in the last chapter, you will have *let go* mentally holding on to any object or point of focus which you had employed to quieten the mental babble. When you let go, I suggested variously that you would be left *just gazing* into a 'serene space' or that you would begin to sink into a 'great silence'.

But just what is this mystical, magical 'serene space?' Many students have asked me questions such as, 'if we really stop thinking or focusing on something, how can there be consciousness, let alone a higher consciousness? What is "there" when the mind ceases to work?' Good questions ... so let's find out.

What happens to our 'mind' when we stop it being congested with mental debris and then what we gaze into has, in fact, been part of the knowing wisdom of the advanced meditator, the yogi, the Zen master, the enlightened ones and all such wondrous creatures – for countless centuries. Many erudite masters, of various meditative and religious traditions, have tried so hard to communicate the experience of this 'place' ... to describe their own undoubted, but virtually inexplicable, wisdom with words that never quite seem to definitively illuminate this part of the Path.

Over the centuries, for example, you find that the place of supreme inner quietness has been variously called the 'Emptiness', the 'Great Silence', 'the Void' or and even 'the Great Void'. Sri Aurobindo called it the 'Luminous Voidness' (he had a wonderful way with words!). The Zen masters use the term I've mentioned, 'No Mind', to try and describe the place devoid of all the usual mental distractions.

With great respect to the wise ones who have coined such descriptive phrases, most of the words they use 'miss the boat' for me because they hint at, or imply, an experience of 'emptiness' or 'nothingness'. Despite the innate purity of such a concept, to me they also imply a slight 'negativity' in the experiencing of their 'space of nothingness'. My own long journeying into and around this 'space' however, has been an experience far removed from emptiness. Quite the opposite. It has rather been a princely Journey into a vast, inimitable, unconditioned positive '*fullness*' and truly experiencing this inner eternal space of 'all there is' was always accompanied by an enveloping *serenity*. So, as you have gathered, I dare to call it the Serene Space.

Sangharakshita (again from his book, *What is the Dharma?*), sums it up rather beautifully in describing it as a place where …

> '*Consciousness has been fully expanded. It has expanded from the individual to the universal, from the finite to the infinite, from the mundane to the transcendental and from the consciousness of ordinary humanity to that, even of a supreme Buddhahood.*'

Of course, whatever we call this place of Stillness of the Silent Mind really doesn't matter a jot because words eventually become utterly immaterial to its presence – and yours within it.

Only the flurry of minds can be written down … silence cannot!

Many, many writers have also implied that it is a big mystical 'secret' only available to a few. In one way, *the great paradoxical joke is that they are right* … because there is only one difficult, blissful, tortuous, simple Path to this place. It is called The Practice of Meditation and only the truly committed tend to have the courage and inner resources to find the Path and set out on this greatest of Journeys, despite the fact that this Path is right there … within you … and *equally* accessible to all.

The Beacon on the Hill

The Beginning of Authentic Meditation

Letting go the mind-quieting techniques and reaching the meditative plateau of just gazing *is,* in fact, something of a 'beacon on a hill' in your Journey. It signals *the beginning of the experience of Meditation itself* – the experiencing of an increasingly profound 'awakeness' to a higher level of consciousness that is experienced when the clutter of unmastered thinking is left behind.

I call these early practices in the Serene Space, the *Liberating Meditations* for the very reason that you become 'liberated' from trampolining thoughts and associated scattery emotions. The practicing of Liberating Meditations provides the illumination needed to find the entrance to the awesome place where the Journey of 'seeing what really is' commences.

But, despite all such lovely descriptive words and the temporary inspiration they may provide, the oft-asked student question validly lingers: 'in down-to-earth terms, *what really, actually happens?*' So, in this short chapter, I shall firstly offer a few general comments on the Serene Space and then outline some of the more specific, often extraordinary 'experiences' you may well encounter if you follow that 'beacon on your *own* hill'.

Note, though, that everyone's Journey through meditation is unique to themselves so your experiences may well differ in content, intensity and timing to any that I mention in this chapter ... and that doesn't matter one little bit. Your Path is yours alone and your unique Journey is as valid as all others, no matter which side of the mountain you are climbing.

'Experiences' Natural ... Never Harmful

Initially, experiences in the Serene Space may indeed seem 'strange' or 'extraordinary', simply because they are so atypical of your familiar 'ordinary' life. Do not feel discomforted if you feel that 'something different' may be happening to you. 'Something different' certainly *will be* happening to you. You will have commenced reaching back into that unfamiliar wonderment of the authentic *you* ... the magnificent, uncluttered Self!

Nevertheless, I need to re-emphasise strongly that any experiences you may have on this 'leg' of your Journey, as with all your experiences so far, are *completely natural* because you are still *just sitting … just gazing*.

I also assure you (and as gurus through the ages attest in their wise writings and teachings), *no experience during genuine Authentic Meditation can ever be harmful to you in any way – physically, mentally or emotionally.* Quite conversely, although some meditation experiences may be surprising when you first encounter them, they are likely to be soothing, peaceful, joyful – even delightful and, later on in your Journey, quite wondrously … well, enlightening. Whatever experiences you may have, understand completely that you remain conscious, awake, aware, safe and 'knowing' of your presence in your Sanctuary – quietly meditating. So endeavour not to 'pull back' from experiences when they happen – just let them run free.

Very importantly, however, do not deliberately seek or endeavour to repeat 'unusual', pleasant or delightful experiences. As I said earlier, *any* desire for an experience becomes a barrier – a form of attachment that will immediately break down a true meditation, taking it back to just a bland practice of techniques.

Is There a 'Pattern' to Experiences?

Although I describe some of the possible 'sensings' and feelings in a seemingly progressive order of deepening awareness or in a kind of 'flow pattern' of experiences, there is no correct order of, or pattern to, experiences. (I use the word 'sensing' now because these little experiences, whatever they may be, will come to you without accompanying thoughts and simply as an 'awareness'.)

The way I present the possibilities is really an amalgam of my own experiences as well as some that others (students, through to my enlightened teachers) have shared with me. I include them so that you may have points of reference in your own practice and know that your Journey is indeed 'progressing normally'. Any experiences at all within the meditative 'state' are really little signals and signposts that you are awakening to your true, unconditioned consciousness beyond thought. As you become increasingly practiced, experiences may initially arise just for a few moments before fading away or, eventually, they will not occur at all.

Tumbling into the Sacred Silence – 'Experiences' in the First Meditations

As you begin to immerse into your practice without an object of focus, you will find your gaze seeming to go deeper and deeper into the Stillness. One of the first true 'experiences' may well be an intensifying awareness of an extraordinary quietness – a quietness that seems almost tangible – *a sacred silence.*

Only once in 'real life' have I ever experienced such a purity of silence and that was driving across a vast desert area known as the Treeless Plains in the south of Australia. Nothing was bigger than a small stone as far as the horizon in all directions, apart from the car … and me. I stopped the car and walked away from it so I could 'listen' to – be present within – pure silence. I then just sat and meditated until I felt literally part of it – at one with the silence, a truly wonderful, natural, mind-opening experience. When I completed that lovely meditation, I became aware that I was being observed by a large lizard holding its undersized, spiky head quizzically to one side – no doubt wondering about this mad creature who had wandered into his nowhere home.

In my early meditations, the sacred silence was as potent as that 'desert-quiet' and yet I felt that I was gazing into something that seemed so … *substantial.* No other way to put it really. All experiences that followed seemed to originate from my seemingly slow-motion 'tumbling' into this deep inner silence.

'Physical' Experiences

In the early part of tumbling into the Serene Space, there may well be specific sensings and quite physical feelings and 'perceptions' – perhaps a little like those you may have encountered when earlier practicing the letting go of techniques. These sensings may come in little steps and stages or they may come in rushes or 'floodings', or both at different times … it doesn't matter, just go with them.

Wonderment and Awe

One of my own more memorable 'experiences' (still crystal-clear after more than 30 years) was the occurrence of fleeting, darting 'feelings' of deep inner wonderment, a kind of awe, as though someone had taken me to the edge of the universe and, with a grand sweep of the arm, had said, 'Look at *that*, mate!' ... and I could see it *all!* Many have spoken to me of the 'wondrous' and 'awesome' nature of their early forays into pure silence.

Lightness and Freedom

A very common experience is that you will begin to *lose the sense of your body* as a physical entity (leading some fringe stalwarts to think fancifully again about levitation and astral travelling). You may remember earlier when you were learning to let go tension, I said, 'the way to know when you are tension-free is when you no longer know if your hands are facing up or down'. Meditating within the Serene Space will take you to a place at which you are not conscious of your physical body *at all* and cannot actually feel yourself sitting on the floor.

You will have a wonderful sense of lightness and may feel as though you are *floating, moving rapidly or travelling* through space. For the 'earth-bound', this may be a little disconcerting at first, but it soon becomes natural, even welcome, as part of the sense of immense 'freedom' that may begin to envelope you.

The Body Slow-down

As with your tension-freeing exercises, your heart rate will slow, but even further during full meditation, and your blood pressure will perhaps decrease a little more. Have no thought that your body will actually stop! It can't. But it will continue to be deeply thankful for its daily, deeply restful slow-down. Also, at the point of deep meditation, any *pain you may suffer will either disappear completely or be significantly eased.* Remain aware, however, that this effect is only temporary, albeit a valuable experience at the moment.

Inner Sounds

In the early stages, quite extraordinarily, the outer physical senses (such as seeing and hearing) may, for some meditators, seem to develop an inner counterpart. For example, in a deeper meditation, you are most unlikely to hear a mosquito buzzing thirstily around or notice the noises that usually fill the street outside. Nor will your inner quietness be suddenly broken by your favourite Mozart concerto or rock band playing in your head but … you may hear distant, sweet, spiritually seductive musical-type sounds that you've never heard before. In deeper meditation, you may even experience the sound the ancients 'heard' as a kind of undulating hum and interpreted as *aum*! All totally normal experiences.

Inner 'Visions'

During 'closed-eyes' meditation, you can't see your physical environment but in the Serene Space many people experience strong visual effects in which they 'see' beautiful colours, lights and shapes with their 'inner sight'. Some have described to me their seeing ethereal 'glimpses' of landscapes, shadowy figures or clouds in a vast sky, and so on.

One of my own most memorable visual experiences was the 'golden light'. I would seemingly become encompassed by a deep golden-yellow glowing light – a colour I had not known in my 'outer' life. I found it beautiful, peaceful and emanating a 'sense' that I can only describe as 'home'. It seemed to bathe the entire immensity of the Serene Space. The seeing of a particular light is an oft-recurring theme in the writings of meditative people.

Just Inner-body Experiences

In some religious and 'metaphysical' environments that may have a meditative element, many such little 'events' are interpreted as having divine, religious, 'other world' or even 'out-of-body' significance.

The truth is … they do not.

As I have said previously, all such 'encounters' are totally inner body experiences – a by-product of peeping through that little window for a glimpse of the universe of your inner self. If you do have any such or similar experiences (and you may not), they are simply a signal that you have indeed begun entering the meditative depth of the Serene Space – simply, the reality of the uncluttered self.

'Super-sense' Experiences during Meditation

Some experiences however, lack such clarity and can seem quite nebulous and dream-like in their nature … quite distinct from the more tangible 'awarenesses' such as experienced in my 'golden light'. It is as though you have developed a kind of 'super-sense' or 'super-awareness'.

'Gazing' Transforms to 'Presence' – Loss of 'Duality'

One of the early such experiences in the silence is likely to be *losing the actual sense of gazing* into the Space. You will almost imperceptibly seem to just melt into the Space and gradually have the awareness of its *enveloping* you – of being through you and within you. Your awareness will seem to have expanded to 'fill' the Space. In other words, you will lose the sense of separateness between you and the Space, as the sense of Space there, me here, fades. *You lose that sense of duality* I mentioned previously (when you were gazing at an object), as you and the Space seem to become one and the same.

Outer Awareness Becomes Inner Awareness

Gradually, as you *just sit* within the presence of the Serene Space, you may begin to develop the sense that your 'ordinary awakeness', your normal, everyday outer awareness seems to transform to an increasingly profound 'inner' awareness. Your normal senses effectively 'switch off' for a little holiday but are readily available when you choose to activate them again. If, for example, somebody were to call you, your inner 'knowingness' would register the sound as a distant awareness … but without thought.

Expanding the Centre of Awareness to the 'Real Mind'

As you progress, the 'ordinary' sense of your mind and your body being separate (you know, the *real me* is up here in my head directing the rest of me – my body, which is down there) also begins to dissolve. Gradually, it will seem to you that your mind is becoming your body and the body your mind – that *the 'you' of your being is one entity.*

In effect, you begin to *extend* your perceived centre of awareness from your brain or your 'mind' to the whole of you – to your entire being – again transcending any concept of duality. It may seem as if your consciousness slowly becomes spread 'evenly' through all of you. This can be said to be an *awakening* of the Real Mind … and that is one of the 'big' awakenings in meditation. Then, perhaps further down the Path, it can even feel as if your consciousness is extending out from you *into* the Serene Space of which you seem to be an intrinsic part because, in reality, you are!

A Reality Beyond 'Reality' – the Elemental 'One-self'

As you meditate further, you may then also have inner glimpses, or even a welling consciousness, that this whole-being awareness seems to be a *you* or a *self* that is somehow *beyond* your previous understanding of 'you' (the 'you' that has thoughts and feelings). The self in this 'beyondness' somehow seems more open, omnipresent and more acutely conscious than the 'normal', outer, conditioned 'you'. For me, this experience of a 'self' distinct from the 'outside' self gradually nurtured into a sense of an immense 'new reality' that seemed far beyond the familiar conditioned and illusory reality – the one driven and daily maintained by the five 'ordinary' senses.

Sensing this beyondness, or a deeper self and a more profound reality, is the beginning of glimpsing the purity of the very core of you – *the authentic, elemental, unspoiled oneness of the fully integrated, complete self that has always been within* but has been gradually hidden and buried by layers and layers of 'conditioned' living. In so doing, you are beginning to 'divine' or *awaken* to, the One-self. It can be said that you are again sensing the singular purity of the child-consciousness within. For the first time since you were a very small child, you begin to 'transcend the muddle' … *just like the child watching the willy wagtail.*

Experiencing the 'Eternal Moment' in the Superconscious.

Finally, a rising perception of a 'deeper self' signals the beginning of your transcendence of the old fragmented, *samsaric* 'you' with its daily mad flurry of memories, thoughts, habitual responses and unrestrained feelings. In so doing, you are beginning to unveil the elemental Self, *as it really is*. You return to *what is actually there* of 'you' when that 'you' is no longer smothered under the lifetime-piles of mental rubble.

This I call 'experiencing the eternal moment' … the point in meditation when you are fully embedded in your … *just being, utterly and purely experiencing the present … purely dwelling in the essence of your existence.*

You are reaching into the level of *awakeness* that originally, Sri Aurobindo called the 'superconscious'.

Bliss, Rapture and Ecstasy

I have written much on quietness and calmness but, as you progress your meditations, these feelings can deepen into a 'super-sense' experience of a pervasive, peaceful serenity. This feeling may in fact expand into a kind of indescribable bliss that some call *nirvana* (and regarded by some as the completion of the *samsaric* endlessness of life or lives on earth) or even 'rapture'. Such experiences of joy and bliss are natural, as they simply well up from the pure inner self – the pure condition of clear consciousness.

Some believe that the reaching of bliss or rapture is the magic 'enlightenment' they seek, even crave. It isn't. It is a singular sense of bliss that comes from glimpsing the Divine within, as well as being increasingly free from the utterly unnatural burden of the conditioned, unmastered mind. It is at this stage of their awakening that some meditators perhaps choose to 'opt out' of normal life for a while (and occasionally longer) and retreat into the full-time pursuit of this *nirvana* and the deeper experiences of the Oneness that can be associated with the sense of bliss.

They tend to miss the point of meditation.

Yes, it is possible to 'bliss-out' on a good feeling – but that is not authentically meditating, it is just blissing out on a good feeling! That is a long way from fully experiencing the magnificence of reality that meditation opens up to us. However, experiences such as joy, bliss and rapture – all those lovely words – to me are wonderful, freeing and pleasurable. But I regard them as I do a railway station on a long train trip. You can get off the train and stay off or you can enjoy the 'break' but get back on for the rest of the journey.

If you stay off the meditative train to seek *nirvana* in bliss, the danger is that you do not, *cannot*, become a meditative person of true enlightenment and graciousness – *you just remain advanced practitioners of the techniques of meditation.* As I have said, to me, Authentic Meditation is about renewing, integrating and enriching our inner core of wellbeing so that we may be truly enthralled by living with unified consciousness – not just 'hooked on a feeling'.

* * *

Ultimately, there will come a time on your Journey when you transcend any 'experiences' at all … a time when you gradually just *become* the totality of the experience of a fully expanded consciousness – *samadhi* – *silently at one with, and within, the 'isness' or the Divine.* The further aspiration of the 'enlightening' meditator then becomes the turning back to the world as an enriched, awakened being, to freely offer the true Self's *unveiled* inner well of love, compassion and kindness.

With deepening practice as you advance along your Path, you may then experience profound insight and wisdom that seem to 'well up' from within, simply by allowing yourself to immerse in the space that remains behind when you completely let go the rubble of your 'ordinary' consciousness.

Completing Liberating Meditations

The golden rule, *the longer the meditation, the longer the completion,* really now applies to your practice. If you have been actually meditating, you probably won't be able to just jump up anyway.

To complete the liberating meditations, when you are ready, take your mind-focus to your breathing, becoming deeply absorbed again in the deep, beautiful rhythm and then just complete in the usual manner. When you have completed, just sit quietly in your sanctuary bathing in the calmness that will be spilling from your 'inner' to your 'outer' being. If possible, spend some time there before re-engaging your outer routine. This provides you with the optimum opportunity to take the meditative serenity with you into your day.

Your Daily Practice of Meditation

Your formal daily practice for the foreseeable future is to reach into the Serene Space and abide there. The aspiration is to persist in your practice until you are able to meditate 'through' all by-product experiences and rest within your expanding inner awareness. I can no longer suggest the length of time for your practice because you will now know what is right for you in each session. It matters not any more whether it is 20 minutes or two hours. The only rule left for the genuinely absorbed meditator is that the practice is now daily.

How Do You Feel After Meditating?

For a short while after completion, you may feel 'out of it' – a little like the luxurious feeling you enjoy after a deep massage. That is why I suggest you just sit quietly for a short while, bathing in 'where you are'. However, when you have resumed life outside your sanctuary, you are almost certain to feel more invigorated with additional energy – simply because you have given your body a period of deep restfulness that is more powerful than sleep, a 'liberating' period in which you have been free of the usual energy-draining worries and stresses.

In my experience, meditators also enjoy a general feeling of wellbeing following a liberating meditation – a further good measure of 'afterglow'. Others have little 'risings' of peacefulness and joy that come and go over a period of hours afterwards when they are not actually meditating in their sanctuary. Some say they 'just feel different as though something has changed'.

A tiny word of caution. In the period of deep peacefulness that often follows a meditation, some folks have the quite understandable desire that this unique experience continues, preferably 'forever please!' In the earlier stages of your Journey (and, I really emphasise, only in the earlier stages) the 'afterglow', in whatever form it may take for you, will not linger very long, for the simple reason that after completing a meditation, you will again become immersed in ordinary life, which can slowly swamp the residual 'good feelings'. Again, this is normal, but only until your practice deepens. When it does, you will find that, as you continue and develop your meditation, the difference you feel will begin to spill for increasingly longer periods of time into the normal-life time when you are not meditating.

If you dedicate yourself to daily practice, the *whole of your life may gradually seem to change* as you begin to *awaken*. Quite simply, if you are now becoming the 'genuine article', an authentic meditator, the effects of your daily practice will gradually begin to sift and seep into every nook and cranny of your life. Any positive effect at all you may notice 'happening' in your daily life really is yet another little signpost telling you that you are 'on track' in your continuing Journey. Eventually, of course, the practiced meditator finds the effects of meditation permeating their very existence as they *become their meditation* ... when living as a meditative person becomes the 'normal state of being'.

Don't 'chase' the effects, though, because that is like trying to catch up to the shimmering mirage on a hot summer's road – it always stays ahead (much to my utter bafflement as a child wanting my grandma to 'drive through the water' I could so often see in front of us). If ever 'just go with the flow' has meaning, this is the time to apply it.

Over-meditating

At the stage of becoming proficient at the liberating meditations, some novitiates may be tempted to 'over-meditate' for the simple reason that the sensings and experiences within meditation may feel better than the spectrum of their outer life.

If you feel the temptation to practice meditation on the false premise 'more is better' ... don't. Over-meditating is of no value to your Journey whatsoever. You see, the practice of *the Way* or the Path is about *awakening*, and then *living as*, a purity of being – not trailing along just looking for good feelings. If you just want that transient, good-feeling 'hit', go to the pub or go shopping.

It is *just practicing* which ultimately unfolds a total, ongoing 'way of living' that infinitely surpasses the temporary pleasure of a 'bliss' experience. Just meditate for the period of time that your innate wisdom tells you is 'right'. Any endeavour to try and 'hide from life-pain' in meditation is as negative as all other negative behavioural patterns and denies you the opportunity to open yourself to the true wonderment of resolving difficulties in a mature, natural and permanent way.

Chapter Sixteen

'Advanced' Meditation?

> *'Meditation is not freedom of the mind.*
> *It is freedom from the mind.'*
>
> *– Author Unknown*

There are a few of you who came straight to this page when you saw this chapter in the Contents list, perhaps having 'done' a little 'meditation' already and thinking you don't need all that preliminary 'stuff'. True? Want the *real* truth though? *There is really no such thing as 'advanced' meditation …* as in that which is reserved for a select few or for the enlightened … but it sure sounds attractive to our competitive being, doesn't it.

Oh, sure, there are techniques of 'letting go' that require some very serious practicing to master. Indeed, the long-term Authentic Meditation practitioner will certainly be reaching into an inner wisdom-level that is not immediately available to the beginner. But the difference between the beginner and the Teacher Yogi, is … just time and practice … not a deep understanding of some secret, non-existent 'mystical knowledge'.

My dear Suni Kaisan particularly used to delight in suddenly pointing to the heart region of a student or tapping them on the chest and yelling, 'in there is the answer – find it!'

So, dear student, beware any so-called gurus making extraordinary claims or books with special 'sealed' sections on 'advanced techniques'. Laughably, they have nothing to do with Authentic Meditation. I tell my students that '*advanced meditation' is, in fact, about living the rest of your lives magnificently as meditative people* – not learning 'secret stuff'.

But, yes, I want to 'round out' your formal practice repertoire with some techniques of letting go that I wasn't allowed to be privy to until I had satisfied my dear Suni that I could be silent of mind within the Serene Space for enduring periods of time (up to six hours – a good way to spend a rainy Saturday afternoon).

But, far more importantly, he needed to be assured that a student's intent in continuing meditation was 'pure' – that he had 'walked the walk' of not only the discipline of long and hard practicing, but also had a serious *understanding* of the practice itself. He needed above all to 'divine' that a student's *ongoing aspiration for enlightenment was for the eventual benefit of others* rather than satisfaction of the I-consciousness or 'ego'.

He knew, of course, that ego-tripping in meditation is the fast way off the Path onto a very muddy, slippery sidetrack that sends the less-than-humble crashing all the way back down to the beginning. (I know, because I indeed had my foot poised precariously over that track a time or two.) I didn't have to pass any special tests to be introduced to later techniques of practicing 'letting go' (except washing pots endlessly, scrubbing floors until you could eat your rice off them, tilling gardens with a less-than-adequate hoe – all probably a fair test of intent in Suni's eyes!).

Now, dear one, I don't know of course, how many pots you've scrubbed or what your aspirations are in continuing your practice. But, I'll make an assumption, I hope a perceptive one, that if you have a) read this far and, b) practiced wisely by only taking a new step after mastering the previous one, then you are likely to have pure 'intent'. I know Suni would say to you as he said to me from time to time, 'sit – we shall go on'. Anyhow, if your motive is not 'pure', you will surely find yourself back at the beginning of the Journey with a wet and muddy backside staring ruefully up the mountain.

From The Serene Space to Mastery – 'Just Do It'

As you journey onwards, the aspiration becomes reaching into a level of mastery where you can enter the Serene Space without using any mental tools or techniques to get there – *to immerse yourself in the silence of the Serene Space at will by ... just doing it!*

Now, *that* degree of mastery, although totally possible for all true seekers, doesn't just 'happen' – it also requires training. So, for a little while, I shall guide you in some practices that are breathtakingly beautiful in their simplicity (which, of course, may make them seem devilishly difficult ... but just for a little while).

Exercise 47. *'Command' Meditation*

When I was ready (meaning sufficiently practiced), I found that a wonderful way to achieve rapid stillness of mind was simply by using the word 'still' as a kind of mental 'command' to my brain. This is how you can bring it into your practice.

> *In your sanctuary, having become tension-free along with adopting rhythm breathing, begin to become aware of the miscellaneous thoughts straggling by. It is at this point that you would normally 'adopt a technique' to achieve single-pointed focus before then letting go the technique, thus opening yourself to the Serene Space.*
>
> *This time, though, observe your thoughts and then simply bring the word 'still' to mind as a command to your thoughts to do just that – 'be still'! Soon you will find them simply ceasing on command. Now try it.*

How easy is that?

After being 'commanded', all thoughts may seem to just rapidly reduce to nothing – as if transfixed by the very concept of being – still. This will take a little practice to master. Early on, you may find your thoughts disappear instantly on 'command', but just as instantly, begin to pop back again. As with mastering all your meditation exercises, repetition is the key. As thoughts try to 'start up' again, just repeat the command. After several repetitions you will find the stillness between thoughts extending longer and longer until, lo and behold, you are simply dwelling beautifully within the Serene Space.

Active Meditation

Over time, this 'mind-stilling' word and its use as a meditative practice, became very positive for me because of its intrinsic implication of serenity. In fact, for several years, I used 'Still!' as an Active Meditation. I would mentally whisper it to myself from time to time when I felt my 'self' under duress or my mind wandering off into babble. I found that just saying the word began to have a lasting 'meditative effect' of calmness as I conducted my day. You will find the same with practice.

The Practice of *Shikantaza* – 'Contentless' Meditation

To the Western person, meditation with some kind of focusing point (such as a *mantra*, gazing at an object or chanting) is usually necessary early in the Journey because most are total strangers to the concept of resident tranquillity and stillness. However, these concepts are innate in most Eastern cultures, particularly in Japan, where the practice of meditation attained its most pure form in Zen. In its most 'advanced' form, the masters practice *mokusho* Zen (*silent enlightenment*). Within this tradition, meditation is practiced *without any overlay of religious practices and, most importantly and simply, without subject and without object.*

When moving into the higher reaches of the meditative Path, the use of any 'support system' gradually becomes unnecessary as your mastery enables you to just 'let go' at will and reach into the meditative state virtually in seconds. The practice of such 'contentless' meditation is known as *shikantaza*, which literally means 'nothing but precisely sitting' (nothing but – *shikan*, precisely – *ta*, sitting – *za* … '*za*' as in *zazen* – *sitting meditation**).

So, in the *Soto Schu* Zen tradition, which I was schooled in, no supporting techniques at all are used. Such techniques are regarded as valuable, but only as stepping-stones to help the practice of beginners until they can 'let them go'.

This most pure form of *zazen* was introduced to Japan from China by Dogen Kigen (1200–53 CE), the Zen Master regarded as perhaps the greatest of all, who said that *shikantaza* is,

---

* From the *Shambhala Dictionary of Buddhism and Zen.*

'resting in a state of bright, alert attention that is free of thoughts, directed to no object and attached to no particular content'.*

It is said to have been practiced by all Buddhas of the past and is considered the shortest, but the steepest, Path to self-realisation or 'enlightenment'. The aspiration of *shikantaza* then is to be able to become clear of mind virtually immediately and ... *at will.* The practice is to become *utterly absorbed in the higher consciousness* as naturally as having a cup of tea.

It's the 'virtually immediately' bit that may seem to be something of a deep chasm on the Path for a while and that is just fine ... there is much wonderment and 'self-realisation' to go on with in the meantime. Be prepared for this last practice to be 'advanced' in a slightly staccato fashion – little step by little step. It's just a matter of will and keeping at it daily – as you well know now.

So, how to 'do' it? You don't ... you just let it happen! Like this ...

Exercise 48. *Contentless Practice*

> *In your sanctuary, when you are completely settled and ready, your attention is allowed to just permeate the Essences of relaxation and breathing – together – just dropping tension from you at the same time as your breathing deepens and slows – almost as if you 'collapse'.*
>
> *Now what to do with the mind? Already of course, your rapid absorption into the first two Essences has slowed the mental babble. But, the 'effort' then (or 'non-effort') is to gaze into the 'nothing' for a moment, stilling thought as if you had 'commanded' quietness of it.*
>
> *Then, as an act of mind-will, let go the gazing which, soon enough, will leave you just utterly aware (eventually with a superconsciousness) of your absorbingly profound presence within the Serene Space.*

In your first efforts, you will almost certainly find it difficult to just focus on 'nothing but letting go'. You have been training with a point of focus

---

* From the *Shambhala Dictionary of Buddhism and Zen.*

(body, breathing and techniques for mind quieting) and you may find yourself switching focus rapidly from one Essence to another and back again. On the other hand, you may find that you can reach into the Perfect Stillness easily – for a moment or two – but then thoughts begin to flood in ('like annoying Aussie flies', as one student wrote). That, in fact, was my own early experience – an initial inner awareness that 'this is a piece of cake' and then a rapid avalanche of thoughts.

The 'avalanche effect' is quite natural, because the suddenness of becoming still in your whole being is like a little shock – and your first reaction can be something like 'how wonderful' or 'this is strange' or something similar. Know that such a mental reaction is normal and it is a matter of continuing the practice until, soon enough, it becomes a fluidity of '*just immersing*'.

Exercise 49. *Contentless Absorption – Authentically Meditating*

The practice of *just immersing* is effectively the final step in *zazen* meditation (although not the final step in *becoming your meditation* or *becoming a meditative being*).

> *For this exercise, you simply sit in sukhasana and just completely 'let go' – tension, wrong breathing and all mental activity in just moments … without steps, process, techniques, content or purpose.*

The effect or experience of this practice is monumentally difficult to describe, but I can say that, at the moment of 'willing' to, you 'just go within'. It is as if all your practice culminates in one single moment.

The whole practice is an experience of just seeming to 'expand' into the lovely inner awareness. I use the word 'expand' deliberately because just letting go and fading from your external awareness brings an almost physical sense of 'swelling' into the universe. It is as if you 'soften' into a state of complete awareness, a crystal consciousness, an absolute awakeness of your 'true inner existence', seemingly without body or mind but solidly, knowingly, part of all.

Of the writers who have tried to describe experiencing the meditative state in this way, I feel that Sangharakshita has perhaps 'nailed it' best. I quote again from his insightful *What is the Dharma?*

'It is ... the withdrawal of one's attention from the external world. You no longer see anything – well, your eyes are closed. But you no longer hear anything either, or taste anything, or smell anything ... Your attention is withdrawn from the senses and therefore also from the corresponding sense objects and you become centred within. All your psychophysical energies too are no longer scattered and dispersed but drawn together, and centred on one point ... So all your energies have been concentrated within, unified and integrated.

And at this second stage, the energies start to rise and there is a gradual raising of the whole level of consciousness, the whole level of being. One is carried up away from one's own physical body, away out of the ordinary, physical material universe that one knows. One ascends in one's inner experience up to successively higher stages of superconsciousness.

As one becomes more and more concentrated, more and more peaceful, more and more blissful, the world becomes more and more distant. Even mental activity fades away until only stillness and silence is left, within which one begins to see with the inner vision and hear with the inner hearing.'

He has described the effects of *zazen – just sitting,* quite beautifully. It is at this stage that you have become truly immersed in *purposeless practice* that I mentioned back in the passage on 'Experiencing'.

Your daily meditative practice of *zazen* then is to 'become present' in contentless absorption within, and (repeating the words of the great Dogen Kigen some 800 years ago), *resting in a state of bright, alert attention that is free of thoughts, directed to no object and attached to no particular content.*

Culminating Experiences and Insights within the Serene Space

Revelation of the Absolute

When you become practiced at 'being absorbed' within the tranquillity of the Serene Space, you may begin to experience sudden insights, without thought – a kind of 'knowingness' or, what are known as *Realisations,* which are cultivated to fruition through your blossoming inner sight. *You may feel as though you are unveiling or unfolding your Self –* that you are beginning to experience the 'pure Self' of you. This of course is the very beginning of the ultimate dwelling within the original self – or, it can be said, *the inner light beginning to permeate the whole of you.*

Eventually, all practice of Authentic Meditation converges into a 'culminating point' or the Culminating Realisation (a lovely way of saying '*enlightenment*') – the summit of 'the steep hill' that the Zen people talk about. This is the point of becoming free of all conditioning – the point of the inner and outer self ('divided' only by conditioning), reintegrating as the natural one-self (the 'Integrated Self' as Aurobindo expressed it). *It is the point of no return* when, as One Being, you are no longer able to go back to the 'old inner and outer' being, the old *samsaric* way of life.

Many have tried to describe the Culminating Realisation of the Great Journey although again, much limited by having 'just words' as explanatory tools. The wonderful Tibetan monk, Sogyal Rinpoche, majestically called this inner luminosity the 'knowledge of all knowledge'. The Quakers refer to it humbly as 'the still, small voice within'. 'The kingdom of heaven is within you', Jesus of Nazareth said. The Hindus call it 'Atman' and the Buddhists 'the pure Buddha-mind'. It is the place of No Mind, the place of dwelling permanently in perfect harmony with all existence, the very heart of the original, unspoiled self where your ultimate wisdom dwells.

As an unknown master once said, 'one does not disappear from a consciousness of world existence but goes where personal being and eternal state are inseparable and are one reality'.

And, Sangharakshita again …

> '*You wrap yourself in a purified consciousness that insulates you from all harm. The dust of the world cannot touch you.*'

I say simply that the Culminating Realisation is your finally stepping *through* the 'gate' to your inner garden in which you can dissolve back into the Divine Oneness – experiencing the revelation of the Absolute … the final *awakening.*

* * *

A Little Story of Encouragement

'It Dawned on Me, I Knew How to Live'

'It was a great relief for me to drop out of my degree and join the fascinating strangers who partied through the shadows, into the bleached, blur-grey morning. In an attempt to side-step a persistence of tension, fatigue and anxiety, I found "respite" in the form of a new, raucous yet fun-loving group of friends. We were always laughing and hugging each other, telling hilarious stories and tripping over in the street. Work was boring but that was ok 'cause it gave me enough money to get trashed several nights a week.

But beneath the enjoyment, I felt a swamp-like misery. As time went on, my "infallible" optimism lost its strength and couldn't be bothered lifting me up any more. I did, and said, all kinds of things which weren't "me", until I found myself unable to find a single thing worth caring about. It was then that I decided I had one more chance to redeem myself and, despite my inner grimace of disdain, I committed myself to at least try to follow my doctor's recommendation and join a meditation class.

I took to meditation with a wholeness of commitment, but little expectation. I meditated every day and began to apply meditative practices like Mindfulness into my daily life. The effect was immediate in the sense that I began to make changes in my life right away. I did a huge throw-out of "stuff" that I didn't need any longer; I stopped going out with my raucous friends; I ended a destructive relationship, and I set about quitting smoking.

These changes did not make me feel better straight away. I was consistently miserable, completely unmotivated at work and now isolated from those with whom I used to love spending time. It took about three months for me to notice that the morose cloud of apathy was beginning to thin. Now instead of walking home with a headache and staring at the ground the whole way wishing I was already home, I started to enjoy the colour of the sky, the sway of the tree or the sound of my footsteps.

I found it very easy to be alone. I was happy to just sit and observe the tiny perfections of the natural world. Just like when I was a child, I might find myself riveted by the sight of sunlight warming the cement in my backyard, with the spider-like shadow of the Hill's hoist cast across. And soon, *it dawned on me that I knew how to live*, that I had always felt a deep compassion for the world and a real affinity with the simple joys of life.

I realise that I had spent a long time trying to convince myself that happiness couldn't be simple, or that I didn't deserve to have it easy. Fulfilment, meaning and satisfaction were the facets of some far-away dream. Rewards which I might collect after a good many years of suffering; working my way up the various ladders of study, career, house, partner, children ... Then ta-da! I might just graduate with a diploma in "life-well-lived", graced with the glittering prize of Contentment!

What I have realised is that life is not something you are working for, it is what you have *right now*, and how you spend it is completely up to you. In knowing that the quality of life is in my hands, I felt a deep sense of relief. Today, I feel stronger and calmer than I ever have, and I feel no longing for the past. Now I can fully appreciate the power of the present.'

– Sarah

* * *

There are many things Sarah didn't say in her story above. Since I have known her, I have discovered her outstanding ability as a brilliant, lyrical and creative writer (I now call her the Sanctuary's D H Lawrence), painter, poet and photographer.

Sarah didn't tell you that she has returned to university to study English language and literature. Nor did she mention that she is one of the very few genuinely, spiritually advanced people (other than my teachers) I have ever met nor that she has a natural depth of wisdom and a pure, uncluttered clarity of 'being'. She didn't mention that in discussion with others, she inevitably illuminates any issue or topic with her innate wisdom.

Sarah didn't tell you she is just 22 years old.

Chapter Seventeen

Mindfulness – the Mystical 'Sixth Sense'

'Perfect mindfulness is perfect meditation.'

– Brahmasamhara

If you have read any books on Eastern 'philosophy' or travelled in Asia, you certainly will have encountered tantalising phrases dripping with mysticism such as 'the third eye' or 'the middle eye' or the 'sixth sense'. For countless centuries, many believed that a timeless assortment of gurus, yogis, Zen monks and various other spiritual mystics (bit like a mixed bag of jellybeans really) had, or have today, a special divine gift to see and know 'things' that others, the 'ordinary' folk in global street, could or cannot see or know.

You may have seen ancient drawings of iconic figures such as Hindu gods or the Buddha, which actually feature another 'eye' drawn on the forehead, above and between the real eyes, signifying their 'possession' of allegedly extraordinary spiritual gifts. For centuries, ancient writings and poetry across Asia and the Middle East have extolled the extrasensory virtues of such mystics who were said to have 'god-like' insight, wisdom and even divine perception and powers.

And it is all true!

There have indeed been, and are, mystics and masters who have a kind of 'inner sight' (insight) – a seemingly extra-sensory perception and a deep spiritual discernment that seems to set them apart. These mystics are the ones who can just 'look at you' and instantly know you better than you know yourself – seeing into the very depths of your inner being!

'However', I tell my wide-eyed students, 'all of you have this same, natural 'god-like ability' of the profound 'sixth sense' – this spiritual insight of the 'third eye'! The difference between most people and the mystic, however, is that in almost everyone the power of the 'sixth sense' has not been *unveiled and awakened*. It is left languishing, usually forever, under a huge pile of mental life debris shovelled onto the 'self' during the conditioned, but illusory, life-long, insane chase after the mirage of 'stuff' – whatever that may be for each person.

So what is this 'sixth sense' – the one portrayed so beautifully in the written and visual tradition of the mystical 'middle' or 'third eye'? Quite simple really.

The sixth sense is … *purity of mindfulness.*

Do you recall what Sangharakshita said about *inner meditation?*

> *'Your attention is withdrawn from the senses and therefore also from the corresponding sense objects and you become centred within.'*

Mindfulness is the other 'perfect half' of Authentic Meditation. It is the ability to have your entire sensory being fully awake in the moment … not just 'present in the moment' but *wholly awake* to *experiencing each moment of life with crystal-clear consciousness*. It is 'possessing' a transparent awakeness that leaves us open to seeing and purely perceiving the reality of ourselves, life, others and the universal environment – with our whole being – the whole time – without the intervention of conditioned thought or reflex behaviour or imposition of attitude and judgement.

In its most pure form, mindfulness really means the ability to 'see' with inner sight, as the mystic does … *as a little child does*. Remember the child on the blanket transfixed with unconditioned wonderment at the antics and songs of the little bird? He was seeing what *is* – without preconception … *he was seeing with his 'sixth sense'.*

* * *

The practice of true mindfulness, within an authentic meditative context, can take you into a completely different realm of seeing and understanding.

Mindfulness is effectively meditation in action, enabling a permanent, transcendent engagement with the totality of your existence – not just 'making it through the day' without too much pain (although in today's world, that is not a bad start, is it).

You see, dear reader, mindfulness is really the same as our formal practice of *zazen* which, as I said before, is the 'illumined experiencing of the self in the moment', except that mindfulness is the practice of meditation *as we go about our daily business.* It is being profoundly conscious of each moment of life *as we actually live it,* rather than being oblivious to reality as we sleepily stumble along, *thinking* our life away.

A wonderful woman and Zen monk, Geri Larkin, says in her book, *Stumbling Towards Enlightenment* (such a brilliant title) …

> [*the practice of mindfulness means*] … '*not missing a moment of this extraordinary Journey which is your life. Even the smallest segment can teach you unfathomable lessons – not to mention the peace, understanding and even joy in the face of all the storms that come our way*'.

Sounds like the way to go, doesn't it? Surely it follows that, if a little child can 'do it', the practice of mindfulness must be pretty simple. But the truth is, dear reader, having left our unconditioned, perfect being back there with our childhood, without dedicated meditative practice the reawakening of our natural mindfulness is very difficult indeed (but not impossible). This is why, of course, so very few people genuinely unveil the not-so-mystical 'sixth sense' of *seeing what is* with a crystal-clear, unconditioned consciousness.

In reality, the vast majority of folks have no concept of such higher reaches of consciousness that can be unveiled when we let go conditioned thought and behaviour. For this reason they tend to be awestruck (as they have been for countless centuries) when they encounter someone with the perception of a 'mystic', someone who has 'the sixth-sense' – in reality, someone who has simply practiced *pure mindfulness*, someone who has *awakened.*

Of course, there is no need to be amazed at the 'powers' of others. The sixth sense of total awakeness is within us all *in equal measure* and, as I have said, requires nothing more than the *genuine* practice of mindfulness to unveil it.

Practicing Mindfulness – Being Awake to Your Life

'There is no mystery whatever – only an inability to perceive the obvious.'

– Author Unknown

Stop now. I want you to reflect for a moment. Do you remember feeling the soothing water warming your body in the shower this morning … or were you so busy *thinking* about the worries of the day ahead that you were barely aware of even being in the shower? Did you sit and pleasurably enjoy each sweet, life-giving mouthful of your breakfast … or were you too busy *thinking*, already stressed out as you shoved a half-burned bit of toast down your suffering throat as you hurried to your employ? Did you offer a good-bye kiss that gave nourishment to your love-heart for the day … or did you nearly kill him/her in the rush to get out the door, too busy *thinking* of the bus coming/your being late/meeting the deadline today?

In fact, have you really 'felt' the 'joy' of *any* moment of your day so far?

No, I don't mean the usual emotions attached to the 'doings' of your day but just walking/standing/sitting/lying there and feeling the magnificence of just 'being'. The truth is, dear one, being *masterfully mindful* in the meditative sense … being awake to the joyfulness of existence … involves every single second of your life, *no matter what you are doing!*

With that in mind, I am reminded that the standout writer of exceptional genuineness on mindfulness is the gentle Thich Nhat Hanh, the Viet-namese monk exiled in France. When you get a chance, read his 'essay' on *just washing the dishes* in his lovely little book titled *The Miracle of Mindfulness.*

You see, most people are so busy rapping ceaselessly in their brains, so preoccupied with the mental intricacies of surviving, *that they don't even use their senses* effectively to perceive the profound and glorious substance of their existence. They can, in fact, just about go through an entire day without really seeing, hearing, smelling, tasting or feeling almost anything, unless there is a gross stimulus (a loud car horn sounding behind them, for example) that so startles their 'chattering monkeys', it brings them moment-arily to the present.

Accordingly, most people remain oblivious (usually for a lifetime) even to *the possibility of uncovering or awakening their sixth sense* – never knowing that there is another level of consciousness available to them through … just being mindful.

Practicing Perfect Awakeness

I said earlier that the practice of mindfulness is the ability 'to have your entire sensory being fully awake in the moment', not just being 'present in the moment'. It is a sad fact that the average person, for the majority of their life has only about five to 10 per cent of their senses available to them because the full capacity of their sensory perception is literally drowned out by unmastered thinking.

Sadly, this means that most people are so 'conditioned' to be brain-occupied that they actually never perceive about 90 per cent of the available 'existence-information' available to them … about themselves, their various relationships, life in general or the lovely universe of which they happen to be a part!

So, in order to witness and experience the wonderment of our existence, *it is necessary to fully awaken our sensory gifts.* Even my dear grandmother used to know about this. She was fond of saying to me, 'for heaven's sake, come to your senses!' (although now, I'm not quite sure whether that was a reflection of her expertise in mindfulness).

You see, dear reader, the wonderment of the 'sixth sense' or the 'middle eye' or the 'third eye' exhibited by all those amazing gurus, mystics and yogi types is simply the fact that they have unveiled the entire capacity of their core faculties and have them *all* 'in play' … the whole time. Having all their core faculties 'open' at the same time (which can become habitual for the genuine ones) enables them to dwell permanently in pure sensory mindfulness.

When these awakened ones 'see', they are so finely 'tuned' that *they see everything* because they are not looking through a warping veil of conditioned thought, opinion and judgement that, in most people, lies between what they 'see' and *what really is.* When they listen, they really hear each wave of sound. When they eat, they eat slowly and taste each morsel with thankful joy. When they smell, it is with an aware pleasure that they can. When they touch an object or a person, each time it is as if for the first time.

But, although difficult, it is eminently possible for anyone to see and know what others cannot see and know – in other words, to be fully awake to the present, the whole time, just like the 'mystics'. In effect, I am saying that everyone has the potential to live with pure mindfulness – to perceive with your 'sixth sense' by accessing the 'missing' 90 per cent of the senses buried under the life debris of your busyness.

Ultimately, pure mindfulness is pure meditation – infinite, glorious, divine awakeness to the experience of existence.

We shall begin practicing mindfulness now with little steps until later maybe, your practice too can become applying mindfulness to your entire life – the whole time. Now there is a truly yogic aspiration.

Listening Mindfulness

If I asked you to write down the sounds you remember having heard in the past half hour (without stopping and listening right now), you would actually list very few – probably not more than two or three in that whole period. When I ask students to do this exercise in class, indeed they mostly list very few – usually my voice, the background music and perhaps a car that has roared loudly down the hill outside. I would like you now to do the very revealing exercise that I ask my Sanctuary students to practice.

Exercise 50. *Practice Really Hearing*

> *Just sit anywhere, close your eyes and give attention to listening for as many different sounds as you can possibly hear in the next 10 minutes and write them down as you hear them. (I tell my dear students that the 'record' held for the number of sounds heard in that short time is 30!)*
>
> *Try now to become single-pointedly aware of 'just listening' – really giving mind-focused attention to identifying sounds.*

You are soon likely to astonish yourself by realising that the world 'out there' is abuzz with sound – as if the whole universe is resonating with noise. For a few minutes, you are unlikely to stop writing at all.

Of course, what you write down is of no import at all. Nor is the number of sounds. At the end of the exercise, I have to confess to the freshlings that I 'exaggerated' about the record being thirty. That was just to get their competitive spirit going (which it does beautifully) so they would really listen with an intensity of will – so they would listen with 100 per cent of their sensory capacity. Most students (and probably you) fill half a page or more with their list of sounds identified in the time allotted. How amazing!

The extraordinary experience that many report is that, in closing their eyes and 'straining' to listen, they are so focused that they *stop thinking* for a moment ... until they hear, identify and write down a sound.

However, in writing down the sounds, or counting 'how many you have' (and then telling yourself 'this is amazing'), *you are still having some thoughts.* You *are* 'moving towards' being mindful, but still reflecting a 'conditioned mind' by the very act of identifying each sound with a name and then writing it down. The child listening to the bird on the blanket did not know the name for the sound so – *he just listened with his entire being!* Refining your mindfulness of listening then, becomes the next step.

Exercise 51. *Listening Without a 'Conditioned Response'*

If you have a music player and a collection of favourites, select a gentle, beautiful track from one of them. For this exercise in class, I often use Chopin's beautiful Concerto in C or sometimes a recording of bird sounds. If you have no music – no matter. Go to a park and choose a place free of people where you can sit and just listen. For the exercise, I shall write now as though you have music.

> *Go to your sanctuary and take your posture. Reach your Essential Stillness while maintaining enough awareness to start the music playing when you are ready. When it begins, take your awareness to your inner listening, but this time, there is no writing down ... just immerse yourself in the sound.*
>
> *Try not to think about what you are hearing. Just 'open' yourself to the sound as if you are listening with your whole being – your ears, feet, lungs and the rest of your body.*

> *When you have attained focused mindfulness, you will begin to experience the feeling of 'oneness with the sound'. You will feel that you are the sound! If thoughts do intrude, just use the music as your point of focus until they fade.*

Hearing with the perceptiveness of your 'inner mind' adds a dimension to listening that you didn't previously know existed. Some students experience such a sense of joy when they first begin to experience 'mindful listening', they sit before me with tears welling in their eyes. In really experiencing the sense of oneness, you open your aural sensory perception to an entirely different level – the level of 'superconscious hearing'.

One of my little joys to this day is taking a cup of tea into the garden in the country cottage on a Sunday morning at dawn to *just listen* for the different, day-greeting bird songs as the little ones awaken to the rising sun. Mindful listening … No Mind … fully awake.

If you too, really 'give yourself' to just listening, your awareness will have an increased sharpness because you are practicing being really here, now – not wandering off in your head. You too, may have the utterly pleasurable experience of your whole inner being just seeming to expand, as if becoming 'one with' the sounds you hear.

In practicing this exercise, you will have awakened *one* of your senses 100 per cent and so begun to open the 'sixth sense'. *Can you imagine what it would be like if you were experiencing life with all your senses fully present – all tuned perfectly to here and now?*

Active Mindfulness

You can begin practicing mindfulness wherever you go. Begin by stopping and … *just listening*. As you just listen, without 'thought judgements' on what you are hearing, you will slowly become aware of a beauty in sound that has not been there before. You will become *awake* to sound and gradually, will uncover a joy in really hearing *everything* with your 'inner hearing'. Most every sound can then become *a powerful sensory experience of delight*, from a guitar in concert to a child laughing; the sound of skis on snow and even, for some, the palpable sound of a beautifully engineered engine, all just by … awakening to mindfulness of listening.

Later, the truly mindful being grows to appreciate, and then nourish, a love of the most perfect sound of all … the sound of silence! Remember, I said the ancients felt they could hear the song of the universe (*aum*) in the purity of silence. Maybe you can too, if you listen with mindfulness!

Opening Your Inner Sight

Although students may have spent many hours in the Meditation Hall, I tell them that there are at least 1000 'things' in there that they have never seen before. I ask them to rest in their stillness for a little while, then open their eyes, look about and start writing down all the objects or items they have never noticed.

They have, in fact, seen *everything* … but have been too busy thinking to be *awake* to most of the objects. They then write non-stop for 10 or so minutes before I ask, 'how many of you saw the reflections and shadows on the [polished board] floor?' Few do, which demonstrates just how hard it really is to begin to ignite the sixth-sense of really 'seeing' with our inner' sight – or just being mindfully awake!

Try this 'eye-opening' exercise for yourself.

Exercise 52. *Opening Your Inner Sight – Finding a Miracle!*

> *In a familiar environment, rest in your Essential Stillness for a while and then open your eyes. Look about you and start writing down all the objects or items you have never 'noticed'.*

I'm sure you'll be surprised at the length of your list. The lesson is there of course. Just as you have begun to really listen, you now need to give real attention to reawakening this extraordinary sense of 'just seeing'. It is another sense that, when awakened, can give you a 'sixth-sense' wealth of life-data, appreciation and pleasure. When practicing mindfulness of seeing, a different world begins to appear – *the world that is really there* – not the one you *thought* was there.

I call this … finding a miracle!

Seeing 'What Is' Without Intervention of Thought

The most difficult aspect of 'mindful seeing', of course, is the endeavour to see *what is* without the usual, automatic intervention of thought, opinion, judgement or intellectual assessment of the subject of your 'looking'. For your whole life to this point, becoming aware of 'seeing' anything is just a trigger for opinionated thinking, not 'sixth-sense appreciation' ... 'oh, the coffee shop is busy today – mmm, smells lovely ... where's the fire engine going – that siren is so loud and annoying ... and so on, endlessly ... assessment, opinion and judgement!

But, just as a child sees, I want you also to practice *just seeing* what there really is without that intervening veil of conditioned thought and judgement. Begin to work on being aware that you are imposing thought onto that which you look at and then practice bringing your attention back to – *just seeing*. Over weeks and months, you will find that you are truly beginning to see with an 'inner' sight.

Therein you will begin to 'find the miracles' – all around you.

Seeing as a small child does will be a revelation. You will find yourself examining everything, gently, intently, deliberately and gracefully. You will see everything 'out there' totally afresh and even ordinary 'things' will have colour, depth, dimension and a newness that you have not perceived before. Remember, I told you of Ajahn Brahm's stopping in the middle of a talk to stare transfixed at a simple glass of water and smiling at its beauty. He was truly seeing 'what is'.

The fascinating fact is that the objects you now view with mindfulness haven't changed, although they will seem totally different. It is your perception of them that changes. As it does, you are continuing the process of ... *awakening* as you further develop 'thoughtless consciousness' ... true mindfulness.

Mindfulness in Tasting

Exercise 53. *The Taste of Things*

You have eaten countless meals in your life and probably appreciated many of them, particularly when you were really hungry or when others have cooked for you or when you have visited a restaurant to titillate the taste buds with 'good food'. However, I suspect you have never used your taste buds while in a state of thoughtless consciousness or being mindfully awake to *just tasting*. Therein awaits another experience of wonderment, pleasure and … *awakening*.

I shall give you a little exercise to 'kick off' a mindfulness practice that hopefully you will take with you for the rest of your life.

> *Prepare a small plate of natural (rather than processed) food – perhaps little pieces of several fruits that you like and, say, a small amount of cheese cubes. Take these to your sanctuary, along with a glass of fresh cool water.*
>
> *When you are ready, enter your Essential Stillness until you have let go thought but without going further into the Serene Space. When you have reached whole-being stillness, slowly place a piece of fruit or cheese into your mouth. Chew it gently and gracefully as though it is the only mouthful available to you in this meal.*
>
> *Take loving, savouring time over this mouthful, feeling the texture of the food – tasting it and knowing its goodness as it goes into your body as nourishment and energy. Endeavour to utilise your whole mind in the act of tasting and appreciating – without thought or mental response to what you are doing.*
>
> *When you have completed that, take some fresh water into your mouth and hold it there for a moment. Feel its coolness, taste and freshness and then sense its goodness as you take it in to your body when you swallow.*

Although you have done this simple little activity countless times before, I promise you that, if you have maintained your inner stillness and mind-focus, you will have found this one mouthful of food and water a totally new experience. Consciously take this practice with you as an Active Meditation, remembering to repeat it whenever you eat and drink. Soon enough, eating food and quenching your thirst (now with your 'open' inner mind) will become a delicious habit in your life – even if the food and drink is only rice and water. You too, may find that you always become the last to finish at the table as you become absorbed in the mindful, simple pleasure of … *just tasting* each life-nourishing mouthful.

Changing Food Habits

With your increasing mindfulness, you will begin to find that, no matter what your food preferences in the past, natural foods such as fruit and vegetables, will begin to appeal to you increasingly more than processed foods.

As a child, I had the 'over-love' of a dear grandmother who provided too many sugar goodies and it was only years later, through the senses exercises of mindfulness with Suni, that I began to develop an appreciation of natural foods. I have no sense of righteousness about health foods or unprocessed foods. From time to time, when I so choose, chocolate on a winter's night or a bowl of ice cream on a sweltering summer's day can be delicious!

You will gradually, however, begin to seek out foods that have a natural taste rather than a 'created' taste. In the garden I endeavour to maintain, I now reserve a corner for the year-round growing of vegetables and find that there is little as satisfying as the taste of chemical- and additive-free food that you have grown, picked and prepared. Try growing a few things yourself – tomatoes, for example – even on a balcony. You will find this both enjoyable and beneficial, far more so than consuming the processed, aged, non-nutritious garbage, albeit so attractively presented, in your local supermarket and for which an uber-amount of money is charged.

So, *do* practice mindful tasting now – and forever! You will slowly develop a complete knowingness about the foods that please, not only your taste but your body as well, while you continue the journey of *awakening the sixth sense*.

Aroma Mindfulness

Did you know that we have millions of receptor cells in a small patch of mucous membrane high in the nasal passage that are able to distinguish about 10000 different aromas? Smell is the main way in which we recognise flavour and hence the food we are eating. How many aromas can you remember smelling today? If you can actually recall five, you are doing wonderfully well because, again, most people are so busy thinking their lives away that they 'think' they have no time to 'stop and smell the roses'. Well, we don't have to stop – just introduce the *mindfulness of smell* into our daily experience.

You can awaken your sense of smell with your inner consciousness in the same way as your other senses by again developing the practice of mindfulness. You will begin to find exquisite subtleties of fragrance that were there all the time, but you didn't know even existed. One of my favourite mindfulness practices, even to this day, is to stop and *just smell* the vegetables and fruits picked from my garden.

Exercise 54. *Stop and Smell the … well, Everything!*

Take a perfumed flower or a stick of incense to your sanctuary and, upon dwelling in your stillness, gently place the item where you can take in the aroma for a few minutes.

Then, wherever you are outside your sanctuary, practice constantly and mindfully taking in the aroma of your favourite foods, the smell of trees brought to you as a gift on the wind or even the hand, hair or skin of a loved one.

I have already mentioned one little caring deed that I have treasured for a long time when Janene, the Sanctuary's 'Mother', brings flowers to ensure that all the meditators have sweet-smelling beauty before them on their mats. Such a simple practice of mindfulness but … so lovely. Try it.

Touching Mindfulness

Exercise 55. *Awakening the Physical*

The sense of touch is the least appreciated. Most people use very little of this sensory capability in a mindful way, mostly limiting themselves to using the sense of touch with fingers to gauge such 'essentials' as the temperature of, say, water. With 'touching mindfulness' though, you can open to the luxurious sense of touch *through your entire body* with your inner mind.

Again, reaching into a quietness of mind, try really feeling the texture and even beauty, of everything – fabrics, metals, woods, plastics, leaves, fur, skin, anything! ... just letting your fingertips dwell and thoughtlessly enjoy. Walk barefooted on grass and sand, just immersing yourself in the sensuousness of being awake – truly awake – to the feeling.

As you stir your sleeping consciousness, it will become increasingly beautiful to do the *simplest* 'touching and feeling'– such as putting your hand in a pool of water and gracefully moving it from side to side or holding your hand in a cool running stream. You'll find it lovely to run your hands across the bark of a tree and through the hair of your child or your lover and feel the vibrancy of natural life – all the things that you have probably done so many times before but without the mindful awareness of being open to your sense of touch *with clear mind*.

Your Body – Your Temple

An important element of fully awakening is beginning to understand the structure and workings of your body. In Authentic Meditation, we regard the body as the physical temple, the 'home', in which your entire consciousness of existence is experienced.

Authentic meditators have a sacred task in both understanding the 'temple' and spending time in its nurturing and nourishment. I have discovered that most people have very little knowledge of their body apart from how it looks and how to adorn it to make it look 'better'. That's all reasonably fine – many animals and birds do the same, some quite elaborately. The difference between the animal kingdom and 'us', of course, is that they have an innate knowledge of *right nourishment* and care as they are so 'in tune' with the naturalness of their existence – something that the non-meditative species of *homo sapiens* (that's us, folks) has long, long forgotten!

Exercise 56. *Knowing Your Body*

One of the important 'touch' exercises we do in class is slowly feeling the inner 'structure' of our own hands and head through gentle feeling, kneading and self-massage. It is a refreshing and lovely exercise you can do in your own sanctuary.

Using a fragrant oil, gently massage your whole body, exploring the bones, muscles, tendons and organs (deeply, but always gently … never pressing too hard).

Another beautiful, awakening experience is to …

reach your inner quietness and then gently, gently massage the body of a 'heart-tie', a loved one, with a purity of mindfulness – being utterly present while you immerse yourself in the wonderment of the other with loving gracefulness.

That is really 'making love' – mindfully, divinely!

Exercise 57. *Mindfulness – Mudra-touch With a Loved One*

This is another sweet exercise of mindfulness you might like to try.

Make a mudra with your hands in the classic prayer position (palms together and fingers pointed to the sky). Take them a little apart and put them each side of the face of a loved one. Close your eyes, then quieten your mind for a moment while feeling the vibrancy of their life-love within you as you offer yours to them.

This beautiful yogic practice can also be 'used' as a loving comfort to a distressed child and to the sick or dying.

'Advanced' Mindfulness – Fully Opening the 'Sixth Sense'

So far, I have given attention to each sense individually. For a while now in your practice, you will find your attention inevitably 'moving' from one sense to the other. For example, if you are walking down the street practicing being 'thoughtlessly aware' of your environment, you will see with great clarity that bird over there pecking at the bark of a tree. You will become absorbed in it and it will delight you (because you probably haven't noticed such things since you were a child).

However, at this stage of singular absorption, you are unlikely to be *equally aware* that the church bells have just begun to ring or *mindful* of the smell of fresh coffee wafting from the cafe nearby, even though you really *do* hear and smell them. 'Seeing' the bird will occupy your whole awareness. After a while, when you became aware of the other stimuli, you would probably then lose your focus on the bird. So, in the beginning, you will mostly find yourself 'being mindful' with just one sense at a time – which is fine.

As I said earlier, however, pure mindfulness is the extraordinary level of sensory perception the mystics and all such lovely beings have (which you can also experience, of course) when all the senses are fully awake *at the same time!* I shall now guide you in the key exercises we practice in the Meditation Sanctuary that will enable you to awaken the 'sixth sense' – the 'yogic specialty' available to all who have the intensity of will to … just practice!

Exercise 58. *Being Mindful With More than One Sense*

You will need a smooth, rounded stone and the piece of music you played previously when practicing mindful listening.

> *Take both to your sanctuary, assume sukhasana and drop into your Essential Stillness. When quiet of mind, begin playing the music softly, opening yourself to listening with the thoughtless awareness of your whole being as you did before. When you feel as though you are the music, endeavour to hold that deep awareness of the music within.*
>
> *Then, at the same time, begin to feel the stone slowly with your fingers. Become aware of its texture, weight, coolness or heat. Perhaps rub its smoothness against the back of your hand or on your cheeks but try not to bring your natural mental responses to mind as thoughts. The endeavour becomes not saying to yourself, 'isn't it lovely and cool', for example, but just 'feeling' smooth coolness from within … with your whole being.*

Oops – you've just let go awareness of the music! And therein lies the difficult part of the training. Having let go any mental response to the music so it just becomes a 'presence', you need to mindfully practice remaining open to thoughtless awareness of both the music and the stone – *at the same time.*

Mindfulness of the Five Senses

I won't spend your reading time going through all the steps of adding each of the senses to your exercises – because the process is as you have done with the first two senses, listening and seeing.

> *So, in your sanctuary, you may find yourself listening to the music and you can then open to your sense of touch by feeling a lovely object (all with your inner being). When the awareness of those two senses overlap, you may then open your eyes and gaze at a lovely object (flower, feather, marble, anything at all really) that you have placed before you. After practicing until the third sense overlaps the others (meaning that you are now awake to the three at the same time), perhaps you can add, say, the aroma of some lovely incense and then, a little later, maybe hold a little spicy cardamom pod in your mouth.*

For a while, you will find you can hold two or three senses 'open' for a few seconds, before your awareness begins switching from one to the other again. Worry not – with practice, the 'switchings' will become closer and closer until eventually they will just overlap and you may have the quite indescribable experience of being fully awake to all your senses at the same time. It may feel like you are internally 'expanding' or 'opening'. This is a natural response but initially, it can just about take your breath away as an astonishing experience of being fully, mindfully awake to your senses with crystal-perfect clarity, washes through you. (At this very moment, my favourite willy wagtail, the one with the unusually crooked, little white stripe down his cheek, just came and sat on the back step near where I am writing and began his morning melody!)

In your practicing, do not strive for any such extraordinary 'feelings' and do not be agitated when first finding it hard to quell the 'switching'. You know my advice off by heart now … just sink into the practice and happily tumble along for the ride. If you do, I promise you, eventually you will be able to open your total sensory mindfulness and perceive with the 'sixth sense', just as the mystics do!

Taking Sensory Mindfulness with You

Of course, true mindfulness becomes effective when you are taking it with you, beyond your sanctuary and into the wider world of your daily life. There, the full, playful sensory kaleidoscope gradually opens before you as the practice you have been doing grows into maturity.

As you widen your practice of being awake to the moment with your sensory mindfulness, *the outer world will simply begin to change.* As you let go the blather of your mind and allow your expanding senses to reveal your life environment, you will begin to have the feeling that you inhabit a whole universe of which you've simply not previously been aware.

In the early stages, you will just be continually amazed, for example, at the vibrancy and variation of colours (yes, there are countless thousands), the sweetness of natural sounds such as birdsong and church bells carried on the wind to you from the other side of town ... excitingly, endlessly. When you have awakened to your senses, it is virtually impossible to go back to 'sleep'.

After quite some practice, you may well develop a sixth sense of *a oneness – with everything!* One of my 'extreme' and lasting experiences of mindful 'inner sight' was awakening to a sense of 'belonging' ... no, not just belonging *to* 'my family', 'my country' or 'my culture', but a breathtaking sense of the 'self' fading as I became aware of the clarity of *belonging 'in' everything* ... where the whole being is in conscious harmony with elemental existence. This *absolute presence,* resulting from the practice of purifying mindfulness, is the beginning of unveiling the Innate Wisdom that begins to bubble up from within – an electrifying, unconditioned, irreversible awakeness to all that *is.*

The Joy in Mindfulness ... and Tranquil Equilibrium

Just as I spoke of joy and bliss being a state of experience in the liberating meditations, so too can one have such a response to moments, minutes or enduring mindfulness. The experience of sensory awakeness can become so intense that it becomes a 'psycho-physical' experience where one can cry with joy or have the hairs on your arms or body stand on end. Some call this a state of rapture where one is overwhelmed by a kind of ecstasy.

However, for the authentic meditator, such extreme responses of emotional joyfulness slowly 'mature through' to a balanced equilibrium – like the 'calm after the storm'. After all the 'thunder' and 'lightning' quietens, a beautiful inner peacefulness simply begins to warmly radiate.

* * *

As with all the experiences you have encountered on your Journey to date, you now need to 'travel on' – to continue practicing until you unveil the next, deeper experience – at this stage, that experience being the tranquillity of just dwelling in absolute awakeness *as your natural state*.

In reaching a state of tranquil equilibrium, however, you do not 'let go' the blissful joy of your existence – quite the opposite. You begin to open the inner door to a transcendent understanding of your inherent place within the eternal existence of everything.

Chapter Eighteen

Mindfulness – a Blowtorch on Your Self!

'Meditation does not change you – it reveals you.'

– Author Unknown

I said at the beginning of the book that the whole of meditation (including mindfulness) is really about how *you live your life* – how you 'use' your wonderful meditative practices to see, understand and let go all that inhibits your profound engagement with the 'reality of the self'. It is about letting go the morass of the superficial, the conditioned, the mirages and the illusions in which so many are needlessly embedded – just 'thinking' they are alive. After developing sensory mindfulness, the steepest part of your Journey is, nevertheless, ahead of you … *opening to crystal-clear mindfulness (perfect meditation) of you and your life – the whole time.*

I want to tell you a story – an important one from more recent times. A Tibetan monk was gaoled for opposing not just the invasion of his land by China but the exceeding brutality inflicted upon his people. He volubly protested the mass murder of monks, the rape of nuns and the destruction of things precious to his country, including many of their sacred monasteries and icons. He protested about it becoming an offence to possess a picture of the Dalai Lama.

So the monk found himself in gaol where he continued to protest, earning himself solitary confinement, repeated beatings and then a 10-day diet of water. During his solitude he noticed that his guard was young, frightened and also appeared to be hungry. On the ninth day of solitary confinement, the door suddenly opened and a bowl of grubby rice was put before the monk. Without hesitation, he immediately offered half to the guard.

End of the known story – almost.

Most teachers of meditation, either within a religious environment or more secular places of practice, as well as countless self-help book have, as the core aspiration of 'meditation', an end point of 'being happy' or at least 'happier'. *I, however, am not at all interested in your just being happy.*

I WANT YOU TO BE MAGNIFICENT!

The monk in gaol wasn't 'happy'. He wasn't waking each morning whistling as he exercised and he wasn't doing little dancy jigs with the joy of just waking up and looking forward to a hearty breakfast. The man was starving, past exhaustion, in pain and dying. Yet he was actually way beyond 'happy' – *he was absolutely magnificent.*

He had reached into the very depths of his being to find the truth of his existence – the very core of his elemental self … love, kindness, compassion and concern for the welfare of all others.

With that one caring gesture, he confirmed that he was a man who had *become his meditation.* His very existence *exemplified* those absolute inner qualities – *he had become his love, kindness and compassion. Above all, he had become his concern for the welfare of others.* In one act of offering to share his bowl of rice with his captor, even though he was starving, he showed that he had reached into his Buddhahood or Christlikeness or had become what I call a Being of Graciousness.

In a moment of grace he had reached a State of Grace.

Soon after, this magnificent monk, whose name I don't even know, died. I light a candle in my heart every day for this Buddha-man – this Christlike being, whoever he was.

It is not necessary to suffer as he suffered to find the opportunity to be magnificent or to exemplify the true qualities of your essential being. *Every moment of your life provides you with that opportunity.* In order to 'see' that, however, it is time to take your mindfulness to another dimension.

It is time to turn your increasing mindfulness back on yourself like a blowtorch!

* * *

So far, you have worked exceedingly hard in practicing the once-natural techniques of 'inner' meditation (liberating meditation) and sensory mindfulness in which you practice 'paying attention' to your existence ('outer' meditation).

However, to the authentic meditator, all the accomplishments of practice are largely a waste of time if there is not *a conscious aspiration to progressively dwell in existence as an awakened person.* Now, I don't expect you to become a monk or live a life of deprivation that many might think is a natural consequence of becoming a meditative person. It isn't, except for those who so choose to find and express their magnificence in that way.

But … I *am* saying there is not much point in getting all 'blissy' in your sanctuary and all mindfully weepy about the loveliness of the flowers in spring if you continue to 'offer' yourself to others as the 'old' self; the one who greedily puts self first, snarls at employees, abuses the poor old street-guy for getting in your way … or *any* such non-meditative, non-caring behaviour.

Certainly, the practices you have undertaken so far may already be rippling through your life in both expected and unexpected ways. Perhaps you have found yourself becoming calmer, less stressed and even more alert and energetic. You will undoubtedly have a higher level of general wellbeing and may well have already begun to identify useless excesses in your life and started to unravel them (having perceived that they would have unravelled you).

You may have indeed gone further and begun to have little 'awakenings' and 'realisations' enabling you to begin letting go some of your 'old' conditioned thinking and behaviour. If so, wonderful – you are ready for the 'steepest' climb. Some dear and good people do seemingly exemplify some such effects or happenings but these can just be the relatively unconscious, almost incidental 'by-products' of practicing or even study, and not the result of an awakening aspiration to reach towards and then *become* their inner true being.

For example, I have met numerous and various meditators, monks, ministers and an assortment of 'religious' people who have spent a lifetime of 'spirituality' and are 'good' souls but who, in reality, are far from *truly* reaching into and expressing their inner magnificence. Many remain spiritually asleep because, although they may have studied and achieved great knowledge of various doctrines and scriptural dogma and adhere to various 'teachings' devotedly, *they have not opened the final gate to their inner divine magnificence.* They have not grasped the fact that the simple, eternal truth of *all* the great spiritual teachers is … that the gate to the *kingdom of heaven* is only fully and finally opened by actually *living a life of love, kindness, compassion and concern for the welfare of others* … and doing so *because you can't help it.*

It is not difficult to discern those who *illuminate* our Way and those who need to *find* their Way. We can all be guided by the illumined ones and, as you continue the journey to *your* own inner garden of divine magnificence, perhaps it is possible for *you* to become a tiny spark of light in the dark for others through *your* living a life of love, kindness, compassion and concern for the welfare of others … because you can't help it.

But, just how to take this step … well, perhaps more of a little leap … along the Path?

True Self-Awareness – the Practice of Everything

You, dear reader, are a long way from base camp now. To climb this next part of the Great Journey means that you start the Practice of Everything. The aspiration is to start practicing the *awakened living of your life.* The aspiration is to practice reaching into the wonderment of your inner qualities, allowing them to filter into your 'outer' being so that, in your becoming mindful of them and *applying them too,* they illuminate your whole life by enlightening *everything you say and do … all the time.*

Sogyal Rinpoche, the delightful Tibetan monk and respected writer I previously mentioned, has said that meditation is really just common sense.

He is right, of course. Applying meditative mindfulness really *is* a matter of common sense! But it is a little like the common sense of being told to 'be kind to everyone – *all the time*'. How obviously 'common-sensical' and simple is that? But … how very nearly impossible to do. It's the *all the time* bit of course (ironically, the most crucial and important bit) that most often proves to be the hardest, seemingly sheer cliff face that needs to be scaled on the Journey. Naturally, that becomes one of the final aspirations of the spiritual warrior – not only to *be* your inner magnificence but also to live the 'truth of your being' *every precious moment* of your life.

* * *

My task from now is perhaps to shine a little light on this Zen-like part of the Journey. But you, dear traveller, must walk on alone because the Path now varies for everyone. Only you will know the prevailing 'weather conditions' on your Path as you go along. Only you will know when you are awakening to the higher qualities of your 'inner' being and when they begin to bubble into, and integrate with, your 'outer being'. Only you can really *know* whether or when you are beginning to lead a more illumined life. Only you can know when you are returning to your original, fully-awake, One-being.

All this *does* await you – if you look down at the Path beneath your feet and … continue walking!

Active Mindfulness – Practice Living Every Moment

The following thoughts and exercises are designed to hopefully, not only offer that small light I mentioned but also, offer a modest hand in the meditative living of your life along the Way.

Nourished Thinking – Nourishing Emotions

I have just spent most of a book guiding you in how to be still of being and mind but, of course, not only *do* we think but we *must* think. We cannot survive life without thinking. As we have seen, though, the *way* we think is when we tend to get messy.

Our aspiration as meditative people is to be able to develop Right Thinking, which I call Nourished Thinking or Intentional Thinking.

The aspiration of Intentional Thinking is to gradually *master your thinking* to a point of thinking only when you *choose* to think and then to give focused attention to whatever you choose to think about. The need is to practice *becoming mindful of your thinking* rather than allowing it to be just driven along mindlessly like tumbleweed in the wind.

This is such an important part of the Journey because, as we have seen, our thoughts are the 'controllers' of our emotions and behaviour – they affect the whole of us. So mastering your thoughts when you need to think is another dimension of mindfulness that can profoundly help develop and maintain emotional balance.

Exercise 59. *Mindful Awareness of Thought*

The initial step to mastering Right Thinking takes you back to an earlier exercise … *true awareness* of exactly what you are thinking. Remember, you can begin by asking yourself, 'what am I thinking right now?' After all your good work to date, it will be so much easier now to 'pin down' just where your mind is.

When you are aware of what subject matter is, or has been, occupying you, the exercise then is to ask yourself, what ideally could I be thinking about right now that advances my practice, my Journey, my life, for both myself and for the benefit of others?

Try and answer that in a very positive way. For example, could you be thinking about how you might be more helpful to others, do a better job at work, planning where to take the kids for a treat or what your partner might need you to bring home tonight (without asking!).

So then, do it! Deliberately give thought to a positive chosen subject. Try to be aware of when you wander off subject and bring yourself back (like bringing yourself back to your point of focus).

Practice hard at staying in that state of mindful presence until you become aware of miscellaneous thoughts beginning to crowd in (and, of course, you will gradually become a master at this). As soon as you do become aware of them, repeat the whole process … awareness, a 'meaningful' subject to contemplate, then contemplate it 'single-pointedly' and conclude by returning back to right here

... right now. In other words, when you have completed contemplating your 'subject', let it go and return to mindfulness. Repeat ... and repeat!

Impossible? No! *Difficult?* Yes! *Practice?* The only Way!

This is part of the yogic practice of Harmlessness, in which we practice doing no harm to ourself or to others. *This includes harmlessness of thinking* so, above all, *we need to become awake to negative thoughts about ourself or others.* Negative thoughts only harm ourselves and, if we remain unaware of them and allow them to simmer and infiltrate our being with anger, jealousy, resentment or any of the other little 'nasties', we may well harm others.

The benefits of being able to select *when* we think and then confining ourselves to *what we want to think about* are immeasurable. The main one, of course, is that it stops our emotions being dragged uncontrollably from pillar to post. As you have seen, this happens in the ragged thinking of the meditatively untrained, because emotions are hopelessly entwined with thought.

Calm, rational, nourishing, intentional thinking can enable a measured steadiness in your emotional state and eventually, a Suni-like tranquillity!

Nourished Thinking dispels the mirages of the mind created by 'wrong' thinking. It will come to you naturally when you have let go your 'old' way of thinking completely and are able to 'know' and *apply all your thoughts consciously, knowingly, mindfully, lovingly and wisely.*

Exercise 60. *Mindfully Listening to Your Self*

Your speech is the most immediate reflection of the 'state of your mind'. There are two elements to this – how you speak and what you say when you do speak.

Your Voice

Have you ever listened to yourself? Have you ever heard a recording of your voice? Have you ever caught yourself talking and asked, 'I wonder what that would have sounded like to him/her?' Do you have any idea whether you speak quickly or slowly? Is your voice squeaky, shrill and loud, or soft, measured and gentle? Do your words come out garbled and mumbled or with well-spoken clarity?

Most people haven't the faintest idea of just how they speak because they have never actually considered listening to themselves. Worse still, they have no idea of how to use their voice as an instrument of beauty and cadence. I have written already about the benefits of breathing to your gift of voice and speech. So start there.

> *Breathe through your words while hara (tummy) breathing – in other words, continue to breathe while you are speaking rather than giving each sound a little burst of air to ride on before cutting it off in your throat (called, wonderfully, the 'glottal stop') after virtually each one. Your voice will soon begin to have a richer smoothness to it.*

The meditative person actually listens to how they speak. They are constantly mindful of how they sound to another and mindful of the manner in which they address another – not to 'make an impression' (although a 'beautiful voice' does) but because they are expressing themselves naturally. So, how do you speak?

What You Say

> *Begin listening to what you say. Then ask yourself some serious questions. How was it said? What emotion were you expressing? Was it really important or was it babble? Do you think it mattered to anyone other than you? Did it show care or concern for the person to whom you were talking? If you were responding to or answering someone, was your response considered and meaningful or just reactive? Did the emotion of another cause your response to be equally, but inappropriately, emotional? For example, if they were angry with you, did you snap back with a harsh tone and word?*

The meditative person is mindful of *what* they say ... the *content* of their speech. They endeavour to speak the truth. They endeavour to be *calm of word* in all responses. They endeavour to exemplify their real inner qualities in the content of their speech. See if it is possible to become so aware that you can have a tiny pause before you say something or answer someone.

Could that pause enable you to say something a little wiser, warmer or kinder than you would if you just instantly responded?

My best 'yogic secret' on speech is, if you have nothing positive or emotionally and spiritually nutritious to say … say nothing!

The meditative person never babbles for attention. When they speak, you listen. They have something to say. From this moment, start listening … to *yourself.*

Harm no other with your voice or the content of your talking! Mindfully practice every aspect of your speaking. You have ample opportunity … like, every single time you open your mouth to utter a sound! That's a good place to start. Wouldn't it be lovely to know that people want or choose to listen to you because you have something 'luminous' to say – not always 'wise and knowledgeable' – perhaps just a meaningful 'good morning!' to a lonely person walking by.

Let your voice and words reflect the glorious rhythm of your existence.

Exercise 61. *Self-observing Mindfully*

Our thinking is not only the driver of our speech but also of our actions, activities and even the way we physically move – our behaviour. Within the great yogic principle of Harmlessness, the Buddhists, for example, call mindfulness of our actions, Right Living. Just as you practice Right Listening as a meditative person, so do you practice mindful Self-observation.

> *Begin to bring your attention to just how you go about your daily 'busyness'. Firstly, become aware of just what you actually do every day. Being mindful of what you do might come as a shock when you begin to wake up to just how much 'life-time' you actually waste … daily! Now turn the blowtorch of mindfulness on how you conduct yourself. Quite simply and no more than this, ask yourself whether all your actions have an underpinning of kindness to both yourself and to others or are they just a reflection of self-absorbed self interest. You know the answer!*

In practicing focused mindfulness on your behaviour, you may find yourself bringing inner disquiet 'out into the open' because aspects of the way you conduct yourself and your life are less than acceptable to the increasing graciousness of a meditative person. In other words, you may find that many of your activities and actions resonate less and less happily in your life as the 'perfect qualities' of the true elemental self begin to well up from within through the scrutiny of your meditative practice.

You may go through periods at this stage of 'seeming to be two people', a time when your 'awakening inner' and 'former outer' beings may seem to be 'at each other's throats', vying for the attention of 'you'. I reassure you that any such feeling is natural and is, in fact, just another little secret yogic sign peeping out from behind a boulder along the Path, whispering that you are not lost but very much into your Journey. There may also be some apprehension about 'change' as virtually everyone is conditioned into socially patterned behaviour.

You will *just know* when it is time to accommodate the nagging voice of the emerging inner 'wise one' by gradually transcending your 'old ways' with action and activities that increasingly become 'right' to you. The meditative person transcends their *samsaric*, former outer being so that *everything* they say and do, and the *way* they say and do it, is a true reflection of their inner magnificence.

What did I say before? *Impossible?* No! *Difficult?* Yes! *Practice?* The only Way!

Some Secret Keys to Mindfulness

The secret key to mindfulness of action and activities is to *slow down*.

The very way you physically move is the place to begin self-observation because *the action of your body is also a mirror-perfect reflection of your state of mind* and will provide great clues to the 'rightness' of your actions and activities. If your life is a mad physical rush, the very way you move will reflect that crazy busyness. Go sit in a mall or in a street cafe or a park. Look at people just about anywhere. Most are moving hastily, clumsily, thoughtlessly – uncoordinated and unattractive in their physical jerkiness in just about everything they do, from shovelling food into their mouths to being dragged on a walk by their dog.

This almost comical mode of erratic physical behaviour doesn't accord with the yogic principle of Right Living. Gradually, the student of meditation begins the practice of moving with peaceful deliberateness and a 'knowing' gracefulness … until they do so naturally, the whole time.

Both my Teachers, Bashayandeh and Suni, for example, were the epitome of grace in their quiet, gentle body movements. If they were painters, their style would be called minimalist. Even when conducting martial arts classes, Suni particularly, would seem almost exquisitely lazy in moving his arms and legs – but never lost a practice bout. As a man of nearly 80, he could easily up-end young, very fit men, including me, and he was so poised you could not predict the move he would make that brought you undone! By practicing a purity of physical mindfulness, his body was *always* in the right place at the right time.

By being mindfully deliberate and gracefully conservative with your body and your energy, you will increasingly find that, with less effort, you seem to be 'doing' much more and *that* 'much more' will increasingly begin to seem a natural fit with the emerging self.

You will increasingly find your heart, your activities and actions, just like Suni, to be in the 'right place at the right time'. As I said way back there, I tell my students that being mindful of the self enables us to effectively live four whole lives in this one life – usually with less exertion and struggle than most people expend (and usually, waste) leading their 'one' crazy-busy life. So, slow down … be graceful! Give attention to this life, as if assuming it is the only one we've been allocated. (If there *is* a next one, you'll have plenty of time to worry about it when you get 'there'.)

Next, try to stop doing everything in a mundane, bored and automatic way. If you conduct *any* activity *thinking* it is mundane or boring, you have just spilled moments of your life on the floor, like tipping over a glass of milk. It is wasted and gone. Given the sacred nature of this precious life, *we do not have the right to spill any moment with wrong activity or action.* That is anathema to the meditative person.

This is your life … every, single, precious second of it. Once that precious second of life has passed, it has gone forever. The meditator regards every second of life as another precious moment to practice mindfulness, no matter what the activity. Meditate upon *that*, until it becomes a known Realisation deep within you.

Begin to *listen* to the voice of the inner magnificent being. That's the one with the wisdom of the universe. Do what it tells you. It is always right!

Mindful 'Realisations' of the Universal Environment

Increasing your mindfulness to the 'now' of your life will bring with it an increasingly acute awareness of not only your self, but also of your life environment, the universe of nature and … the nature of the whole universe!

As practicing *mindful observation* begins to seep across your life, there will be a series of Realisations about the wider environment that bubble up from the wisdom within. You will begin to realise the truth of nature – that season after season it offers freely of itself to provide us with food, water and shelter. You will realise that it gifts us with the resources for our brains to turn into 'things' that we think we need/want. You will also, sadly, realise that in our lack of understanding and appreciation of this bounty however, we just close our eyes and haphazardly discard our waste, shoving it back at nature without apology for choking it to inefficiency with our mindless polluting.

Your awakening consciousness will begin to set you apart from the multiplicity of destroyers in most societies on earth who only see the elements of the natural world as a resource to be plundered for profit. (In simply opening my eyes daily upon this world, I am rudely reminded that humans are the only species on earth to act with this sickening selfishness.)

As you awaken to your meditative Being, you will realise that the environment is not there to be owned or 'taken'. It has been and will just *be* … eternally … in some form or other, and actually 'belongs' to everyone and … *we to it*. It *is* yours … but, to the meditative person, 'yours' means the sacred duty of taking only what is needed and no more. It also means that the meditative being has the divine task or responsibility of caring for the environment on behalf of all beings to follow, so that it may be handed on with only the lightest of footprints left behind.

There is, of course, the other minor matter of the exquisite joy in the meditator's eventual Realisation that *everything matters*, every particle of dust, every leaf, every living thing (including us!), as well as every non-living thing. All are part of our universe and part of all universes – a Divine part of all there is, of the Absolute … of our self!

Your task, dear one, is to practice mindfulness of the gift of your environment *at every moment for the rest of your life*. I won't give you a chapter now that reads like a 'Right Things to Do' to help you fulfil your care-responsibility as an increasingly magnificent, meditative person. *Your inner wisdom knows them implicitly* because *caring* is one of the innate, core qualities of your true being.

The Mindfulness of Love, Compassion and Kindness — True Enlightenment

After we have put a flame to the conditioned debris of our life, we can peep in to see what there really is at the very core of our being and, lo and behold, we stumble across a 'secret' cache ... an eternal well of love, kindness, compassion and concern for the welfare of others about which I have been talking. I have said that the ultimate practice of the meditative being on the sacred inner Journey is to unveil those innate qualities at the core of our existence.

However, I have also indicated that the Path to Enlightenment is not just unveiling those qualities, or simply having the Realisation of this truth, but is the *becoming* of love, compassion and kindness ... the moment of *true enlightenment* when we turn to the world as an expression of these precious qualities because we can't help it ... *and can no longer turn back*.

I said something akin to that to a senior class just recently. I looked around at the heads resting to one side (encouraging sign that they were listening) and the nice, soft expressions on the students' faces. I said softly and gently, 'they are lovely words aren't they. Such pretty words'. There were placid smiles of agreement, tender little nods of heads and quiet sighs. Yep, aspirational, even inspirational ... by the looks on their sweet faces.

Until I suddenly yelled, '*they are not just pretty words! They are useless as words!* Love, kindness and compassion are qualities at the very core of you to dig into with both hands — to discover, unveil, feel, know, practice and begin living ... *as of now*'.

Practicing love, kindness and compassion, dear reader, is the hard end of the meditative scale, the deep end of the universe's pool. It's like boot camp ... only much tougher. I kid you not. Few get as far as trying it, let alone trying it *all* the time. But, *actually becoming* love, compassion and kindness then ... surely that is a pipe dream of those crazy Zen types ... isn't it?

Yes, just about. Few are those who really try and fewer are those who reach into their enlightenment ... although it is just in *there*, within, silent, eager, hopeful and far from impossible to uncover ... just waiting for you to *awaken* to it! There is no magic formula that I can offer, no short cut to this 'super level' of wisdom and understanding. The Way 'there', though, is really not difficult and the fact that only few attain their enlightenment of becoming the magnificent, loving and compassionate self, the whole time, is simply because ... *so few try!*

But, if you are one who still truly seeks this extraordinary, divine, illuminated *Way of Living*, I shall offer you ... the 'final secret' ... all I have! It is very simple. It is a matter of ... practice! Just through practicing being loving, kind and compassionate, *you will find that unattainable 'enlightenment' is eventually, actually attainable.* Wahoo!

Let's get back on the Path now.

Exercise 62. *Practicing Loving Kindness!*

The authentically awakened being ultimately assumes the truly transcendent responsibility of turning back to the world, offering of the self, in whatever way, with Luminous Love ... because they can no longer help but do so! Therein lies your final practice.

> *Begin by practicing loving everyone (including yourself) and everything, selflessly and unconditionally without expectation of a 'return'.*
> *Begin by practicing unreasonable kindness for no reason at all.*
> *Begin by offering compassionate care to others without discrimination and at whatever cost to you.*

I have said 'begin by'. The next important step in the practice then is ... *repeat the beginning step*, over and over, *ceaselessly, without question, for the rest of your life.* Therein lies the Path to the Divine within you. Therein you release the magnificent 'You'. Therein you will *awaken* to Heaven on Earth.

There you have it. There is no more.

Chapter Nineteen

The End ... and the Beginning

I was standing in the small, quiet, sensuously lavender-laden garden of Suni Kaisan's monastery one soft, late-spring afternoon. I remember luxuriating in peacefulness and the rare feeling of being 'at home', having been part of the monastery's life in different ways for nearly three years. I saw Suni emerge slowly from the building, meander across the low verandah, partly masked by a white veil of a flowering Chinese wisteria, and watched as he walked gracefully towards me along the crunchy pebble path. He had a gentle, half-smile on his face. Puzzled, I turned towards him as he came up to me.

He took my hand, like a father holding the hand of a child, and led me to an old wooden bench where we sat ... and he began to talk. Suni told me that my time with him was completed. He said that it was time to 'go away now and test your practice in the world'. He told me I would know whether, or when, I had 'become my meditation'. He told me that when I experienced that moment of Realisation, I was to become a teacher.

I was astonished ... and instantly saddened, definitely not yet free of 'possessive attachment' ... wanting to, *needing to* hold onto '*my*' Dear Teacher – my 'spiritual' security blanket.

When he finished talking, Suni just sat with me awhile, lost in ... well, *mindfulness* ... listening to the spring birds and drinking in the sweet scent of the garden on which I'd spent much 'growing' time. He stood up and slowly led me through the monastery to the front gate. He let go my hand

and said, '*no self, no mind, then happiness*' and turned quickly away. But, I had already noticed that his eyes were moist, as were mine. I never saw him again. From his point of view, there was no need to. In those few words, he had given me all he had … all there was … to give.

At the time, I neither fully understood what he meant nor the life-long implications of his extraordinary words. I did understand that he seemed to 'believe' in me – probably more than I did. I missed Suni. I missed him for years until, a long time later, and after many tortuous 'mountain climbs' along the Path, I finally Realised his teaching of the ancient understanding that we all, and everything, are utterly connected in the Oneness of the eternal existence and, when we 'lose our Self' in the Serene Space of No Mind, we may experience our Oneness with the Divinity – of the Absolute. As one Zen master said, 'if you have your mind, you must practice. If you have No Mind, already you are a Buddha'.

I eventually realised that Suni and his wisdom hadn't let me go. My dear, enlightened Buddha-man had been, and is, with me – at one with me – the whole while, now and forever.

Time now for me to walk with you to the 'front gate' and encourage you to 'take your practice out into the world'. *Be inspired and inspiring.* Reach in deep and begin to release the magnificent You. Somewhere, sometime, you *will*. Then, in expressing your love, kindness and compassion, you will again rediscover your own innate wisdom, freedom, and tranquillity.

If you get 'lost in the world', remember to *just look down*. See! The Path is still beneath your feet! Take another step and don't stop until you are in love with everything that moves and … everything that doesn't! Then you may live the illumined life of the enlightened.

Bless you on your Sacred Journey.

Until one day perhaps …

– Brahm

Postscript

What Happened to Nathan?

Dear Nathan practiced with us uncomplainingly and hard. He didn't leave his job but received yet further promotion. Today, Nathan spends his lunch hours taking meditation to the corporate world, guiding his colleagues and others of the 'business fraternity' in the practice of Authentic Meditation. After our conversation in the Meditation Sanctuary on that twilight evening long ago, he has never again mentioned 'enlightenment'. I suspect he may have 'found' it.

Dossier of Exercises

Dossier of Photographs

The Meditation Sanctuary

Enquiries on content may be addressed to the Meditation Sanctuary at
yb@meditationsanctuary.com
or
www.meditationsanctuary.com.

Brahmasamhara

Yogi Brahmasamhara (Brahm) is the Meditation Master at the Meditation Sanctuary which he established in an inner-city suburb in Sydney, Australia, in 2001. He has practiced Authentic Meditation for more than 37 years. He initially spent five years studying Integral Yoga with Indian Yogi, Misra Bashayandeh, who himself had been a student of the internationally renowned philosopher and Yoga Guru, Sri Aurobindo, at Pondicherry in India. He then refined his practice within the classic *Soto-schu* Zen tradition of meditation at the monastery of Japanese Zen monk, Suni Kaisan, on both a visiting and full-time basis over three years.

Brahmasamhara was born in Griffith, NSW, Australia, to farming parents. At 16, he became a radio announcer before moving to Sydney to study theology. Meeting Bashayandeh gradually shifted his intended 'spiritual path' away from formal religion to exploring and studying the 'enthralling profundity' of meditation. Later, it was his Zen Master, Suni Kaisan, who sent him into the world 'to experience life to prepare him' for teaching.

He did just that, working in various fields. He taught English Language and Literature at the University of New South Wales; produced some 30 documentaries on Australian artists; tasted the corporate world with a three-year stint in an international oil company and then established his own award-winning graphic design company. During that time, he co-authored a book on William Balmain (with Dr Peter Reynolds) and wrote poetry prolifically. He also spent much of his time competing around Australia as a motor racing driver – which he describes as 'an extremely meditative activity'.

In the mid '90s, he turned to teaching meditation as his Teacher had foretold and today, the Meditation Sanctuary attracts hundreds of students each year.

*'Make Kindness Your Cause and
Inner Peace Your Passion'*